The Travels of
Sir John Mandeville

Translated with an Introduction by
C. W. R. D. MOSELEY

T0176493

PENGUIN BOOKS

PENGUIN BOOKS

Published by the Penguin Group
Penguin Books Ltd, 80 Strand, London WC2R ORL, England
Penguin Group (USA) Inc., 375 Hudson Street, New York, New York 10014, USA
Penguin Group (Canada), 10 Alcorn Avenue, Toronto, Ontario, Canada M4V 3B2
(a division of Pearson Penguin Canada Inc.)
Penguin Ireland, 25 St Stephen's Green, Dublin 2, Ireland (a division of Penguin Books Ltd)
Penguin Group (Australia), 250 Camberwell Road, Camberwell, Victoria 3124,
Australia (a division of Pearson Australia Group Pty Ltd)
Penguin Books India Pvt Ltd, 11 Community Centre,
Panchsheel Park, New Delhi – 110 017, India
Penguin Group (NZ), cnr Airborne and Rosedale Roads, Albany,
Auckland 1310, New Zealand (a division of Pearson New Zealand Ltd)
Penguin Books (South Africa) (Pty) Ltd, 24 Sturdee Avenue, Rosebank 2196, South Africa

Penguin Books Ltd, Registered Offices: 80 Strand, London WC2R ORL, England

www.penguin.com

This translation first published 1983
Reprinted with a revised Introduction, new Notes and Bibliography 2005

021

Printed and bound in Great Britain by Clays Ltd, Elcograf S.p.A.
Filmset in VIP Palatino

ISBN-13: 978–0–141–44143–6

www.greenpenguin.co.uk

dilectissimis pignoribus
Antoniae Justinoque
qui mirabilia Domini videant

CONTENTS

INTRODUCTION

When Leonardo da Vinci left Milan for France in 1499, he had an inventory made of his library. His books reflected his wide interests, and the depth of his reading. He owned several books on natural history, on the sphere, on the heavens. But out of the multitude of travel accounts Leonardo could have had, in MS or from the new printing press, the list records only the one: Mandeville's *Travels*. At about the same time, Columbus (according to Andrés Bernáldez' *Life*) was treating Mandeville with great seriousness as a source of information on China and the East while he prepared for his voyage; and in 1576 a copy of the *Travels* was with Frobisher as he nosed into Baffin Bay. The number of people who relied on the *Travels* for practical geographical information in the two centuries after it first appeared demands that we give it serious attention if we want to understand the late medieval and Renaissance mental picture of the world. But in 1605 Bishop Joseph Hall can speak of 'whetstone leasings [lies] of old Mandeville'; in 1640 Richard Brome can hang a satiric comedy (*The Antipodes*) designed for the popular theatre entirely on the book – which suggests just how widely it was known – and assume (rightly) that virtually nobody then would regard it seriously. The dismissive attitude to it that prevailed through most of the last century descends from this later tradition; but the *Travels'* astonishing popularity (continuing even after it had ceased to command respect as a work of information) can be shown to depend on genuine merits. Ironically, both the earlier uncritical acceptance and that later dismissal are based on a distorted view of what the author seems to have been trying to achieve.

1 The Book and its Author

The *Travels* first began circulating between 1356 and 1366. Originally written in French, by 1400 some version was available in every major European language; by 1500, the number of MSS was vast – including Czech, Danish, Dutch and Irish versions – and some three hundred survive. (For comparison, Polo's *Divisament dou Monde*, of *c*. 1298, is represented in about seventy.) The many early printed editions, *incunabula*,

9

indicate both the importance attached to it and its appeal to printers seeking profit in the new trade.

The MS history is extremely complicated. Briefly, the MSS divide into two groups, a Continental and an Insular version. (The Anglo-Norman variety of French was still current in English aristocratic circles.) The Insular version does not mention a story in the Continental which links the author with one Dr Jean de Bourgogne (author of an extant treatise *De Pestilentia*) and a wordy, industrious Liège notary, Jean d'Outremeuse. There is no serious doubt that d'Outremeuse handled a text and considerably influenced the scribal tradition of the Continental version, but there is not a shred of evidence to compel the conclusion that 'Mandeville' was either de Bourgogne's or d'Outremeuse's *nom de plume*, as was confidently suggested at the end of the nineteenth century. If d'Outremeuse is unreliable (as we know him to be from elsewhere) and if the references to de Bourgogne depend on d'Outremeuse, one might be inclined, with proper caution, to regard the earliest MSS of the Insular version as closer to the author's original. (The parent MS from which the Insular Version derives could of course have been written on the Continent.) But here is not the place to go into this complex matter[1] – and what I have just said makes Alexander the Great's cutting the Gordian knot look irresolute; the text I have chosen for this translation is one of the three early English translations – Cotton, Egerton (each represented by a single MS) and the unhappily named Defective (see p. 38) – from the Anglo-Norman of the Insular version. (All are extant in late fourteenth or early fifteenth century MSS.) Its relation to the others is briefly indicated below, pp. 35ff.

So who was Mandeville? Despite much scholarly ingenuity, nothing is known of the author apart from what he tells us or may be deduced from his book – and he is certainly creating a fictional *persona*. Josephine Bennett suggested he might have been a Mandeville of Black Notley in Essex: not impossible, but her evidence is unconvincing. Christiane Deluz broadly accepts the story of the MSS, arguing that he was a liberally educated noble. However, Dr Seymour (1994, p. 27) lists five conditions he deduces from the book any candidate for authorship must meet, and concluded (2002, p.173) that those conditions would be met by a Benedictine who had studied in Paris like Jean le Lonc, a Benedictine of St Bertin, whose compendium of books about the East seems certainly to have been related to the *Travels*.

Mandeville claims he was an English knight, and that he travelled from 1322 to 1356 (1332 to 1366 in some texts), during which time he saw service with the Sultan of Egypt and the Great Khan. These details range from the quite possible to the improbable but *just* possible. Nevertheless, the case for an English author is not unreasonable, and was strong enough for most of the English readers of the book to accept it without demur for centuries: the narrative is wholly consistent in its references to 'this country', 'our country', the discussion of the peculiarly English letters þ (*thorn*) and ȝ (*yogh*), the barnacle geese reputed to breed in Britain, and so on. The consistency of such details is persuasive.[2] The chronicler Thomas Walsingham, writing between 1370 and 1396, in his discussion of famous people connected with his abbey, St Albans, as Mandeville reputedly was, clearly accepted the author was English, and the abbey (which has a memorial to Mandeville) seems to have been one centre of dissemination for MSS of the *Travels*. Walsingham, of course, may simply be drawing on the story in the book. The original's French is no argument against English authorship: the natural language for literary endeavour of a secular (non-religious and non-scholarly) nature for an Englishman born in the early 1300s would be Anglo-Norman French – even if, like Henry of Lancaster (or John Gower) he felt the need to apologize for his handling of it.[3] But the really interesting question, not yet satisfactorily answered, is what conceivable motive the author had in so cleverly pretending to be English if he was not. And if he was not, then our opinion of his skill in his book must be the higher.

How far he travelled (if at all) is a similar problem. The post-Renaissance view of Mandeville sees him as the archetypal 'lying traveller'. (It is easy to forget that ideas of truth, and of what travellers' reports ought to do, change.) He claims to have travelled to China, though not, interestingly, as far as the Japan visited by Marco Polo in the late 1200s. Though very unusual, such journeys were not in themselves improbable. The Franciscans, such as Odoric of Pordenone or John of Plano de Carpini, and a few merchants, such as the Polos and Balducci Pegolotti, penetrated in some numbers during the period of Tartar hegemony – roughly the century after 1220 – to the Far East and lived to write their memoirs. But two factors have severely damaged Mandeville's credit. First, since the European voyages of discovery, we have a completely different picture of the world and no longer accept the stories of monsters and marvels that descended to the medieval mind from Pliny, Aethicus, Solinus and Herodotus, which were so expected – usual – that no account of the East that omitted them could be held to be serious. For a later age, if Mandeville reported them, then he was a liar. But this argument is weak; for what you see (and can write about) depends considerably on the conceptual and methodological structures you have in your mind. The fact that we see lepers as victims of a disease while ancient writers reported them, often second hand, as 'flatfaces' (or sufferers from elephantiasis as sciapods) depends on our respective assumptions. The twentieth-century cargo cults of the Pacific illustrate this: to us, a prosaic aeroplane, yet to a different mind – and equally 'truly' – a great silver bird bringing gifts from the gods. What Mandeville's first readers would have found convincing, confirming what 'everyone knew' was in the utter East, for us works in the opposite way. Second, Mandeville's dependence on a large number of earlier accounts of the East has been convincingly demonstrated: consequently, some have said roundly that Mandeville's longest journey was to the nearest library. But, again, not conclusive: the medieval convention – not only accepted but admired – of reworking 'olde feeldes' for 'newe corne', 'olde bokes' for 'newe science', the reliance on *auctoritas*, would make a book of this type that did *not* rely on others unusual in the extreme – and untrustworthy. 'Plagiarism' is a concept still centuries in the future; borrowing is an accepted, expected, practice, and Mandeville is working within a perfectly usual pattern. Marie de France, for example, reworks Robert of Flamborough's *Poenitentiale*, keeping the first person and thus claiming experiences she could not have had, without any unease.[4] More to the point, later travellers – such as Johann Schiltberger, captured after the debacle of the Nicopolis Crusade in 1396, about whose wanderings there is absolutely no doubt – demonstrably borrowed freely from Mandeville to flesh out their own accounts. Even the estimable Polo, like Herodotus before him, repeated hearsay and what he, and his readers, expected of the marvels at the margins of the known. Neither factor, then, rules out the possibility of Mandeville's having travelled. Indeed, some details just *could* be firsthand reporting. The story of Ypocras' (Hippocrates) daughter at Cos, for example, has no known source; yet Felix Fabri says it was current on the island when he visited it in 1483. Moreover, Mandeville says the walls of the Great Khan's palace were covered with the sweet-smelling skin of 'panthers' (p. 142), a detail not in his source Odoric of Pordenone, who mentions only leather. The detail is included for no obvious reason. Commentators have discoursed about the sweet smell the Bestiaries attached to the panther; but the red panda does smell of musk, and the Nepali word 'panda' could easily be misheard as the Latin *panthera*. Finally, it would be odd indeed if someone with such an interest in far countries should have found no way of getting at least as far as the Holy Land in a century when (just as on the Muslim Hajj to Mecca) relatively large numbers of people of all social classes used the pilgrim routes thither.[5] These were organized almost as comprehensively as the modern package tour – even to commercial renting to pilgrims of sleeping rolls and cooking utensils for the voyage from Venice by entrepreneurs who could be found in Piazza San Marco.[6]

The motives for going, then as now, were never entirely pure. Some just liked 'wandringe by the weye' – whatever Chaucer meant by that; some went out of genuine devotion; all looked for souvenirs. Amusingly, Mandeville reports a Saracen solution to problems of tourist pressure on ancient monuments identical to that adopted by many modern conservation bodies (p. 77). None of this, of course, proves Mandeville travelled; but equally one cannot entirely dismiss his claim. And if this man did *not* travel, our opinion of his literary ability must be the higher: his book conveys a superbly coherent illusion of a speaking voice talking of firsthand experience, even to the important (and often amusing) disclaimers when he cannot tell us something: 'Of Paradise I cannot speak properly, for I have not been there; and that I regret' (p. 184). Ironically, the more one questions Mandeville's truthfulness, the higher one must rate his literary artistry.

But these questions, though interesting, are relatively side-issues. Many people wrote travel narratives; only this one achieved an enormous, lasting popularity. The reasons for that popularity[7] and the influence it exerted must be sought in the nature of the book and how it treats its material – and in the handling of the audience's assumptions. To a modern reader, the form seems loose and inconsequential. This is deceptive. The journey narrative has the great advantage of being inclusive of many diverse elements (a quality greatly to medieval taste in literature as in scholarship – consider how popular were the *summa* and the compendium) and provides a basic structuring for the material against a landscape (in the first half of the book at least) geographically and politically recognizable to fourteenth-century eyes. At least in part, too, the narrative caters for the same sort of taste as the *Alexander Romances* and Prester John's letter (which latter had lost, by Mandeville's time, some of its initial political urgency). Mandeville uses elements of both. The language and form are accessible to a wide audience, and thus provide an ideal medium for a *haute vulgarisation* of authoritative 'geographical' thought. Mandeville was a serious writer, taking his matter from sources he believed (generally correctly) to be the best available; his book was as accurate and up to date an account of knowledge of the world as he knew how to make it. He deliberately integrates material of very different kinds not readily to be found elsewhere; but unlike the compendium writer – for example, Vincent of Beauvais, whose *Speculum Naturale* and *Historiale* he used – he does not just compile. One of his most remarkable and interesting achievements is to have

Introduction

Introduction

synthesized so many sources so that the joins do not show. He adapts
and shapes to fit his plan, unifying all with the stamp of a valuing sub-
jectivity. The medieval ideal of *lust* and *lore* – pleasure and instruction –
seems to be the goal. We should remember, too, the medieval (and
indeed Renaissance) assumption that all serious writing should have a
moral dimension discoverable by intellectual understanding penetrat-
ing the surface of the text. The earth, likewise, is to be understood as a lit-
eral place first; therefore we have the careful and authoritative account
of the size and shape of the earth; but it is also to be understood morally,
and so we have the curious story of the reproduction of the diamond followed by its moral significance from the lapidaries (pp. 118–19), or an
emphasis on there being a *significacio* for fish coming to land to be caught
(p. 133). We must not only know but judge experience: 'Let the man who
will, believe it; and leave him alone who will not' (p. 144). The medieval
view of the world, as of literature, was that it was polysemous, carrying
many meanings; the physical world itself was the *umbra* from which
Faith could be supported by Reason:

> Yit nevertheless we may haif knawlegeing
> Off God Almychtie, be his Creatouris . . .
> (Robert Henryson, *Morall Fabillis*, ll. 1650ff.)

Henryson's adaptation of Romans i, 19–20 converges with St Paul's
assertion that 'All that is written, is written for our profit.' And so
Mandeville's impeccable geographical thought (in the sense in which
we use the term 'geographical' in our methodology), despite its intrinsic
interest for us as the picture of the world that a well-educated medieval
man could have held, is only part of the *Travels'* importance, just as is the
delight 'to hear strange things' (p. 44) that Mandeville assumes in his
reader or hearer (p. 189).

It is really the difference in our mental maps and assumptions governed by them that makes a just assessment of Mandeville's impact in
his time and later so hard. We simply do not look at the world in the
same way. So it is worth pausing briefly to glance at medieval conceptions, and representations, of space: after all, a travel book can hardly
be indifferent to such things. While areas close to home – microspace –
might be precisely known and the relationship between places exactly
understood, and while this sort of knowledge might extend along main
lines of communication, clearly, without an overall agreed convention
for a descriptive or pictorial system, one will have an infinitude of more
or less overlapping but in the last analysis distinct spatial models. The
further from home, the less detailed the microspatial picture will be,

14

and the more the macrospatial, which will work on quite different principles, will come into operation. In Appendix II I have described the formula of the 'T in O' *mappae mundi*: such maps are useless as ways of finding one's way, but treat the world and the places and the events that occurred there as moral symbols placed on a land space symmetrically disposed round Jerusalem. On the macrospace they represent are inscribed the legends and marvels, the myths and monsters that are beyond the mental margins. Their importance is far more mnemonic and moral, and historical – within the linear model, itself moral, of Time from Creation to the Last Judgement that was usual till long after the Middle Ages – than descriptive or orientational. The distinction is illustrated by contrasting the sea charts of the Middle Ages, the portolans, which are perfectly satisfactory tools to find your way from one haven to another – across microspace – with *mappae mundi* like the Hereford Map: a map of moral history, where space becomes symbol.

This dichotomy is apparent in literature. The Canterbury Road Chaucer's pilgrims ride is microspace – even so, their journey is symbolic. But the landscape of romance, for example *King Alisaunder*, or the *Roman de toute chevalerie* of Thomas of Kent – or even the Arthurian romances – is not interested in physical sequence and detail: the focus is on the moral tests and prowess of the hero as he goes out into the macrospace. Mandeville's first chapters describe plausible routes to Jerusalem – the routes many followed. But the East is another matter: here we are in the world where symbol and reality are virtually indistinguishable. Thus it is meaningless to attempt, as editors did once upon a time, to plot Mandeville's journey on a modern map outline, for the rigid spatial relationships of the modern map, for us so important a part of the meaning of map conventions, are simply irrelevant. We easily forget how much the relatively modern inventions of coordinates and the compass rose unconsciously affect our modes of understanding our world. Even direction is vague to the medieval mind: north and south can be, as required, up or down. But that we see the world differently does not imply that the medieval model was in its time unworkable – clearly, it was not – nor that we are more 'right' than they were. Indeed, the root from which our way of thinking has grown lies in the work done in the medieval centuries. Mandeville's insistence that had he found company and shipping he too could have girdled the entire globe (and it is, incidentally, a modern slander that the medievals believed the earth to be flat) played, with his discussion of the Pole star, some important part in the dissemination of important geographical concepts and in preparing for the great voyages of the next century on which our world-view is partly based.

So, learned though it is, the book is not simply 'a compendium'. It also includes Romance elements and stories, which I discuss below. It shares to some degree that element, easily forgotten by us, in all Western writing about the East after 1164, when the *Letter of Prester John* began to circulate, of political interest in a strategic linking with the Tartars and Prester John against a menacing Islam. (This strategic concern was one of the three motives that spurred Prince Henry of Portugal to sponsor the voyages of discovery – and it is one reason he was so interested in Mandeville.) The book provides, too, a moral and political perspective for Europe (for example, pp. 149, 156). European assumptions of superiority in politics, law, virtue and religion are either directly or ironically challenged. And last, it is, at least partly, a careful and quite genuine pilgrim's devotional manual for the journey to the Holy Land. One owner of the Cotton text apparently so used it (see p. 22). Now these different genres, homogenized by the journey narrative, result in a complex and subtle book which can very easily make a fool of an inattentive or incautious reader. These elements, including the handling of sources, will need some discussion later, after we have looked in more detail at the structure and control of the book.

The tight categorical and proportional structuring of narrative, where everything relates to everything else, where balanced structure is an important clue to meaning, that we find in, for example, Dante, Gower or Chaucer, is largely lacking. There are, however, certain topics Mandeville refers to frequently – the insistence on Christians' unworthiness to possess Palestine, the corruption and complacency of the Western Church, the goodness in works of non-Christians. These are the thematic keys of the work. Almost exactly half-way through, the division is clearly marked between the parts dealing with the Holy Land and the Far East. Both parts open and close with a repeat of their first ideas – the ways to the Holy Land, and the division of the world by the four rivers of Paradise. The last pages echo the ideas of the prologue. The narrative is clearly signposted, the signposts marking divisions of the matter (for example, pp. 44, 103, 111, 188). I also see a thematic link between the repeated insistence on the inability of the Christians to take Palestine (not recognizing their need for moral and social reform before so doing) and the impossibility of Mandeville himself reaching the balm near Alexander's Trees of the Sun and Moon (p. 181, cf. p. 66), or the impossibility of great lords with all their power attaining to the Earthly Paradise (p. 185), because of the opposition presented by the very nature of the world. So a simple formal structure is supported by a thematic one.

In crucial places, the response of the audience is controlled by the intervention of a first-person voice. Though not as complex as, for example, Chaucer's, Gower's or Langland's *personae* – and after all, his aims and engagement with his audience were palpably different – Mandeville's *persona* is crucial. He sets him up as a somewhat sceptical reporter, firmly rooted in firsthand experience. He introduces him(self) with an engagingly modest protestation of his unworthiness, as an experienced pilgrim who travels in good company (p. 45); he possesses a thorn from the Crown of Thorns (a king's ransom!) and *implies* he was given it by the Byzantine Emperor; he served as a soldier with the Sultan, and was offered a princess in marriage – 'but I did not want to' (p. 59); he is experienced in the tests for good balm, and shows a sturdy independence of mind at the monastery of Saint Katherine on Sinai (pp. 66, 71). The Sultan gave him special letters of introduction ('to me he did a special favour', p. 80) to the Temple authorities. He has a 'private' talk with the Sultan (p. 107). He is ready to disclaim knowledge ('I never followed that route to Jerusalem, and so I cannot talk about it', p. 103). He is very plausible in relating what is supposedly his own experience in seeing the southern stars (p. 128). The diffident boasting is amusing; but gradually his trustworthiness as a guide for us in our response is built up. He is made to be detached about his own job as a narrator; he is cautious about the Ark on Ararat (pp. 113–14), and about the supposed cross of Dismas in Cyprus and other relics (pp. 46, 55). He is sensible about the pepper forests (in fact he contradicts his source, p. 123, because it is talking patent nonsense) and reflective about the problems of belief in unfamiliar material (p. 144). When going through the Vale Perilous, there is a semantic emphasis on seeming, illusion, fantasy – a distrust of his own cognition (p. 173) – and, by implication, ours, and our response to his material. Almost the last remark in the book is deliciously ironic: 'I shall cease telling of the different things I saw in those countries, so that those who desire to visit those countries may find enough new things to speak of for the solace and recreation of those whom it pleases to hear them' (p. 188). This *persona* can generate a neat ironic tone, sometimes simply by the positioning of a clause. I have already quoted his apology for not telling us about Paradise, but he did drink of the Well of Youth, and characteristically claims not the instant rejuvenation one would expect from the (interpolated) *Letter of Prester John* but 'ever since that time I have felt the better and healthier'. Going through the Vale Perilous (one of the stimuli, by the way, for Bunyan's

Valley of the Shadow) he and his companions were much afraid: 'We were more devout then than we ever were before or after' (p. 174). In Lamory, he reports the 'evil custom' of fattening children for the table; but our expected horror is pointed by the deadpan, sardonic positioning at the end of the paragraph of the simple remark: 'They say it is the best and sweetest flesh in the world' (p. 127). The statement that '[Hippopotami] eat men . . . no meat more readily' is carefully booby-trapped by the insertion of the clause 'whenever they can get them' (p. 167).

But most important are the occasions when the *persona* involves himself in dialogue. During his confidential talk with the Sultan his laconic unease introduces the Sultan's fluent indictment of Christian conduct, and he is wrongfooted at every turn (p. 108). This episode is comic in precisely the same way as the *persona* Gulliver is comic when talking to the King of Brobdingnag. But he can also be used not only to trigger a moral assessment of his own culture but to point out false values in others' – for example, his expostulation at the obscurantism of the monks on Mount Sinai (p. 71). Or he can modify our initial reactions in the direction of sense and understanding; for instance, when he asks Judas's question of the monk of Cassay (p. 139) who is feeding the animals, it elicits two things: the good organization of a state so that the poor do not exist and the fact that there is a rational explanation for a very odd act. (His source, Odoric, merely 'laughed heartily' at this pagan piety.) And is not that act exactly parallel to the European custom of Masses for the dead? At the Great Khan's court, the *persona* is confident that the marvels are not 'diabolic' as Odoric said, but capable of rational explanation on terms he can understand. And, finally, the *persona* can direct our moral response in a quite unambiguous way. The approval and admiration for the Gymnosophists is supported by a second reference to the important figure of Job (p. 180, cf. p. 115). All the accumulated authority of this figure is behind the remark 'we know not whom God loves nor whom He hates' – a generalized statement subsuming all the hinted warnings against too uncritical a judgement or too ready an acceptance of the unusual and strange. The creation of this credible *persona* is clearly an important element in the design of the book and a significant factor in its success. And while in the early versions the *persona* is carefully made to question and to refuse to give an opinion, as well as, occasionally, to affirm the truth of the material, it is very noticeable that later redactions are marked by a multiplication of truthclaims and asseverations, often in a style much more emphatic than what we find in the earlier – 'I, John Mandeville, saw this, and it is the truth.'

2 *The Sources and their Use*

We must now look at the sources used and the way they are handled. Apart from those mentioned above, there are important details and stories for which no source is known. Some, like the story of the Castle of the Sparrowhawk, have analogues that can be found in romances; some, like the story of the circumnavigation of the world, are without parallel. But Mandeville apparently used a lot of books:

Albert of Aix, *Historia Hierosolomitanae Expeditionis*
Caesarius of Heisterbach, *Dialogus Miraculorum*
Haiton of Armenia, *Fleurs des Histors d'Orient*
Jacopo de Voragine, *The Golden Legend*
Jacques de Vitry, *Historia Hierosolomitana*
John of Sacrobosco, *De Sphaera*
Odoric of Pordenone, *Itinerarium*
pseudo-Odoric, *De Terra Sancta*
William von Boldensele, *ltinerarium*
William of Tripoli, *De Statu Saracenorum*
The Letter of Prester John
Vincent of Beauvais, *Speculum Historiale* and *Speculum Naturale*,
    including extracts from John of Piano de Carpini, Pliny and Solinus;
Pilgrims' manuals
Alexander Romances, including 'Alexander's letter to Aristotle';
and, possibly:
Brunetto Latini, *Livre dou Tresor*
Burchard of Mount Sion, *Descriptio Terrae Sanctae*

Quite a reading list. Even allowing for the fact that several are gathered in Vincent of Beauvais's encyclopedia, and that many of the travel accounts occur conveniently in the compendium of travels made by Jean le Lonc of Ypres (which Mandeville quite possibly used), Mandeville still did a good deal of research. But the sources are used with quite remarkable assurance: there are certainly verbatim liftings (as there are in many medieval and Renaissance writers) but the joins are pretty seamless – one is never conscious of leaving one source and moving to another. Mandeville moves backwards and forwards between sources with complete confidence, dovetailing Haiton into Odoric and mixing in Vincent exactly as he requires.[8] To say this, however, suggests a mere scissors-and-paste job; the impressive thing is the freedom with which the sources have been altered and shaped. Where he found reported speech, it is often transposed into the more arresting direct – for example, when Mandeville reworks Haiton's story of the advice of the dying Great Khan (p. 148). Many elements are amplified with considerable ingenuity. Three examples will show the different levels on which this is done.

First, Odoric,[9] that homespun Odysseus, has one sentence (Yule, p. 114) on his trip on one of the stitched ships (see endnote to p. 120). Mandeville uses the story twice: once, briefly, in describing Ormuz (p. 120) – the right region for them, in fact; again, as a result of one of the many perils of the sea off Prester John's land. Odoric's single sentence is blown up into a circumstantial account, vastly more interesting, full of personal observation. Second, Odoric's story of the Vegetable Lamb of Tartary (Yule, p. 240f.): Mandeville again expands, and alters the whole tone of the incident. Odoric merely mentions an unusual 'melon' he has been told of, which story (he feels) may be true, as 'there are trees in Ireland which produce birds'. Mandeville's description is much more vivid: not only is the fruit described more fully, but also the persona is given a credible reaction, and – a nice touch – the Tartars to whom he describes the marvels of the West react with wonderment:

> There grows there a kind of fruit as big as gourds, and when it is ripe men open it and find inside an animal of flesh and blood and bone, like a little lamb without wool. And the people of that land eat the animal, and the fruit too. It is a great marvel. Nevertheless I said to them that it did not seem a very great marvel to me, for in my country, I said, there were trees which bore a fruit that became birds that could fly; men call them barnacle geese, and there is good meat on them . . . And when I told them this they marvelled greatly at it. (p. 165)

The *persona's* intervention emphasizes by implication one of Mandeville's key ideas: that the same Nature rules everywhere and what is impossible in Europe is impossible in Cathay. If the impossible seems to happen, either our knowledge or our interpretation is at fault. Just as the East looks odd to the West, the West looks odd to the East. Not many literary Westerners made that conceptual leap.

Finally, Odoric's journey through the Vale Perilous. His account demonstrates both the problem of assimilating new experience outside normal conceptual patterns, as mentioned above, and the essential qualities of his narrative. Unquestionably, however dull he was, Odoric was a man of great courage, and as truthful a reporter as he knew how to be. The singing sands of the deserts of Asia are quite beyond his previous experience, but the idea of devils is emphatically not; and so the noises and appearance of the Valley become supernatural and threatening:

I went through a certain valley which lieth by the River of Delights. I saw therein many dead corpses lying. And I heard also therein sundry kinds of music, but chiefly nakers [drums] which were marvellously played upon. And so great was the noise thereof that very great fear came upon me. Now, this valley is seven or eight miles long; and if any unbeliever enter therein he quitteth it never again, but perisheth incontinently. Yet I hesitated not to go in that I might see once for all what the matter was. And when I had gone in I saw there, as I have said, such numbers of corpses as no one without seeing it could deem it credible. And at one side of the valley, in the very rock, I beheld as it were the face of a man very great and terrible, so very terrible indeed that for my exceeding great fear my spirit seemed to die within me. Wherefore I made the sign of the cross. I ascended a hill of sand and looked about me. But nothing could I descry, only I still heard those nakers play which were played so marvellously. And when I got to the top of that hill I found there a great quantity of silver heaped up as it had been fishes' scales, and some of this I put into my bosom. But as I cared nought for it, and was at the same time in fear lest it should be a snare to hinder my escape, I cast it all down again to the ground. And so by God's grace I came forth scathless. Then all the Saracens,[10] when they heard of this, showed me great worship, saying I was a baptized and holy man. But those who had perished in that valley they said belonged to the devil. (Yule, pp. 262–6)

Mandeville's version (pp. 173–4) is obviously much expanded, particularly in the development of details. But, crucially, he has made the crossing of the Vale a moral test, of covetousness – the sin which in the first pages of the book, and in the story of the Watching of the Sparrowhawk (p. 112) he makes the besetting sin of Western Christendom. Odoric's picking up and then casting away of the silver is developed into a warning – for some fail the test. Odoric, somewhat complacently, relies for safety merely on his profession of faith; Mandeville insists that to be safe even Christians must be 'firm in the faith . . . be cleanly confessed and absolved' and must 'bless themselves with the sign of the Cross'. Mandeville not only questions the evidence of the senses and judgement based on them – a serious enough issue in itself, and one not insignificant as a motif in the whole book; he also, with some finesse, suggests that he was accompanied by two Franciscans (Odoric was a Franciscan . . .) who sought safety in numbers! Mandeville tempers Odoric's seriousness with a rather pointed humour. Clearly the passage is the work of an extremely competent writer, who knew exactly what he wanted.

This shrewd judgement in the handling of sources cannot, of course, be separated from the use of the *persona*. Too emphatic a commitment to the personal experience of everything would diminish returns rapidly; Mandeville knew that. So the sources are not always *amplified* and, so to speak, re-voiced, but sometimes, as in the case of Haiton's personal experience of the Land of Darkness, abbreviated and objectified. What holds the whole collection of material from many disparate sources together is the device of the journey framework, which provides a plausible sequential order, and the *persona*'s never intrusive but occasionally crucial interventions and reactions.

3 Confounding Expectations: The Arguments of the Travels

The literary modes (and the expectations they arouse) used in this book are an unusual mixture. The hearer or reader initially might easily assume he or she is embarking on a devotional guide, a manual of the pilgrim voyage to the Holy Land: there are many examples in the period. There are striking methodological and stylistic parallels between Mandeville's description of Jerusalem's relics and places and the description of those of Rome and Jerusalem in the pilgrims' manuals, for example *The Stacions of Rome* or the *Informacõn for Pylgrymes into the Holy Londe*, printed by de Worde in 1498. This sort of book was useful as an aide-memoire to the returned pilgrim – a reminder, perhaps, of a period of spiritual intensity now fading into oblivion – a guidebook for the new, and a fireside voyage for the sedentary. In all three cases there was some devotional response – at the lowest level, the detailed recalling of the events and places that witnessed the individual reader's salvation. The actual place is frequently used as a mnemonic stimulus for a biblical text and for a figuring of the Passion.[11] Wherever Mandeville is dealing with the Holy Land or the Saints of the Church and their miracles, this stylistic mode is used. Sometimes, indeed, the details are so vividly filled in – as in the story of Samson, or the detail about the auger hole in the Ark whence the Devil escaped (pp. 57, 113) – that one wonders whether Mandeville is also drawing on another religious mode that exploited the vividness of circumstantial detail, the mystery play. And just as Mandeville certainly used pilgrims' manuals, a number of later works – some much later – borrowed Mandeville's remarks and incorporated them into devotional guides (for example, *The Pylgrymage of Sir Richard Guylford to the Holy Land A.D.* 1506, and the narrative based on it, *The Pylgrymage of Sir Richard Torkyngton*, 1517). One owner of the Cotton text (see p. 37) of the *Travels* tore out those pages that could be used as a pilgrim guide – perhaps so to use them. (The style and tone decorous to this sort of writing is astonishingly durable, still being traceable in Henry Maundrell's *A Journey from Aleppo to Jerusalem at Easter*, 1697.) Of course, the pilgrimage is itself a metaphor for man's earthly life as a journey to the Heavenly Jerusalem, and this idea, specifically picked up in the last words of the book, casts an ironic light on Mandeville's claim to be writing in furtherance of a crusade. (A crusade is a sort of armed pilgrimage, of course.) For the 'Land of Promise' – earthly or heavenly – can only be won if Christians reform themselves according to the truth they profess. (There is an ironic backward glance at Christian pilgrimage when Mandeville speaks of the devout pilgrims to the shrine of the Juggernaut, pp. 125–6.) And when appropriate, Mandeville can adopt the quite recognizable style of the sermon (e.g. p. 180, with its careful array of biblical texts). This devotional interest is accompanied by a great deal of practical advice on the various routes, of observations on tourist attractions and on a tourist vandalism familiar to us today (pp. 77, 99). A choice of which pilgrimage to follow could quite sensibly be based on Mandeville's description of the different journeys.

But the first half of the book, on the ways to Jerusalem, does not deal only with devotional material. Here, as later, the narrative is frequently suspended by digressions into other modes. Mandeville liked a good story, and he took them from elsewhere as well as the appropriate *Golden Legend*.[12] They rarely remain only stories. The lurid mixture of necrophilia and disaster in the story (current in the chroniclers) of the 'Bane of Satalye' – Adalia in Turkey (p. 55) – is used not simply to account for the *ville engloutie* which fascinated many pilgrims but to make a moral point about the consequences of man's sin in the macrocosm. The charming story of the Field of Flowers is similar to one told of Abraham's daughter; it is paralleled in Machaut's *Dit du Lion* (1342) and has similarities to the Apocryphal legend of Susanna. Mandeville, however, uses it rather like a *Golden Legend* story, to account – a 'just so' story! – for the existence of roses and to demonstrate the saving grace of God. The Watching of the Sparrowhawk (pp. 112–13) is a splendidly told story,[13] which as well as being diverting explores personal moral and ethical choice and behaviour. Later, the Old Man of the Mountains – historically, he founded the extreme Muslim sect of the Hashishi'yun or Assassins – is worked up from Odoric to emphasize the mechanically engineered deceit of his fake Paradise. Europe had heard enough of him to be fascinated by *how* he got his suicidal assassination squads to work – and the story still has a depressingly familiar topicality. Similarly, the long-nailed Mandarin, whom Mandeville again took from Odoric, is first made much more vividly voluptuous and then is set up as an icon of gluttony. (He reappears in *The Further Adventures of Robinson Crusoe*: Defoe trawled widely for that book, and Mandeville was one of his sources.) So the stories generally are used to demand a moral response from the audience. Some actually do not need overt moralizing; the well-known ones, such as the story of the 'hills of gold that pismires

[ants] keep' (p. 183) automatically symbolize the foolish industry of men working to gather for themselves what they cannot possess and another enjoys. The digressions, then, are functional supporters of the central ideas of the book.

Those central ideas spring essentially from two concerns: the moral state of Christendom, and the nature of the world we inhabit. Paul Hamelius, one of the earlier editors of the Cotton text, was so impressed by the remarks about Christendom that he saw the *Travels* as no more than 'an anti-papal pamphlet in disguise'. (He also with unwarranted lack of reserve, or evidence, attributed it to Jean d'Outremeuse.) This is reductive to a degree of a very complex book, and virtually every writer in this century (even the churchmen) forcefully attacks the abuses of the Church. But while Mandeville is certainly cool towards the papacy – so were many, at a time when the Avignon Popes were in a deeply compromised political position – his more important target seem to be overconfidence in European moral and religious superiority to the rest of the world. I referred above to Mandeville's insistence on the need for moral reform before Christians can hope to possess the holy places. First, it is set out clearly in the prologue: the scheme of salvation has been set up, yet 'pride, envy and covetousness have so inflamed the hearts of lords of the world that they are more busy to disinherit their neighbours than to lay claim to or conquer their own rightful inheritance'. The common people are left leaderless, like sheep without a shepherd. Social divisions and unrest have a moral origin. The issue returns briefly, as a hope for eventual reform, in the most appropriate place, the chapter on Jerusalem (p. 77). Then Mandeville attacks from a different angle. The *persona* is made to suffer the Sultan's comprehensive attack on the gap between Christendom's profession and its practice. He catalogues instances of all the sins, and castigates the behaviour of all three of the Estates – those who work, those who fight and those who pray (p. 107). Direct speech, and making the speaker a Muslim who condemns Christians on Christian terms, increases the force of this. We are made to see the attack as an appraisal from outside the Christian sensibility and *données* of the *persona* – in fact, we feel his embarrassment. Furthermore, the Saracens, benighted as they are, administer justice better than Christians: 'They say that no man should have audience of a prince without leaving happier than he came thither' (p. 61). (This may be deliberate irony: Pope Clement VI, the most pro-French of the Avignon Popes, who had died just before Mandeville started to write, used to say this of his own role.) The pagan monk of Cassay indicates a social system more efficient in preventing poverty than a religion that specifically honours the poor. The 'Bragmans' (Brahmins) take the idea further; here is a detailed account of a people not Christian yet living lives which, in terms of works, Christians ought to envy. The passage (pp. 178–9) is full of echoes of Dominical injunctions. Alexander is said to have wanted to conquer these folk, and Mandeville uses their traditional reply to attack the vainglory and deceitfulness of Western values. Alexander, like the *persona* earlier, is sent away with his tail between his legs. Mandeville is deliberately setting up more or less differing mirror societies as a commentary on Christian practices and failings – just as, indeed, Utopian fiction was later to be employed, often using Mandeville's own travel motif (for example, More's *Utopia* of 1516 itself, or Bishop Hall's *Mundus Alter et Idem*, 1605). The attack starts destructively but gradually becomes more and more idealistic, finally culminating in the deliberate repetition of the account of the virtuous Bragmans in the paradisal innocence (symbolized, as often in medieval art, by nakedness) of Gymnoscriphe (the land of the Gymnosophistae; pp. 179–80). In the process, the good, peaceful government of the Chinese is used as a contrast to the internecine quarrels of Europeans; Prester John's kingdom is the ideal Christian state; the alms-giving of the Saracens challenges the moral superiority of Europe. The account of suttee is used to show that pagans take Heaven more seriously than Christians, and the horrific piety of the pilgrims to the Juggernaut (pp. 125–6) first shocks by its violence, and then by its direct moral: 'And truly they suffer so much pain and mortification of their bodies for love of that idol that hardly would any Christian man suffer the half – nay, not a tenth – for love of Our Lord Jesus Christ.'

This general critique is supported by detailed criticism of the Roman Church. Those who should be the shepherds are specifically criticized. The manner can vary from the open 'For now is simony crowned like a king in Holy Church' to the more oblique suggestion, the thrust of which is pointed by the positioning of the clause and the falter in the rhythm: 'They sell benefices of Holy Church, and so do men in other places.' Both these examples come from the generally accurate account of Greek Orthodoxy, the first of many descriptions of different rites and religions. The summary of the Greek position is remarkably neutral at a time of strained relations with Byzantium. Mandeville quotes without comment a letter of the Greeks to Pope John XXII accusing the papacy of avarice and damning Roman claims to universal authority. It is difficult to see how this would not remind his audience of Boniface VIII's Bull *Unam Sanctam* of 1302, which, building on Innocent III's restatement in 1215 that *nulla salus extra ecclesiam* – 'there is no salvation outside the

church' – did 'declare, say, define, and pronounce that it is wholly necessary for the salvation of every human creature to be subject to the
Roman Pontiff'. His silence suggests approval of the Pope getting his
comeuppance. Similarly, the Jacobites practise a real devotion, despite
their not using 'the additions of the popes, which our priests are accustomed to use at Mass' (p. 79). The Tibetans have a religious leader
(p. 186), 'the Pope of their religion, whom they call Lobassi . . . and all the
priests and ministers of the idols are obedient to him'; the sentence and
the paragraph close with the deliciously sardonic phrase 'as our priests
are to our Pope' – this, in the century of the Babylonish Captivity![14]

The obverse of this critical look at western Christendom is apparent in
the attitude to other religions and societies. His accuracy and lack of
animus in the accounts of the Eastern Churches and Islam are quite
untypical of the period. Despite centuries of contact and trade, it was not
only in 'popular' writing that Saracens were seen, with a total ignoring
of their theology, as virtual devils incarnate. The miracle plays, and
romances like *The Sowdone of Babyloine*, echo the standard idea Lydgate
repeats of Muhammad as a false prophet, glutton and necromancer (*Fall
of Princes*, IX, 53ff.). The scholars (some Mandeville's sources), despite
odd exceptions like Abelard, William of Malmesbury and Roger Bacon,
are rarely better. Few men studied Islamic books at all deeply; those who
did, such as Ramón Lull and Ricold of Monte Croce (who could both
preach in Arabic), either carried little weight or confirmed the prejudices
of their audience. Lull's agonized vision of a vast army of souls trooping
down to Hell for want of Christian doctrine led him to plead at the
Council of Vienne (1315) for centres of Islamic study; the plea was
ignored, and even Lull comes round to advocating military force. Ricold
used his learning to seek points of difference, writing mere polemic.
Jacques de Vitry, Bishop of Acre, shows complete misunderstanding of
Muslim theology; even the remarkably fair-minded Burchard of Mount
Sion gives a less neutral account than Mandeville. The same intolerant
ignorance extends to other religions and peoples; John of Piano de
Carpini, Mandeville's source on the Tartars, loathed them; Ricold,
despite wide travels, abuses them, and William of Rubruck saw all Eastern religions as diabolic aberrations. The politic Greek was distrusted
(not without reason); nevertheless it is chilling to find the gentle
Burchard recommending the seizing of Constantinople and the burning
of all dubious books. Ludolf von Suchem emphasizes that the Pope has
authorized the forcible dispossession of Greeks from their lands and
their being sold as cattle. Now it is fair to object that all these writers are
clerics and have, to some extent necessarily, a *parti pris* position; but else-

where it is clear from the silence that tolerant understanding is not even considered. Gower, perhaps, reveals moral unease at the idea of a crusade (*Confessio Amantis*, III, 2488–96), as did Wiclif; and Langland's Anima hopes Saracens and Jews will alike be saved (*Piers Plowman*, B, 382ff., 488ff., 530ff.). But that is as far as it goes. There is nothing comparable to the Muslim Averroës' assertion that God is worshipped satisfactorily in many ways; indeed, it would have been, strictly, rank heresy.

The importance of Mandeville's position has been largely overlooked. The imaginative leap necessary for his openness is itself remarkable; and because the book was so widely read, many would get their first reasonably accurate account of the Koran from it. His summary of Muslim attitudes to Jesus and Muhammad is fair, sensible and detailed. (It is noticeable how this balance and openness was coarsened, even reversed, in later reworkings of the *Travels*.) Similarly, he treats the Greeks, the Muslims, the Jacobites and the Bragmans as interesting and honourable and worthy of sympathetic respect, not merely as sticks with which to beat European complacency. Diverging from his source, de Vitry, on the Jacobites and Syrians, he describes their rites neutrally, supports their doctrine of confession with a goodly array of biblical texts (pp. 97–8) and concludes merely with the sentence – astonishing in its period – 'all their differences would be too much to relate'. Most of his contemporaries would have revelled in extended castigation of such variance.

The descriptions of Far Eastern cults and societies show the same willingness radically to redirect his source. Odoric was particularly upset by the cannibalism and sexual promiscuity of Lamory: 'It is an evil and a pestilent generation', he cries (Yule, p. 127). But Mandeville delights in expanding the details and provides a biblical text to justify the sexual licence – 'Increase and multiply and fill the earth' (p. 127). Thus he forces his audience to justify the opposite standards they take for granted. He can so easily climb inside the skin of a man brought up in a totally different, even if invented, culture that the preconceptions of Europe must necessarily be questioned. Perhaps the best example of this redirection of material and consequent upending of European religious assumptions is Mandeville's interpolation (drawing, possibly, on Isidore of Seville) in Odoric's account of Tana. Odoric saw only 'idolaters'; Mandeville saw 'a variety of religions' (p. 121) and introduces a long discussion of the philosophical and cult difference between an image ('simulacre') and an idol. It is conducted resourcefully and intelligently, and allows him to view human sacrifice and the worship of the ox with some sympathy. Just because we might be revolted by Jainism, or necrophagy, or the strange use of one's ancestors' skulls in Tibet, does not mean that there is not real piety in the actions. The clear implication is that the intention to worship is more important than any failing in the cult itself. Odoric's 'marvellous and beastly customs' hide universal man. The crucial idea, that men behave rationally according to their lights, is the key to understanding how Mandeville treats all other strange societies. Just because the society of Amazons reverses all our social norms, it does not mean it will not work: and, ironically, Mandeville is at pains to stress that the security of Europe depends on those Amazons, who upend all European ideas of gender roles and proper sexual relations, keeping guard (p. 166) over the Lost Ten Tribes, Gog and Magog, whom Alexander imprisoned, and who will overrun the world in the Last Days.

All these threads of tolerance, understanding, charity and questioning are woven together in a crucial passage linking those Bragmans, who live well by works, with the virtuous pagan Job (p. 180): 'And even if these people do not have the articles of our faith, nevertheless I believe that because of their good faith that they have by nature, and *their good intent* [my italics], God loves them well and is well pleased by their manner of life, as He was with Job, who was a pagan. For we know not whom God loves nor whom He hates.' Not only does that passage carry a warning of the fallibility of human judgement, it is also the culmination of a series of equivocal glances at the doctrine of 'no salvation outside the Church'.

The premise on which Mandeville seems to be working is that the world, however marvellous, is comprehensible by reason. So the final topic we must briefly mention is Mandeville's idea of nature. Nature is a mirror of providence, a reliable guide to understanding. The Dead Sea (p. 89) has qualities apparently 'against nature', yet those qualities are consequences of sin 'against nature', and designed by God so that man's mind by contemplation of the marvel will understand the sterile denial of nature implicit in all sin. (The *Gawain* poet uses the Dead Sea in this way too.)[15] First appearances are a dubious basis for judgement; the pygmies (p. 140) cannot be dismissed as the freaks their appearance might suggest; they are 'very clever, and can judge between good and evil'. So with the dog-headed men who worship the ox (pp. 134–5). This reinserts them into what St Augustine called the 'Family of Adam' and therefore, however bizarre, redeemable. The 'monsters of men', the blemmyes, sciapods (p. 137) and so on whose conceptual lineage reaches back at least to Pliny, are crammed into a single paragraph as 'too numerous to relate', and given much less sensational weight than in most of the sources. They are made to seem in context a mere matter-of-fact feature of the human geography of those regions. Throughout the book there is the implication that nature is ultimately rational. A necessary consequence of this insight that the marvellous is explicable is that men may have confidence the world behaves according to the same rules wherever they travel. And, if they have company and shipping, they can travel everywhere.

The *Travels*, then, is a complex and thoughtful, even radical, book, executed with skill of a high order. Its diverse source material has been made to serve a unified purpose, controlled successfully by clever manipulation of the reader's response. Its immediate popularity rested on its meeting a number of tastes – the interest in the mysterious East, the desire for devotional Baedekers and its provision of a very considerable amount of information. But that popularity could not have been achieved and sustained had the book not had that panache which distinguishes the outstanding from the merely competent. I think much of that continuing attraction lies in the credibility of the *persona's* good sense and good nature. Mandeville, whoever he was, old, certainly, and infirm (and perhaps, too, travel-worn), deserves the prayers he asks for.

4 *The Career of the* Travels

Up to 1750 only Chaucer among other fourteenth-century English works has a comparably large and constant body of readers, and Mandeville's was a more heterogeneous body than Chaucer's, and his reputation more complex. The lack of any certain biographical detail in the earliest texts, or elsewhere, allowed the insertion of such details in growing numbers as time went on, and Mandeville as the doyen of modern travellers – as on Samuel Purchas's title page in 1625 – just had to have a biography. But all old authors and their books suffer the vicissitudes of reputation, and the differing estimates held of a book reveal quite as much about the readers as they do of the book. The response to and use of the *Travels* can illustrate the assumptions, values and perceptions of a given period. There is, unfortunately, not space to go into this entertaining question here. But one can stress that significant shifts in the reputation and use made of the *Travels* need seeing in a wider context. All we can now do is sketch the importance of the *Travels* in Renaissance geographical thought and discovery, and its literary influence.

The happy accident of its being written first in French ensured that it immediately acquired a European readership as well as an English one. By the 1370s the Insular and Continental versions of the book had begun to diverge, with substantial additions in the version in which Jean d'Outremeuse may have had a hand. Within a hundred years of its writing the rapid proliferation of MSS made it available in most countries of Europe; the early translation into Latin – the language, significantly, of scholarship, and thus an indicator of how some early readers felt about its material – allowed it to cross any remaining linguistic boundaries. These MSS do, of course, show a greater or lesser degree of adaptation and what used to be called 'contamination'. Some of them are not so much copies as versions, made for special interests, and it is perhaps worth reminding ourselves that our concepts of the integrity of a text are only just being invented in Mandeville's period. Indeed, it is useful to recognize the applicability of the concept Paul Zumthor called *mouvance*, where a book is continuously recreated in transmission, each recreation spawning others germane to the imperatives of that particular writer or intended audience. Later versions of Mandeville get further and further away from the nuances and values of the original; even as early as the fifteenth century, the *Travels* is reworked as the equivalent of a coarse comic strip. The progressive amplification (or abbreviation), sensationalization and corruption of versions is a major problem in assessing Mandeville's influence on the mind of Europe.[16]

In most cases it is impossible to say which version – which isotope, to use Iain Higgins's helpful image – of Mandeville anyone read, and one must always bear in mind the differences in content between the many versions. However, the spread of the printing press probably tended to standardize the text in general circulation in any country on the first copy text used; thus in England after Pynson's edition of the Defective version (1496) (see p. 38), all subsequent printed editions known in English of the *Travels* in the sixteenth century are offshoots of Defective, and the same process is repeated after the 1478 and 1481 Augsburg editions of Anton Sorg, or the 1480 Milan edition of Comeno. The earliness of these printings is remarkable: before 1500 eight German printings are known, seven French, twelve Italian, four Latin, two Dutch and two English. There are Czech and Spanish editions before 1520. Clearly there was money as well as interest in Mandeville.

An assessment of Mandeville, then, can be based only on an early text of good authority; an assessment of his later influence, by contrast, has to take into account the divergent versions circulating under the same name. Very early on in its manuscript career, the *Travels* was included in the compendia, often collections of important texts on a particular topic. It was included, with Odoric of Pordenone and Marco Polo, in the sumptuously illuminated *Livre de Merveilles* of 1403, an authoritative collection of material on the East made for Jean sans Peur of Burgundy. Michel Velser's German translation, made *c.* 1393, is included in an MS miscellany of astronomical works, presumably because the compiler thought the account of the Pole star important. That practical interest lasts a long time: a couple of centuries later, when Hakluyt made his first edition of the *Principall Navigations* (1589), which was specifically gathered to provide a ready fund of information for his countrymen aspiring to commercial exploits in the Orient – the book is both commercial inducement and geographical information – he includes Mandeville in the version known as the Latin Vulgate (a Continental text). Hakluyt extolled the scholarship and good sense of Sir John, yet uneasily suggests that the text has been corrupted by scribes and printers – neither blanket acceptance nor rejection of the text as fact will do, and only the discerning mind will find it useful. Hakluyt's view of Mandeville's usefulness changed radically as the next ten years saw a flood of information about the New World reaching England from English travellers and translated Spanish sources, and he dropped Mandeville from his second edition (1598–1600). But Samuel Purchas, a most eager Elisha, clawed Hakluyt's mantle down on himself in his publication of *Purchas his Pilgrimes* (1625) – a text which Coleridge loved. His collection is less concerned than Hakluyt's with trade statistics and discovery than with picturesque descriptions and theological and missionary musings. A heavily cut Mandeville appears, and his portrait appears on the title page with Columbus and King Solomon and others who have performed or sponsored great journeys. It is important that two writers, one ostensibly following the other, should, in so short a time, use Mandeville for such different purposes. The *Travels* was also pillaged, extracted or epitomized in such seminal books as the *Nuremberg Chronicle* (1493) and Münster's *Cosmographia* (1544), chiefly for its information on the East. Much of Mandeville's material then flows indirectly through these conduits, as well as directly, into the sum of European knowledge in the Renaissance.

The practical importance of this sort of dissemination cannot be discounted. The *Travels* was anthologized because it was authoritative; it was given new authority by being anthologized, and so it gets into the hands of men who over two centuries drove the European discovery of the East and of America. The *Travels* was used as a source in the outstanding Catalan Atlas of 1375. Abraham Cresques made this atlas for Peter III of Aragon, who was very interested indeed in reports of the East and Prester John, and it incorporates the very latest geographical knowledge. The *Travels* again seems to have been used (as Polo was not) in the Andrea Bianco map of 1434. And the so-called 'Behaim' globe made in Nuremberg in 1492 – the earliest to have survived – quotes Mandeville wholesale, with great respect. Now this is crucial: these maps represent the mental picture of the world the explorers took with them and, clearly, the basis on which their backers financed them.

Prince Henry of Portugal is not unique in being interested strategically, commerically and religiously in the East, nor in having his agents scour Europe for information on the East. The hard-headed German commercial empire of the Fuggers put money into these voyages, and one wonders whether the Augsburg editions of the *Travels* may have some connection with Fugger interest. (It is indeed a curious coincidence that right up to the end of the sixteenth century there are noticeable increases in the frequency of known editions of the *Travels* coinciding with major voyages of exploration.) Several important explorers can be shown to have used Mandeville as one of their sources of information – for example, the principal sources of Columbus's ideas were Polo, Mandeville and Ptolemy. It may indeed be that Columbus's determination to sail west to Cathay was fuelled by Mandeville's story of circumnavigation. Frobisher, in his attempt on the North West Passage, took with him a copy of Mandeville for its information on China. The expectations aroused by Mandeville led the first discoverers to see the New World not objectively but in preconceived terms: Columbus seems, from surviving letters, to have died believing he had found islands off Mandeville's Cathay. Even after America was known to be a new continent, the old legends were still operative, merely being transferred to the unknown interior. When the native Amerindian myth of the regenerative land of Bimini reached the ears of the first Spanish settlers, they eagerly grafted on to it the story of Mandeville's Well of Youth, of which Mandeville had drunk three times, and Ponce de Leon led two expeditions, in 1513 and 1521, to look for it. (They found themselves in Florida instead.) The English descriptions of the Roanoke voyages, again, are full of the *topoi* of the travel literature of the past, and (probably unconsciously) exploit the conceptual and semantic parameters of the icons of innocence from the Bragmans to the Earthly Paradise. Sir Walter Raleigh's *Discoverie of the Empyre of Guiana* (1596) shows clearly his heavy conceptual dependence on these old accounts of the wonders of the East, and, indeed, he quotes Mandeville by name. Once again, the new is misunderstood in terms of the old, as we see with Odoric; and seeking Cathay to satisfy the dreams of their fathers, the voyagers found an image of Paradise for their children.

It is somewhat oversimple to look at the geographical influence of

Mandeville in this way. It is nevertheless doubly useful. First, it shows a deliberate and widespread use of only a *part* of what we saw above as the totality of meaning of the *Travels;* second, the effect of the explosion of geographical knowledge resulting partly from Mandeville and his confident and unusual insistence that the world was everywhere traversable radically altered the esteem in which the book was held and the uses to which it could be put. Although Richard Willes, in his *Historie of Travaile* (1577), can still treat Mandeville as a prime authority, this is becoming less and less possible. Gerard Mercator in that same year, in a letter, accepted Mandeville's story of his circumnavigation (and used him as a source for his map) but seriously questioned his judgement in reporting what he saw – an unease felt, as noted above, by Hakluyt. Although Mandeville's material still found its way into scientific compilations, it did so less and less frequently. By about 1600, his reputation has fallen sharply; he is now outdated by new knowledge and his work often treated with contempt. There are, however, supplementary reasons for this.

Just as the *Travels'* real nature had been adapted to serve the interests of the learned, so it was reworked for other partialities. At the same time that Prince Henry was using it for political and commercial information, it was available in re-editings as a book merely of wonders, as a devotional guide, as a romance. Part (much cut) was put into heavy-footed octosyllabic verse at about the end of the fifteenth century, as a popular account of the East, strongly pointed with a muscle-bound Christianity; another late-fifteenth-century ancestor of McGonagall made a nearly complete version in coarse octosyllabics, as a sort of popular Romance (the *Metrical Version*) incorporating many other legendary wonders. Everything is sensationalized, and the original delicate balance between matter and treatment has completely gone. The *Metrical Version* points firmly to the much later career of the book as a chapbook for children; its popular appeal is enhanced by the dragging in of regular stars like Alexander and the Nine Worthies.

So, by the end of the fifteenth century, 'Mandeville' could mean many different things to different people – or to the same person at the same time. The process intensifies. William Warner in 1586 published his first version of *Albion's England*, an account – much expanded in later editions – in fourteener verse of mythical English history down to the voyages of his time. In Books XI and XII he interlards it with a sugary romance in which Mandeville's travels are reduced to knight errantry resulting from an unhappy love affair. *Albion's England* seems to have been an influential source for the Elizabethan dramatists and also for Milton. It must have been difficult to have taken Mandeville seriously as a source of information or anything else when Warner's bland fourteeners plodded into your consciousness.

It would be even more difficult if you had seen the play of Mandeville which ran fairly successfully in the 1590s; if, as I suspect, the source was Warner and it is to this play Nashe refers in his *Nashes Lenten Stuffe* (1599), the prospect of such vapid drama is alarming. Clearly, by the end of the century, the knight is an almost mythical figure, the archetypal traveller, the grandfather of lies that are like truth. It is exactly in this way that Richard Brome's comedy *The Antipodes* (played 1636) regards him – and the whole comedy depends on the theatre audience knowing not only who Mandeville was but even some details of the book. Significantly, his name can even be used in a book title: *The Spanish Mandeuile of Miracles* (1600), the title given to the translation of Antonio de Torquemada's *Jardin de Flores Curiosas* (1570). The multiple Mandeville tradition plus the revolution in knowledge of the world finally killed the book's serious career as a work of information – even though as late as the eighteenth century we find the odd anomalies of Dr Johnson recommending it to a friend for information on China, and a catchpenny re-editing (claiming Mandeville set out in 1732!) with the travels of the excellent Jonas Hanway and Lionel Wafer issued about 1760 by a consortium of London publishers. Nevertheless, illustrated printed editions and chapbook versions still continue to be made and sold. The knowledge of the *Travels* remains general; the attitude to it changes irrevocably.

It is a labour of very doubtful value to seek out specific borrowings from Mandeville in other authors. It can be done, and a list of Mandeville's debtors, from the *Gawain* poet to Coleridge, is huge. The really interesting thing, which we can here touch on only briefly, is how the *Travels* as a whole fertilized something already in a writer's mind and helped it to fruit. For example, the development of Mandeville's use of 'mirror' societies was clearly a most useful tool for Saint Thomas More, whose *Utopia* (1516) is the parent of all subsequent writing in that important mode. It is significant how often satiric or moral utopias of the sixteenth or seventeenth centuries borrow details and techniques from the *Travels*. Mandeville is the first fully to develop the travel-fiction form; it was enthusiastically adopted not only by More, but also by Rabelais, by Joseph Hall, by Richard Head – whose debt in *The English Rogue* (1671) to Mandeville is large – and by Defoe and Swift. (Oddly enough, the 'I' of *Robinson Crusoe* – especially in *The Further Adventures* – and of *Gulliver's Travels* both seem close to the *persona* of the *Travels*;

Robinson Crusoe appeared in 1719, *Gulliver* in 1725 and the Cotton text of Mandeville in 1725.) Interestingly, such travel fiction depends on complicity between reader and author in taking for granted that what is consistently presented as truth is in fact fiction, and such a sophistication is, I feel, present to some degree in the *Travels*. The final example of this curious symbiosis between the *Travels'* nature and the interests and assumptions of various ages is in fact the beginning of a totally new development in the reading of the *Travels* in the eighteenth century. In the 6 November 1711 issue of the *Spectator*, Addison sounds for the first time the note that will resound in *Les Natchez* and, modulated, in *Ivanhoe*, the 'delight in contemplating those Virtues which are wild and uncultivated'. Steele, in *The Tatler* No. 254 (1710), connects this half-moralizing taste for the outlandish with an escapist delight in travel-books – especially Mandeville: 'all is enchanted ground and Fairyland'.[17]

Here is a revolution indeed! No moral disapproval of the lying traveller, only a delight in fiction as a safe escape. Here is the germ of that curiously sentimental and patronizing early-eighteenth-century delight in old books simply because they are old – a germ that grew into the foundations of serious medieval scholarship as we know it. The publication of the Cotton text in 1725 – the first scholar's text – could hardly have happened without the presence of this taste; and it is extremely significant in itself. For Mandeville is now in the province of the scholar, the dilettante and the bibliophile; the chapbooks and the continuing Defective versions are clearly to be distinguished from an authoritative old text, and gradually we meet growing surprise at the quality revealed when the *Travels* is read in a good text. But that very change in taste and attitude ensures that thenceforward the lively luxuriation of Mandevilliana will stop; as the integrity of the book was at last guaranteed, its power to change and inform imaginative thought was almost killed. Nothing grows in formalin.

Now I, like John Mandeville, am 'now come to rest, as a man discomfited for age and travel and feebleness. I must now cease telling of diverse things so that those who follow may find things enough to speak of.'

5 *The Translations, the Style and the Text*

All three of the extant early English versions of Mandeville are translations descending ultimately from the French original. It is often forgotten that in terms of volume the major literary activity in England in the later fourteenth century is translation of important material written in French, and, indeed, that in the early and middle parts of that century

French is a more important 'English' language than English itself. The use of French as a literary language for Englishmen did not survive more than a generation after the Black Death – possibly due to the dearth of clerical teachers of the language, for the clergy as a class were particularly hard hit by the epidemic. The problem was that secular (as distinct from religious) prose had for the best part of two centuries been written by Englishmen in an increasingly flexible and expressive French, with a resulting development of syntactical, verbal and rhetorical resources. When people came to try to put this material into English, the language structures capable of conveying the full meaning simply were not available. One could hardly deploy the specialized rhetoric of the sermon for the discussion of gold-digging ants. The solution adopted was the wholesale borrowing of French literary and linguistic structures and verbal concepts; the result was the eventual creation of a literary English of unexampled resource. Now by any standards the Mandeville translations are important landmarks in the development of that prose. They are among the first extended prose works in English dealing with a wide range of subjects from the scientific to the devotional, and are a major influence on subsequent English writing.

The very difficulty of the business of translation into English meant that at least at first translators stuck fairly closely to the structures and cadences of the French. Comparison of an early Anglo-Norman text (e.g. British Library MS Harley 4383: see p. 38) with the Cotton, Egerton and Defective translations shows this. Thus it is – unusually – possible to make points about the author's nuances as conveyed by style using the translations, especially where there is a large measure of agreement between them.

Probably because of the French source, the style of the translations is generally more hypotactic than is typical of English prose of the period – though there is still a greater degree of repetitive parataxis than is immediately pleasing or comfortable to a modern ear. (I have deliberately allowed much of it to remain.) Hypotaxis (the subordination of clauses, with consequent complexity of sentence structure) can convey much finer shades of meaning than the repetitive statements of parataxis. Ideas can be structured into an order of importance. Some of Mandeville's effects do indeed depend on such structuring – like the positioning of the clause 'whenever they can get them' in the sentence about the hippopotamus's taste for men (p. 167). The style of the Anglo-Norman is capable of subtle flexibility, its effects varying from complex exposition (the Pole star passage, p.128), to philosophic analysis (idols and simulacres, p. 121) to devotional prose when dealing with the scenes of the

Passion. A *decorum* of style is observed throughout. The most common 'linking' style is an informal, conversational, direct manner well suited to the use of a *persona* whose individuality we must be made to accept if the control mechanism of the book is to work. Moreover, Mandeville is capable of the extended architectonics of the periodic style as well where it is decorous – as in the opening of the book. This feature does not bulk large in the book – indeed that opening is the only really good example – but it demonstrates that the dominance of a mainly simple style is deliberate. The last sentence of the prologue is composed of one complex compound sentence. The proliferation of the list scheme and the accumulation of relative and adverbial (causal) clauses is sustained until the main and penultimate clause unites them all and announces the topic of the book. And if one disregards the modern punctuation, the whole of the prologue can be seen to be constructed on that single main clause: two huge causal propositions, with their own *internal* articulation of main and subordinate clauses arranged – almost as internal glosses – into sentence units are merely preparatory to announcing that main topic. On this analysis, the structure of the whole of the prologue can be expressed thus:

1. 'Since it is so that the land beyond the sea . . .'
2. 'And since it is a long time . . .'
3. '[Therefore] I shall tell you . . .'

Only a writer of real skill could handle this periodic and episodic complex in his mind and express it effectively. Mandeville's ability is clear.

But despite an apparent closeness to the French, all three English versions show hints of the problem we noted above, where later versions of Mandeville begin to lose the nuances and values of the original. Our ideal of translation is of something faithful to the original; one principal medieval concept of *translatio* is more a free reworking of the original to suit one's purpose. (In this sense, I suppose Mandeville's use of Odoric could be called a sort of a *translatio*.) In choosing a text for this edition, therefore, I had to take these problems into consideration. It had to be early; it had to be in English, because of the importance of those early translations, not least in the development of a secular English prose; but it had to allow for the later experience of the book over, say, the first two centuries of its existence. There were three possible texts, representing three distinct but closely related translations. First, the Cotton translation, extant uniquely in British Library MS Cotton Titus c. xvi, of the late fourteenth or early fifteenth century. This is incomplete, having lost three leaves after fo. 53. It was not printed until 1725. Next, the

'Common', 'Defective' or 'Pynson' version, represented in several MSS of late-fourteenth- or early-fifteenth-century date. This is an important translation, as it was edited – cut – and printed in 1496 by Richard Pynson; this edition was the parent of all subsequent printed copies in England, bar two in Latin (Hakluyt's and Purchas's) until 1725. But there is a large lacuna in the description of Egypt, amounting to 12 pages (pp. 59–71) in the text printed here (hence its sobriquet 'Defective'). Finally, the version represented by a single exemplar, British Library MS Egerton 1982.[18] I chose this for a number of reasons. First, it corresponds well to the Anglo-Norman texts of the Insular version, being (despite some howlers) less optimistic about its control of French and less free in its readings than the contemporary Cotton text. In many places it makes very much better sense than Cotton. It also corresponds better than Cotton to the French of the important Paris French text, dated 1371, (Bibliothèque Nationale, fonds français nouv. acqu. 4515) of the Continental version. Second, it is based on a lost MS in French of Defective (as is Cotton) carefully conflated with a lost English translation of the Latin text (independent of Defective) behind the abridged English version (Oxford, Bodleian MSS Rawlinson D.99 and e musaeo 116). The proper names are much less confused than in Cotton. The Egerton text, unlike Cotton, is not divided into chapters; I have followed the divisions in the fourteenth-century Anglo-Norman MSS British Library Harley 4383 and Royal 20 B.X, which correspond to Cotton's, and have supplied chapter titles from these texts.[19] Egerton contains six alphabets against Defective's two (see Appendix I on the alphabets). Now, both Cotton and Egerton draw on the French text of the Defective version. Egerton has a very close correspondence with Defective up to the 'Egypt Gap' and shows a close conflation thereafter. It seemed marginally preferable, therefore, to use Egerton as the basis for this edition. But as how people used the *Travels* is also of interest, I have indicated some significant omissions in Defective (using the good MS in Cambridge University Library, Dd i. 17) by printing the 'Egypt Gap' in italics, and surrounding less lengthy ones with angle brackets.

In the translation I have tried to 'go the middel weie' between wholesale 'retelling' and a mere transcription of the MS. So, as far as is consonant with the modern reader's ease, I have retained the sentence structures of the original; inevitably, in places, this has given a looseness of style. Names – particularly place names and proper names – have on their first mention been glossed in square brackets where necessary and possible; some are not known, others are unidentifiable. In subsequent mentions I have used the modern form where appropriate. The recognition of a correct name lurking behind the distorted form does not, of course, indicate that they could be plotted on a modern map, for some are as mythical as Pliny's Chryse and Argyre. Some of Mandeville's places are mere ghosts; he or his sources found two very different names for a single place and assumed two places on the ground. (See, for example, p. 114, where Ani seems to occur as two cities with different names.) There is at times variation in form within the text even where the names clearly refer to the same place. Corrections of Egerton (mainly slight) against MSS Harley 4383 and Royal 20 B.X have been made where necessary for sense; they, with editorial corrections and translations, have been indicated by square brackets. I have also largely followed Mandeville's usage of 'isle' as a pretty general term not limited to something entirely surrounded by water. Appendix II, on the type of geographical terms the author and his audience might have used, indicates my reasons.

Before letting John Mandeville have his say, I must here acknowledge my debt in making this translation to the editions of the Egerton text by Sir George Warner and Mr Malcolm Letts, and of the Cotton and Defective texts by Dr M. C. Seymour. They have been a light unto my feet, but did not cause my stumbles.

Reach, Cambridgeshire,
Ascension Day, 2004

NOTES

1. The most helpful discussions are by Josephine W. Bennett, Christiane Deluz and Drs Poerck and Seymour: see Bibliography. Mrs Bennett listed, with descriptive details, all the extant MSS known to her, but the list in Dr Seymour's 1994 essay is more helpful.

2. Authors creating a character of different nationality to themselves commonly slip up by inconsistency. In 1708 the *London Monthly Miscellany* published a 'Letter from Admiral Bartholomew da Fonte', purporting to describe a voyage from the Pacific to the Atlantic in 1640. The circumstantial detail is good. But 'da Fonte's' credibility is destroyed as he reckons his dates from the accession of Charles I of England. (Repr. H. R. Wagner, 'Apocryphal Voyages to the West Coast of America', *Proceedings of the American Antiquarian Society* 41 (1931), pp. 179–234.) Similarly, George Psalmanazar (1679?–1763) could not maintain his assumed Formosan nationality, and even the friendship of Dr Johnson could not prevent his passing from ridicule to obscurity.

3. 'Jeo doie estre escusee, pur ceo qe jeo sui engleis et n'ai pas moelt hauntee le franceis' (*Livre de Seyntz Medecines*, ed. E. J. Arnould (Oxford, 1940), p. 239).

The rhetorical figure of *diminutio* – polite apology for real or potential inadequacy – may underlie Henry's and Gower's remarks. But both possibly are aware of the growing fashionableness of 'Frenssh of Paris' as a literary language. Chaucer's remark about his Prioress's Flemish French suggests that one so conscious of what is *comme il faut* might have been more up to date in the matter of a polite language.

4. Mandeville's claim to have served the Khan at Manzi (p. 144) – adopted from his source Odoric of Pordenone – is impossible since Manzi fell at the end of the Sung dynasty in 1278.

5. But a Benedictine monk, for example, would be prevented from leaving his monastery by the Benedictine rule of *stabilitas loci* – staying in one place – unless given leave to travel for study.

6. Jonathan Sumption, *Pilgrimage* (1975), Norbert Ohler, *The Medieval Pilgrim* (1989), Diana Webb, *Pilgrims and Pilgrimage in the Medieval West* (London, 1999).

7. Comparison with the *Libro del Conoscimiento* (*c.* 1350), by a Spanish Franciscan (trans. C. Markham, Hakluyt Society, 1912), highlights this. This man wandered all over Africa and the East, and did not just compile; yet he includes all the traditional monsters and fabulous stories. His ineffable dullness and lack of detail underline how vastly more informative and entertaining is Mandeville.

8. There are naturally occasional awkwardnesses, which modern filing systems and methods of writing books would have avoided. Sometimes sources are not fully digested, and occasionally two conflicting versions of the same event happen – e.g. two stories of Muhammad's prohibition of wine, chapters 9 and 15. Sometimes one single source gets to Mandeville by two independent routes, and is thus doubleted – for instance, the account of Silha and then Taprobane (chapters 21, 33).

9. Translated by Sir Henry Yule, *Cathay and the Way Thither*, Vol 2. See Bibliography. One might just note how different are Polo, Odoric and Mandeville: Odoric plods worthily on his way, Polo observes keenly and accurately, with no literary or doctrinal malice aforethought, while Mandeville creates a memorable fanciful trope. See *The Travels of Marco Polo* (Penguin Books, Harmondsworth, 1958), p. 66.

10. The name most westerners use for any Eastern non-Christian. The Greek word in the later Roman period was used to designate the semi-nomadic peoples of Arabia.

11. The way it was illustrated, among other things, suggests the devotional interest in it. The early-fifteenth-century British Library MS, Addit. 24189, is simply a picture-book, without text; it illustrates each of the Crownings of Our Lord, and Mandeville's first five chapters are expressed in twenty-eight superb illustrations (facsimile, *The Travels of Sir John Mandeville*, ed. Josef Krasa, New York, 1995): Another illustrated Mandeville appears in the compendium British Library MS Addit. 37049, which is entirely composed of devotional material.

Notes

12. Jacopo da Voragine's collection of Saints' Lives (*c*. 1280). William Caxton's translation is available on the Web at
www.catholic-forum.com/saints/golden000.htm.

13. It is a version of the Mélusine romance, which Jean d'Arras in 1378 linked to the House of Lusignan. Mélusine in her dragon mode is depicted flying over their castle in the *Très Riches Heures du Duc de Berri*. A branch of the Lusignan were kings of Armenia.

14. The story of the Pope certifying the book as true is an interpolation, found only in the English versions, that must post-date 1377, when Gregory XI returned the papacy to Rome. See note in text.

15. Compare *Clannes*, in *The Poems of the Pearle Manuscript*, ed. Andrews and Waldron, repr. 2002, ll. 977–1052, and above, p. 34. See also Gollancz and Day, *Clannes: Glossary and Illustrative Texts* (Oxford, 1933), pp. 75, 91–2 and 96–8, and in R. J. Menner, *Yale Studies in English* 61 (New Haven, 1920), p. xlff. It has long been recognized that the *Gawain* poet knew the *Travels*, and I have argued elsewhere that Chaucer and the poet of the Alliterative *Morte Arthur* did too.

16. The process of accretion and alteration continues down to the 1700s: Steele, in *Tatler* 254 (1710), fathers on Mandeville a story from Rabelais which Raspe later borrowed for *The Marvellous Travels of Baron von Münchausen* (1785).

17. Mandeville is here on the way to being bracketed with Münchausen in most people's minds.

18. One owner of Egerton transcribed on the flyleaf a now lost note on the inside of the cover: ' "Thys fayre boke I have fro the abbey at Saint Albons in thys yeare of our Lord m.cccclxxxx the sixt day of Apryll. Willyam Caxton. Richard Tottyl, 1579 – Lond." This book was given to me by the Revd. Hugh Tuthill, a descendant of the above named Richard Tottyl, who was a celebrated printer – E. Hill, M.D., March 22d. 1803.' Dr Hill notes the careful comparison of the MS with the 1727 printing of the Cotton text, and concludes Egerton is the better.

19. Sir George Warner first printed these, in his French text. MS Harley 4383 runs up to the middle of chapter 22. He completed his text with the closely related, contemporary MS Royal 20 B.X.

41

THE TRAVELS OF
SIR JOHN MANDEVILLE

PROLOGUE

Since it is so that the land beyond the sea, that is to say the Land of
Promise which men call the Holy Land, among all other lands is the
most worthy land and mistress over all others, and is blessed and
hallowed and consecrated by the precious blood of Our Lord Jesus
Christ;* in which land it pleased Him to take life and blood by Our Lady
Saint Mary and to travel round that land with His blessed feet. And
there He did many miracles, and preached and taught the faith and law
of us Christian men as if to His children; and there He suffered many
insults and scourgings on our behalf. And He who was King of Heaven
and of Earth, of the air and the sea, and of all that is contained therein,
desired to be called King of that land especially, as the prophet says:
Noli timere, filia Syon: ecce, rex tuus uenit tibi mansuetus, that is to say,
'Thou daughter of Sion, fear not, for lo, thy king cometh unto thee,
duly meek and mild';† and that land He chose before all other lands as
the best and the most honourable in the world, for, as the philospher
says, *Virtus rerum in medio consistit*, that is to say, 'The excellence of
things is in the middle.'‡ And in that land He wished to lead His life and
suffer His hard Passion and death at [the hands of] the Jews for us sinful
worms, to buy and deliver us from death without end, which was
ordained for us because of the sin of our first father Adam and because
of our own also. For, as for Himself, He never deserved any evil; for He
never did evil nor thought ever evil. And He who was King of glory,
mightiest and best, wished to suffer death in that place rather than in
any other. For he who wants to do anything that he wishes to be openly
known to all men, will have it openly cried in the centre of a town or
city, so that it may be known to all parts of the city. In the same way He
that was King of all the world wanted to suffer death at Jerusalem
which is in the middle of the world so that it might be known to men of
all parts of the world how dearly He bought man, whom He had made
in His own likeness, because of the great love He had towards him. For

* See note on the translation, p. 37.
† John xii, 15; cf. Isaiah lxii, 110.
‡ Aristotle, *Nicomachean Ethics* II.

43

a more valuable property He could not have staked for us than His own blessed body and His precious blood, the which He suffered to be shed for us. Ah, dear God! What love He had for His subjects when He who never committed sin would for sinners suffer death! Right well ought men to love and serve such a lord, and honour and praise such a Holy Land, which brought forth such fruit, through which man is saved, except it be through his own fault. This is the land that is promised to us as heritage; and in that land He willed to die, and to be seised of it, to leave it to His children. Each good Christian man who is able, and has the means, should set himself to conquer our inheritance, this land, and chase out therefrom those who are misbelievers. For we are called Christian men from Christ our Father; and if we be true children of Christ, we ought to lay claim to the heritage that our Father left to us, and win it out of strange men's hands. But now pride, envy and covetousness have so inflamed the hearts of lords of the world that they are more busy to disinherit their neighbours than to lay claim to or conquer their own rightful inheritance. And the common people, who would put their bodies and their goods in jeopardy to conquer our heritage, may do nothing without lords. For an assembly of the people without lords who can govern them is as a flock of sheep that have no shepherd, which part asunder and never known whither they should go. But if God would that their worldly lords were in good accord, and with others of their common people would undertake this holy voyage over the sea, I believe that within a little time our true heritage beforesaid should be recovered and put in the hands of the true heirs of Jesu Christ.

And for as much as it is a long time past since there was any general passage over the sea into the Holy Land, and since men covet to hear that land spoken of, and divers countries thereabout, and have of that great pleasure and enjoyment, I, John Mandeville, knight, although I am unworthy, who was born in England in the town of St Albans and passed the sea the year of Our Lord Jesu Christ 1332, on Michaelmas Day, and since have been a long time overseas, and have seen and gone through many kingdoms, lands, provinces and isles, and have passed through Turkye [Turkey], Ermony [Armenia] the Lesser and the Greater, Tartary, Perse [Persia], Sirie [Syria], Araby [Arabia], Egipte [Egypt] the Upper and the Lower, Liby [Libya], Caldee [Chaldea], and a great part of Ethiope [Ethiopia], Amazon[ia], a great part of Inde [India] the Lesser and the Greater, and through many other isles that are about India, where dwell many divers kinds of folk of divers laws and shapes – of these lands and isles I shall speak more plainly, and shall describe a part of those things that are there, when the time comes, according as they come to my mind, and specially for those who desire and intend to visit the holy city of Jerusalem and the holy places that are thereabout; and shall tell of the way that they shall go thither, for I have many times travelled and ridden over it in goodly company of lords.

1

Of the way from England to Constantinople

In the name of God Almighty: he who wants to pass over the sea to Jerusalem, may go by many ways, both by sea and by land depending on the countries he comes from; many ways come to a single end. But do not think I shall tell of all the towns and cities and castles that men shall go by; for then I must make too long a tale of it. But only some countries and the most important places that men shall pass through to go the right road do I briefly intend to touch on. For, if a man comes from the western parts of the world – like England, Ireland, Wales, Scotland or Norway – he may, if he wants, go through Almayne [Germany] and through the kingdom of Hungary, which borders the lands of Polainie [Poland] and the land of Pannony [Bulgaria] and of Allesye [Silesia]. And you must know that the King of Hungary is a very great and mighty lord, and holds much important land. For he holds the land of Hungary, Savoy [Slavonia], Comany [Cumania], a great part of Bulgary (which men call the land of the Bulgars), and a great part of the kingdom of Ruscy [Russia], and that stretches to the land of Nyfeland [Livonia] and borders on Pruysse [Prussia]. And through the land of Hungary men go to a city that is called Chippron [Soprony] and by the castle of Newburgh, and then by the River Danuby [Danube]. This is a very big river which [rises in] Germany below the hills of Lombardy, and it takes into itself forty other rivers; and it runs through Hungary and Cresses [Greece] and Tracy [Thrace] and then enters the sea so powerfully and with such strength that the water is fresh twenty miles out to sea. And afterwards men go to [Belgrade] and enter the land of the Bulgars, and there you pass a bridge of stone that is over the River Marrok [Maritsa]. And then men pass through the land of Pynceras [Petschenegs] and come to Greece to the city of Sternes [Sofia] and to the city of Affynpayn [Philippopolis]; then to the city of Bradenople [Adrianople], and then to the city of

Constantinople, which was once called Bethsamoron [Byzantium], where the Emperor of Greece usually dwells. There is the best and most beautiful church in the world, of Saint Sophia. And in front of the church of Saint Sophia is a statue of Justinian the Emperor, well gilded over; it is made sitting, crowned, on a horse. This statue used to hold in its hand a round apple of gold; but it is long since fallen out of the hand. And it is said there that the fall of the apple is a token that the Emperor has lost a great part of his lordship. For he used to be Emperor of Romany [Romania], of Greece, of Asia Minor, of Surry [Syria], of the land of Iudee [Judea], in which is Jerusalem, of the land of Egypt, of Persia and Arabia; but he has lost all, except Greece, and that land only he holds. Men wanted many a time to put the apple back in the statue's hand, but it will not remain there. This apple signifies the lordship that he had over all the world. The other hand it holds lifted up against the west, as a sign of menace to evildoers. This statue stands on a pillar of marble.

2

Of the Cross and Crown of Our Lord

At Constantinople is the sponge and reed with which the Jews gave drink to Our Lord when He hung upon the Cross. Some men believe that half the Cross of Christ is in Cipre [Cyprus] in an abbey of monks which is called the Hill of the Holy Cross; but it is not so. For that cross that is in Cyprus is the cross on which Dismas the good thief was hanged. But not all men know that, and that is ill done. For in order to get offerings they say that it is the Cross of Our Lord Jesu Christ.

And you must understand that the Cross of Our Lord was made of four kinds of trees, as it is contained in the verse written here: *In cruce fit palma, cedrus, cypressus, oliua.* [In the Cross [are] palm, cedar, cypress and olive.] For the piece that ran up from the earth to the head was of cypress; and that piece that went across, to which His hands were nailed, was of palm; and the block that stood in the earth, in which a mortice was made, was of cedar; and the tablet above His head was a foot and a half long, on which the superscription was written in Hebrew, Greek and Latin, and it was of olive. Of these four kinds of wood the Jews made Christ's Cross for they believed that He would have been hanging upon that Cross as long as the Cross might last. And so they made the foot of cedar; for cedar does not rot in earth or water.

They wanted it to last a long time. And because they thought Christ's body would stink, they made the upright, on which His body hung, of cypress, for it is sweet smelling, so that the smell of His body should not be offensive to men who came by. And the piece that went across, to which His hands were nailed, was of palm; for in the Old Testament it was ordained that when any man had victory over his enemy he should be crowned with palm. And because they believed that they had the victory over Christ, they made the cross-piece of palm. And the tablet of the titles was of olive; for olive betokens peace, as the story of Noe [Noah] bears witness, when the dove brought the twig of olive in her beak, which signified peace between God and man. And so the Jews believed they would have peace when Christ was dead, for they said that He caused strife among them. And you should know that Our Lord was nailed to the Cross lying down, and therefore He suffered the greater pain.

Men of Greece and other Christian men too who dwell beyond the sea say that the wood of the Cross that we call cypress was of the tree Adam ate the apple from, and so they find it written. And they say also that their Scripture says that Adam fell sick and said to his son Seth that he should go to Paradise and beseech the angel that guards Paradise that he would send him some of the oil of the Tree of Mercy to anoint his limbs with, so that he might have healing. And Seth went to Paradise; but the angel would not let him in, but said to him that he could not have any of the oil of mercy. But he took four seeds of the same tree that his father ate the apple from and told him that, as soon as his father was dead, he should put these seeds under his tongue and bury him like that; and from these four seeds would grow trees that should bear a fruit through which Adam would be saved. And, when Seth came home again, he found his father nearly dead; and he did as the angel had told him with the seeds, from which sprouted four trees, whereof a Cross was made that bore good fruit, Jesu Christ, through whom Adam and all who come from him are saved and freed from death without end, unless it be through their own fault. This Holy Cross the Jews had hidden in the earth under the rock of Mount Calvary; and it lay there two hundred years and more up to the time when Saint Helena found it (which Saint Helena was mother of Constantine the Emperor of Rome). And she was daughter of Coel, King of England, that was at that time called Greater Britain. And the Emperor of Rome, when he was in that country and saw her great beauty, took her to wife and begot on her Constantine. And you must know that the Cross of Our Lord was in length eight cubits, and that beam that went across in length three cubits and a half. A part of the Crown of Thorns with which Our Lord was crowned, and one of the nails, and the spearhead, and many other relics are in France in the King's chapel. And the Crown lies in a vessel of crystal, beautifully and richly made. A king of France bought these relics once off the Januenes [Genoese], to whom the Emperor had laid them in pledge for a great sum of gold. And even though men say that this Crown is of thorns, you must understand that it was of reeds of the sea* that were white and pricked as sharply as thorns. For I have many times seen both that which is at Paris and that which is at Constantinople; for they were both parts of one whole, made of reeds of the sea, but men have split them into two parts, of which one part is at Paris and the other at Constantinople. And I have a thorn thereof, which looks like a hawthorn, and it was given me out of great friendship. For many of them are broken and have fallen down in the vessel in which is the Crown, for they break when men disturb the vessel to show the Crown to great lords and to pilgrims who come thither.

And you must know that Our Lord, the night that He was captured, was led into a garden, and was there sharply interrogated; and there the Jews mocked Him and set a Crown on His head and pushed it down so hard that the blood ran down in many places on His face and His neck and His shoulders. And that crown was made of branches of hawthorn; and therefore the hawthorn has many virtues. For he who carries a twig of it on him, no thunder nor any kind of storm shall harm him; and no evil spirit may come into the house or any other place where it is. And in that same garden Saint Peter denied Our Lord thrice. Afterwards Our Lord was led before the Bishop and the officials of the [Old] Law in another garden, Annas's; and there too He was interrogated and ridiculed and crowned afterwards with a thorn that is called barberry, which grew in that garden. And that too has many virtues. And later still He was led into the garden of Cayphas [Caiaphas]; and there He was crowned with a briar rose. And then He was led into the chamber of Pilate; and there too He was accused and crowned. For the Jews set Him in a chair and clad Him in a mantle; and they made the Crown of reeds of the sea, and they kneeled to Him and

---

* 'Reeds of the sea' ('joncs de la mer' in the French) is meaningless in that it does not seem to indicate any identifiable plant. The iconographic tradition in the West suggests a crown made of some plant like gorse, whose French name (*ajonc*) is similar to that of the common reed (*jonc*). The material of the crown has been persuasively identified as the spines of the date palm (*Phoenix dactylifera*) by H. St J. Hart in his important article 'The Crown of Thorns', *Journal of Theological Studies*, N.S. 111, (1952) pp. 66–75.

crowned Him with it and said, *Aue Rex Iudeorum*, that is to say, 'Hail, King of the Jews'. And this Crown, of which the one half is at Paris and the other at Constantinople, Christ had upon His head when He was crucified. And therefore men should honour it, and hold it more worthy than any of the others. The shaft of the spear with which Christ was pierced to the heart the Emperor of Germany has; but the head of it is at Paris. The Emperor of Constantinople says that he has the spearhead; and that spearhead I have often seen, but it is bigger than that at Paris.

3

Of the city of Constantinople,
and of the faith of the Greeks

Also at Constantinople lies Saint Anne, the mother of Our Lady, whom Saint Helena had brought from Jerusalem. And there lies also the body of John Chrysostom, who was Bishop of Constantinople. And there lies Saint Luke the Evangelist; for his bones were brought from Bethany [Bithynia], where he was buried. And many other relics are there. And there are some vessels of stone, like marble, which men call 'ydrious',* which continually drip water and fill themselves each year. Constantinople is a very fair and good city, and well walled; it is three cornered. There is an arm of the sea that men call the Hellespont; and some call it the Mouth of Constantinople, and some the Arm of Saint George. And this water encloses two parts of the city. And further up towards the sea, on this same stretch of water, used to stand the city of Troy; but that city was destroyed by the Greeks.

Around Greece are many isles: that is to say, Calcas [Carki], Calistra [Thera], Oertige [Ortygia, Delos], Tesbiria [Lesbos], Minca [Paros], Flaxania [Naxos?], Melo [Melos], Carpateya [Scarpanto], Lempnia [Lemnos]. And in this region is the mountain Caucasus [Athos] which pierces through the clouds. There are also many other different countries and nations speaking different languages which are tributary to and obey the Emperor – Turcople, Petschenegs, Cumania, Thrace, Macedonia, of which Alexander was King, and many others. In this

---

* *Enhydros*, mentioned by Isidore of Seville and Pliny. Lewis and Short's dictionary glosses as 'an unknown gem'. Certain types of agate contain water occluded in cavities. The phenomenon referred to here may be due to condensation, of course.

region was Aristotle born in a city that is called Strages [Stagira], a little way from Thrace. At Stagira lies Aristotle, and there is an altar upon his tomb. And there men hold a solemn feast each year, as if he were a saint. And upon his altar they hold their great council and assembly, and they believe that through the inspiration of God and of him they will have the better counsel. In that country are very great mountains near the border of Macedonia. And among others there is one which is called Olympus, which divides Macedonia and Thrace; and it is high above the clouds. There is also another hill which men call Athos; and that is so high that its shadow stretches to Lemnos, which is distant from it nearly seventy-eight miles. Upon these hills the air is so clear and so pure that no wind can be felt there; and so no animal nor bird can live there, the air is so dry. And men say in those countries that once wise men went up on those hills and held to their noses sponges soaked with water to catch the air, for the air was so dry. And also up on those hills they wrote letters in the dust with their fingers, and at the end of a year they went up again and found the same letters that they had written the year before as fresh as they were on the first day, without any defect. And therefore it certainly appears that these hills pass beyond the clouds to the pure air.

In that city of Constantinople is the Emperor's palace, very fair and well built; and beside it is a fair place set aside for jousts. There are terraces made all round it, and steps, that men can sit on, one above the other, to see the jousting, so that no one shall get in anybody's way or hinder their view. And under the terraces are stables, well vaulted, for the Emperor's horses; and all the pillars are of marble. And in the church of Saint Sophia once upon a time an emperor wanted to lay to rest the body of his father, when he was dead; and as they dug the grave, they found a body in the earth, and on that body lay a great plate of gold; and thereon was written in Hebrew, in Greek and in Latin, *Ihesus Christus nascetur de uirgine Maria; et ego credo in eum*, that is to say, 'Jesus Christ shall be born of the Virgin Mary, and I believe in Him.' And the date when this was written and laid in the earth was two thousand years before the Incarnation of Christ. And that plate is still in the treasury of the church; and men say that the body was the body of Hermogenes the wise man.

And although the Greeks are Christian, nevertheless they vary from our faith. For they say that the Holy Ghost proceeds not from the Son, but only from the Father; and they are not in obedience to the Church of Rome, nor to the Pope. And they say that beyond the Greek Sea their Patriarch has as much power as our Pope has on his side of it. And therefore Pope John XXII sent letters to them showing them that the Christian faith should be unified, and that all Christian men ought to obey a Pope, who is Christ's Vicar on earth and to whom God gave full power to bind and to loose; and therefore they ought to obey him. And they sent to him many answers; and, among others, they sent one saying, *Potentiam tuam summam circa tuos subiectos firmiter credimus; superbiam tollerare non possumus; auariciam tuam summam saciare non intendimus. Dominus tecum sit, quia Dominus nobiscum est. Vale.* That is to say, 'We well believe your power is great over your subjects; we cannot support your great pride; we do not purpose to slake your great avarice. God be with you, for God is with us. Farewell.' And other answer had he none of them. The Greeks also make the sacrament at the altar of leavened bread; for Our Lord made it of leavened bread when he held the Last Supper. And they say that we err in making the sacrament with unleavened bread. And on Maundy Thursday they make that bread as a token of Our Lord's Institution, and dry it in the sun, and keep it all year and give it to sick men instead of the consecrated Body of Christ. And they anoint only once when they christen children, and dip them but once at the font. They do not anoint sick men; and they say there is no Purgatory, and that souls shall have neither joy nor pain before the Day of Judgement. They say also that fornication is not a deadly sin, but a natural one, and that men and women should only marry once; and, whoever marries more than once, their children are bastards and begotten in sin. Their priests too are married. And they say that usury is no deadly sin. They sell benefices of Holy Church, and so do men in other places; and that is a great scandal and disgrace. For now is simony crowned like a king in Holy Church. God can amend it when it is His will. They say also that in Lent men should not sing Mass except on Saturdays and Sundays. And they do not fast on Saturdays at any time of the year, unless it be Christmas or Easter Even. They allow no man who comes from this side of the Greek Sea to celebrate at their altars; and if it so chance that any do, they wash the altar immediately with holy water. And they say that there should be but one Mass sung at each altar each day. Moreover, they say that Our Lord never ate bodily food, but made an appearance of eating, feigning that He had, showing sign of man's nature. They say we commit a deadly sin in shaving our beards, for they say that the beard is a symbol of manhood and the gift of God. And they who shave their beards do it only to appear well to the world and to please their wives. They say too that we commit deadly sin in eating animals that were forbidden in the Old Law, like pigs, hares and other beasts that do not chew the cud. And also they say we sin in eating meat on the three days before Ash Wednesday, and also in eating meat on Wednesdays, and when we eat white meat on Fridays. And they curse all those who do not eat meat on Saturday. Also the Emperor of Constantinople appoints the patriarchs, archbishops, and bishops, and distributes all the dignities of Holy Church in that country; and he deprives of office and goods those who seem to him unworthy. And so he is their lord both temporal and spiritual.

If you wish to know about the A B C E of Greece and what kinds of letters they use, here you can see them, and their names too:

alpha	beta	gamma	delta	e brevis	epissima	zeta
hetha	tetha	iota	kappa	lappa	mi	ni
xe	o/brevis	pe	cope	ro	sima	tau
gui	fi	xi	spi	o longa	encos	chile

4

Of Saint John the Evangelist; and of Hippocrates' daughter, turned into the shape of a dragon

And although these things do not bear on teaching you the way to the Holy Land, nevertheless they do touch on what I promised to show you, that is to say the customs, manners and diversities of countries. And since the land of Greece is the nearest country that varies and is discordant in faith and writing from us and our faith, I have therefore put it in here so that you may know the differences between our belief and theirs. For many men desire to hear of unfamiliar things and take pleasure in them.

Now I return to teaching the way from Constantinople to the Holy Land. He who will go through Turkey goes to the city which is called Nyke [Nicaea] and so through the Gate of Chivotot [Cibotus, Gemlik] and the mountain of Chivotot, which is very high; it is [one and a half leagues] from the city of Nicaea. Whoever passes from Constantinople to the Holy Land by sea will go by the Arm of Saint George, and then, sailing in the Greek Sea, past a place where lies Saint Nicholas, and many other places. And first men come to an island which is called Silo [Chios]. And in that island grows mastic, on small trees; and it exudes from them like the gum of plum or cherry trees.

Then men pass by the isle of Patmos, where Saint John the Evangelist wrote the Apocalypse. And you must know that when Our Lord died Saint John was thirty-two years of age, and he lived after the Passion of Christ sixty-two years. From Patmos men go to Ephesus, a fair city, near to the sea. And there Saint John died, and was buried behind the altar in a tomb. And there is a fine church; for Christian men used to possess that city. But now it is occupied by Turks, and so is all Asia Minor; and therefore Asia Minor is called Turkey. In the tomb of Saint John many find nothing but manna, for some men say his body was translated to Paradise. And you must understand that Saint John had his grave made there while he was alive and laid himself in it alive; and therefore some say he did not die, but rests there until the Day of Judgement. And indeed there is there a great marvel, for men can see the earth of the tomb many a time stir and shift, as if there were a living thing underneath.

From Ephesus men pass by many islands in the sea to the city of Patera, where Saint Nicholas was born, and then to the city of Marc [Myra] where he was chosen to be Bishop. There grows a very good strong wine, which is called the wine of Marc. Thence men pass to the isles of Grece [Crete], the which the Emperor once gave to the Genoese. And thence men make their way by the isle of Cophos [Cos], and by the isle of Lango, of which islands Ypocras [Hippocrates] was once lord.

And some say that in the isle of Lango is Hippocrates' daughter, in the form of a dragon, which is a hundred feet long – as men say, for I myself have not seen it. Folk there call her the lady of that island. She was changed thus into a dragon from a fair damsel by a goddess who is called Diana. And it is said she shall remain like that until the time when a knight comes who is so bold as to dare to go to her and kiss her on the mouth. Then will she return into her own shape and be a woman; but she shall live only a little time afterwards. And it is not very long since a knight of Rhodes, a bold, capable fellow, said he would kiss her. He leapt on his horse and went to the castle and entered the vault where the dragon was lying. And she began to lift up her head against him; and he saw it in all its hideousness, and he ran away. The dragon followed and took the knight and carried him, despite his struggles, to a sea-cliff, and she cast him over that crag into the sea; and so that knight was lost. Also, a young man, who knew nothing of the dragon, once disembarked from a ship to get some exercise, and took a walk in this island; he came to the castle, and entered the vault. And he found a room, and therein a damsel combing her hair and looking in a mirror, and she had much treasure round her. And he supposed she was a harlot, who had dwelled in that place to catch men who came through the district; and he stood still there, behind her, until she turned towards him and asked him what he wanted. And he said he wanted to be her lover. And she asked him if he was a knight, and he said no. And she said he might not then be her lover; but she told him to return to his companions and get himself knighted, and to come again the next day; she would then come out of the vault. And she told him that he should kiss her on the mouth and have no fear of her, whatever shape he saw her in, for she would do him no harm, however ugly or hideous she was to his sight. For, she said, it was done by enchantment, for she was just as he saw her at that moment. And she told him that if he kissed her, he should have all that treasure and be lord of her and of those islands. And he left her and came to his companions by the ship and had himself made knight, and went again in the morning to kiss the damsel. And when he saw her come out of the vault in the likeness of a dragon, he had such great fear that he fled to the ship, and she followed him. And when she saw that he did not turn back, she began to wail like a thing in great sorrow. To the ship she followed him and when he had gone aboard, she turned back with a terrible cry; and soon after the knight died. And from that time on no knight has been able to see her without dying soon afterwards. But when a knight comes who is bold enough to dare to kiss her, he shall not die, but he shall turn that damsel into her proper shape, and he shall be lord of her and of the islands.

From this island men pass to the isle of Rhodes, which the Hospitallers hold and govern. This isle they won from the Emperor of Constantinople. It was once called Colos and so the Turks still call it. And Saint Paul wrote to the people of that isle in his Epistle to the Colossians.* This isle is eight hundred miles from Constantinople, going by sea.

* Colossae, in Phrygia, was frequently confused with Rhodes, whose alternative name, after the Colossus, was Colos.

5

Of different things in Cyprus;
of the route from Cyprus to Jerusalem;
and of the marvel of a ditch full of sand

From this island of Rhodes men pass across to the isle of Cyprus, where there are many vines, of which a very strong and noble wine is made; the first year it is red, and after a year it turns to a white, and, the older it gets, the whiter it becomes and the clearer and stronger, and the better the bouquet it has. On the way to Cyprus men pass by a place that is called the Gulf of Cathaly [Adalia], which was once a great and fair country, and there was a fair city in it that was called Adalia. And all that country was lost through the folly of a young man. For there was a beautiful damsel whom he loved well, and she died suddenly and was laid in a tomb of marble; and on account of the great love he had for her he went one night to her grave and opened it and went in and lay with her and then went on his way. At the end of nine months a voice came to him one night and said, 'Go to the grave of that woman and open it, and behold what you have begotten on her. And if you go not you shall have great evil and suffering.' And he went and opened the grave, and there flew out a very horrible head, hideous to look at, which flew all round the city; and forthwith the city sank, and all the district round about. And around there are many dangerous passages.

From Rhodes to Cyprus is near five hundred miles; but men may journey to Cyprus and not touch at Rhodes. Cyprus is a fine island, and a big one; there are many good cities, but principally four. There are also three bishops and one archbishop. The Archbishop's see is at Nicosia. The principal city of Cyprus is Famagost [Famagusta]; and there is the world's best harbour. Christians and heathen and men of all nations land there. And in Cyprus there is another harbour at the city of Lymettes [Limassol]. In Cyprus too is the Mountain of the Holy Cross, where there is an abbey of monks, and there is the cross of the good thief Dismas, as I said before. And some believe that half of the Cross of Our Lord is there, but it is not so. In Cyprus lies Saint Genovefe [Sozomen], for whom men of that country hold a great and solemn festival. And in the castle of Amours* lies the body of Saint Hilarion,

* The Franks called the castle of Saint Hilarion 'Deudamor' (Dieu d'Amour) – a corruption of the Greek name for the mountain on which it stands.

and it is kept with great honour. In Cyprus men hunt with papions [hunting leopards or cheetahs] which are like leopards; and they catch wild beasts very well – better and more swiftly than hounds. And they are somewhat bigger than lions. In Cyprus it is the custom that all men, lords and others, eat their food on the earth. For they make pits in the earth around the hall, knee-deep, and have them well paved; and when they want to eat, they go into these pits and sit down. And this is in order to be cooler, for that land is hotter than it is here. At great feasts, and for foreigners who go there, they set tables and benches as men do in this country; but they would rather sit on the earth.

In Cyprus there is a lake half a mile from the sea, whose water at a certain time congeals into good salt; and therefore ships coming from the Holy Land go thither to load up with that salt.

From Cyprus men may go by sea and land to Jerusalem; and in a day and a night he who has a good wind can make the harbour of Tyre, which is now called Surry [Sûr]; and it is the port of entry for Syria. There was once there a fine city of Christian men, but the Sarzenes [Saracens] have destroyed a great part of it. And they guard the harbour very strongly because of the fear they have of Christian men. People could pass directly to that port without touching at Cyprus, but they go gladly to Cyprus to rest and refresh themselves on the land, and also to load the ships with salt, as I told you before – and to buy other things they have need of for their victualling. On the shore at Tyre, every so often, many rubies are found. And there is also the well of which Holy Writ says thus: *Fons ortorum, puteus aquarum uiuencium.** In this city of Tyre the Samaritan woman said these words to Our Lord: *Beatus uenter qui te portauit et ubera que suxisti*, that is to say, 'Blessed be the womb that bore thee and the paps that thou hast sucked.'† And there Our Lord forgave the sins of the woman of Canaan. In front of the city of Tyre was once the stone on which Our Lord sat and preached; and on that stone was founded the Church of Saint Saviour.

And eight miles from Tyre on the coast is the city of Saphon, or Sarepte [Sûrafend], towards the east. The prophet Helyas [Elijah] used to dwell there, and there the Lord Jesus raised the widow's son from the dead. And five miles thence is the city of Sidon, of which city Dido, who was Eneas's [Aeneas] wife after the destruction of Troy, was Queen. And she founded Carthage in Africa, which is now called Dydoncato. In the city of Tyre ruled Achilles [Agenor], Dido's father. And eighteen miles from Sidon is the city of Beruch [Beirut]. And three

* 'A fountain of gardens, a well of living waters': Song of Solomon iv, 15.
† Luke xi, 27.

days' journey from Beruch is the city of Sardyne [Saidenaya]. And five miles from there is the city of Damasc [Damascus].

Anyone who wants to travel further by sea and arrive near Jerusalem will go from Cyprus to Jaff [Jaffa] for that is the nearest port to Jerusalem. From that harbour it is only a day and a half's journey to Jerusalem. There is the city of Jopp [Joppa]; but it is called Jaffa after one of Noah's sons, called Japhet, who founded it. And some men say it is the oldest city in the world, for it was founded before Noah's flood. And there are the bones of a giant there who was called Andromeda, and one of his ribs is forty feet long. He who arrives at the first port, Tyre (which I spoke of before), may go if he wants by land to Jerusalem. He will go to the city of Acon [Acre], which was sometime called Tholomayda [Ptolemais], a day's journey from Tyre. And once it was a city of Christian men, but now it is mostly destroyed. And from Venice to Acre is by sea two thousand and four score Lombardy miles; and from Calabre [Calabria] or from Cicil [Sicily] to Acre is one thousand three hundred miles. And the isle of Crete is directly on the way. Near the city of Acre, towards the sea, some six score furlongs thence, on the right to the south is Mount Carmel, where Elijah the prophet lived. And there was the order of Carmelite friars first founded. This mountain is not very big or high. At the foot of the mountain was once a goodly city of Christian men, which was called Cayphas [Haifa], because Caiaphas founded it; but it is now all deserted. At the left of the hill is a town called Saffre [Seffûrich] and it is set on another hill. There Saint James and Saint John were born; and in the place of their birth there stands a fine church. Also from Acre to a hill that men call the Ladder of Tyre is one hundred furlongs.

And beside Acre runs a little river, called the Belyon [Abellin], and near there there is the Fosse of Mynon, all round, roughly a hundred cubits broad; and it is all full of gravel. And however much be taken out in a day, on the morrow it is as full as ever it was, and that is a great marvel. And there is always a great wind in that pit, which stirs up all the gravel and makes it eddy about. And if any metal be put therein, immediately it turns to glass. This gravel is shiny, and men make good clear glass of it. The glass that is made of this gravel, if it be put back in the gravel, turns back into gravel, as it was at first. And some say it is an outlet of the Gravelly Sea. People come from far countries by sea with ships and by land with carts to get some of that gravel.

From Acre a three days' journey is made to the city of Palestine [Philistia], which is now called Gaza, and it is a very fine city, full of wealth and people. From this city to a hill outside, Samson the Strong carried the gates of the city, which were made of brass. And in that city he slew the King in his palace, and about three thousand other folk, and himself with them. For they had captured him and put out his eyes, and cropped his hair, and put him in prison. And at their festivals they brought him forth before them and made him dance before them and entertain them. So, one great day of festival, when he was weary of dancing before them, he asked the man who was leading him to take him to the pillar that supported the whole building; and he took the pillar in his arms and shook down all the house on top of them, and so he slew himself and all who were inside, as it is told in the Bible, in Judges xvi. From this city you may go to the city of Gerare [Caesarea], and so to the Castle of Pilgrims, and then to Jaffa, and so to Jerusalem.

He who wants first of all to go to Babylon [Cairo] where the Sultan dwells, to get leave to travel more securely through the region, and to go to Mount Sinai before he gets to Jerusalem and then to make for Jerusalem, will go from Gaza to the castle of Ayre [Darum]. And then a man passes out of Syria and enters the desert, where the route is very sandy. The desert lasts for eight days' journey. Nevertheless men can find all they need in the way of supplies along the road. This wilderness is called Acchelek [Et-Tîh]. And, when a man comes out of this desert, he enters Egypt, which is also called Canopak; and in another language it is called Merfyne. And the first good town men find is called Balbeor [Belbays], and it is on the border of the kingdom of Halope [Aleppo]. And from there men go to Babylon and to the city of Cairo.

6

Of several names of the Sultans; of their estate;
and of the Tower of Babylon

In Babylon [Cairo]* is a fine church of Our Lady; she sojourned there eight years when she fled out of the land of Judea for fear of King Herod. And there lies the body of the holy virgin Saint Barbara, and Joseph dwelled there when his brothers had sold him away into Egypt. And there also King Nabugodonosor [Nebuchadnezzar] had the Three Children put in the fire, because they kept the true faith. And these Children were called Anay, Azary, and Mysael, as says the psalm

* Cairo had the Arabic name Bab-al-yun, which went out of use in favour of Al Kehirah, but the Copts retained it. The confusion with Babylon, 'that great city', in Mesopotamia, was inevitable.

[Canticle] *Benedicite*. But Nebuchadnezzar called them other names, that is to say, Sydrak, Mysak and Abdenago [Shadrach, Meshach and Abednego], which is as much as to say, God glorious, God victorious, God over all kingdoms; and that was because of the miracle he saw, when he saw God's Son walk with the Children up and down in the fire. At Babylon is usually the residence of the Sultan, in a fair, strong castle, set on a high rock. In that castle there are always more than eight thousand men, to guard the castle and to serve the Sultan, and they are maintained in all their needs by the Sultan. I should know the organization of his court pretty well, for I lived for a long time with the Sultan and was a soldier with him in his wars against the Bedoynes [Bedouin]. And he would have arranged a rich marriage for me with a great prince's daughter, and given me many great lordships if I had forsaken my faith and embraced theirs; but I did not want to.

And you must understand that the Sultan is lord of five kingdoms, which he has won by conquest and appropriated. And they are these: Egypt, and the kingdom of Jerusalem, of which David and Solomon were once kings; Syria, of which the city of Damascus was head; the kingdom of Aleppo in the land of Dameth [Hamath]; and the kingdom of Arabia, of which one of the Three Kings who brought gifts to Our Lord when He was born was King. The Sultan rules many other lands. And he is called Caliph, which is a name of great dignity and honour, and is equivalent to 'King'; for the Sultan is of as great authority among them as the King is among us here. *And you shall know that there were once five Sultans, according to the number of the five kingdoms that belong to the present Sultan. But now there is but one Sultan, who is called the Sultan of Babylon.*

The first Sultan of Egypt was called Yaracon [Sheerkooh] and he was Saladyne's [Saladin] father; who was Sultan after Sheerkooh, at the time when King Richard was in those parts with his army of Christian men. After Saladin reigned his son Boradyn [al-Afdal], and after him reigned his nephew. When he was dead, the common people of Egypt thought themselves oppressed and enslaved, and saw that they were strong because of their numbers; and they went and chose one of themselves to be their Sultan; and he was called Melechsala [as-Salih Ayub]. And in his time Louis the King of France went to the Holy Land and fought with the Sultan, and there the King was captured and put in prison. This same Sultan was later slain by his own servants and another was chosen in his stead, who was called Tympieman [Turanshah]. And he ransomed King Louis and freed him from prison. Afterwards, one of the common people, called Cothas, murdered Turanshah, and was made Sultan in his stead; and he had himself called Melechomethos [ad-Din Aibek]. Soon afterwards, another commoner, Benochdaer by name, slew him and reigned in his stead; and he was called Melechdaer [Baibars]. In his time the good King Edward went to Syria and did a lot of harm to the Saracens. This same Sultan was poisoned at Damascus and died there. And after him his son would have reigned as the next heir; he had himself called Melechsayt [Baraqa]. But soon another fellow called Elphy [Qalawun] came with many people and drove Baraqa out of the country, and made himself Sultan. He took the city of Triple [Tripoli] and killed many Christian men there in the year of Our Lord 1279. Afterwards, Qalawun was poisoned by someone else who wanted to be Sultan; and he too was slain soon after. And then the son of Qalawun was chosen to be Sultan, and he was called Melechesserak [al-Ashraf Khalil]. He took the city of Acre and drove out of it all the Christian men there. Afterwards he died of poison and his brother reigned in his stead and was called Melechinasser [an-Nasir]. Soon after that a man called Guytoga took this Sultan and imprisoned him in the castle of Mount Reall and reigned as Sultan in his stead; and he was called Melechadell [al-Adil]. Because he was a foreigner – that is to say, a Tartar – he was driven out of the land; and another called Bathyn was made Sultan and was called Melechynanser [an-Din]. And one day, as he was playing chess, his sword lying drawn beside him, he fell to quarrelling with his opponent, who took up his own sword and slew him with it. And afterwards there was great discord among them over the choice of another Sultan. At last they all agreed that an-Nasir already mentioned, whom al-Adil had imprisoned in the castle of Mount Reall, should be their Sultan. This same an-Nasir reigned a long time and governed very wisely, so that after his death his eldest son was chosen Sultan, and he was called Melechinader [al-Mansur]. His brother had him secretly slain and reigned in his stead, and had himself called Melechimandabron [al-Ashraf]. And he was the Sultan when I left that land.

The Sultan can lead out of Egypt more than twenty thousand men at arms; and out of the realm of Syria and Turkey, and out of the other realms that are under his rule he can gather more than fifty thousand. And they all get their wages and all that they need from the Sultan; that is to say each man gets yearly six score florins; but each man must maintain three horses and a camel. And there are appointed among them in different cities and towns certain persons who are called admirals, and every admiral [emir] shall have at his command four or five or six [hundred] men at arms, and some command more. And every admiral will have for himself as much as all those beneath him get together. And therefore, when the Sultan is pleased to advance any good man who is with him, he makes him an admiral. And if any scarcity happens in that country, then poor knights and soldiers sell their equipment out of poverty.

The Sultan has three wives, of whom one shall be a Christian and the other two Saracens. And one of those wives shall live at Jerusalem, another at

Damascus, and the third at Ascalon. And whenever it pleases him he goes to visit them, and sometimes takes them about with him. Nevertheless he has concubines, as many as it pleases him to have; for, when he comes to any city or town, he has brought before him all the noblest and fairest maidens of the neighbouring region, and he has them looked after with nobility and dignity. And when he wants any of them, he has them all brought before him, and whoever is most pleasing to him, to her he sends, or takes a ring off his finger and throws it to her. And then she will be washed and perfumed and richly dressed and after supper she will be brought to his bedchamber. And he does this whenever he wants. No stranger must come before the Sultan unless he be clad in cloth of gold or tars [cloth of Tartary] or camlet – a fashion of clothing the Saracens follow. And whenever he sees the Sultan, at a window or elsewhere, he must kneel down and kiss the earth; for such is the manner there of doing reverence to the Sultan when anyone wants to speak to him. And when any foreigners come to him as messengers from far lands, his men stand round with drawn swords in their hands, and their hands raised on high to strike him down if he say anything displeasing to the Sultan. No stranger shall come before him to ask anything without having his request granted, if it be reasonable and not contrary to their law. And so do all other princes and lords in that country; for they say that no man should have audience of a prince without leaving happier than he came thither.

Do understand that this Babylon which I speak of at the moment, where the Sultan lives, is not Babylon the Great, where happened the Confusion of Tongues, when the Tower of Babilon [Babel] was being built. The walls of it were sixty-three furlongs high, and it is in the deserts of Arabia as you go towards the kingdom of Chaldea. But it is a long time since anyone dared approach that wretched place; for it is waste, and so full of dragons and snakes and other venomous beasts that no man dares come near it. The circumference of the Tower, with the extent of the city that was once there, is some twenty-five miles round, so they say in that country. And though it is called a tower, there were once within it many fair buildings, which are now destroyed; there is nothing but wilderness. And you should know that it was made foursquare, and each side was six miles or more long. Nembrot [Nimrod] made this same Tower; he was King of that land. And men say he was the first earthly King ever. He also had an image made in memory of his father, and commanded all his subjects to worship that image. Other great lords round about did the same; and thus began idolatry first. That same city of Babylon the Great was set in a fair plain, which was called the Field of Sennaar [Land of Shinar], on the River Euphrates, which ran through the city at that time. And the walls of the city were twenty cubits high and fifty cubits thick. But later Syrus [Cyrus], the King of Persia, cut off the water and destroyed the city and the surrounding country.

He diverted the great River Euphrates, and made it flow in three hundred and forty different channels. For he had made a great oath, and sworn very seriously, that he would bring it to the point where women could wade over and not wet their knees; and so he did. And the reason was that frequently in that river many of his worthiest men had been drowned.

From that Babylon where the Sultan dwells to Babylon the Great is forty days' journey, travelling north-east through the desert. And Babylon the Great is not subject to the Sultan but in the lordship of the King of Persia. He holds it of the Great Caan [Khan], who is a great emperor – indeed the greatest in the world, for he is lord of the great land of Cathay and many other countries, and of a great part of India. His land marches with Prester John's land; and he has such great lordships that he knows no end of them. He is greater and beyond comparison mightier than the Sultan. Of his great state and majesty I intend to speak later, when I come to it.

In the great deserts of Arabia is the city of Meek [Mecca] and there lies the body of Muhammad, much honoured, in a temple that the Saracens call Musket [a mosque]. And this city is thirty-two days' journey from Babylon where the Sultan dwells. You should know that the realm of Arabia is very large, but within it there are many deserts, which cannot be much inhabited because of the lack of water. For those deserts are so dry and sandy that nothing can grow in them. But where the land is inhabited there are very many people. Arabia stretches from the end of Chaldea to the end of Africa, and it adjoins Ydumee [Idumea] towards Botron [Bosra]. The chief city of Chaldea is Baldak [Baghdad]; and of Africa the chief city is Carthage, which was founded by Dido, who was the wife of Aeneas, first King of Troy and later of Italy. Mesopotamia also marches with the deserts of Arabia, and it is a great country, in which is the city of Aran [Harran], where the Patriarch Abraham once dwelt. From this city came the great scholars Effrem [Ephraim Syrus] and Teophill [Saint Theophilus the Penitent], whom Our Lady delivered from the slavery of the Devil, as is found written in the book of the Miracles of Our Lady. Mesopotamia stretches from the River Euphrates to the River Tigris; the realm lies between those two great rivers. And beyond the Tigris is the kingdom of Chaldea, which is a vast great country. In that country, as I said before, is the city of Baghdad where the Caliph used to dwell – he was Pope and Emperor of that people, that is to say lord of temporalities and spiritualities. And he was successor to Muhammad and his kindred. This city of Baghdad was once called Susis, and Nebuchadnezzar founded it. There dwelt Daniel the prophet, and often saw visions from God; and there he interpreted the King's dreams. Since the Sultan Saladin, the Caliphs have been called Sultans.

Babylon the Less, where the Sultan lives, and the city of Cairo that is nearby, are both fine big cities. And one of them is situated on the River Gyon [Gihon],

that is also called the Nile, and it comes from the Earthly Paradise. Each year
when the sun enters the sign of Cancer, this river begins to rise, and it rises
continually as long as the sun is in that sign and in the sign of Leo. It rises so
that sometimes it is twenty cubits deep, and then it inundates all the land and
often does much harm to places that are near the river. For no man may at that
time see to the cultivation of the land, and so there often happens a great scarcity
of corn in that country because of too much wet. And, similarly, there is great
shortage when the river rises only a little, because the land is then too dry. And
when the sun enters the sign of Virgo the Nile begins to fall, until the sun enters
Libra, and then it keeps within its banks. This river, as I said before, comes from
the Earthly Paradise and flows through the deserts of India, and then it sinks
down into the earth and runs a great way underground; it comes up again below
a mountain that is called Alloche [Atlas], which is between India and Ethiopia –
some five months' journey from the march of Ethiopia. And then it runs all
round Ethiopia and Mauretania, and so through all the length of Egypt to the
city of Alexandria. There it enters the sea, where Egypt ends. Along this river
there are very many birds, which are called ciconie or ibices in Latin [storks or
ibises].

7

Of the country of Egypt; of the Phoenix of Arabia;
of the city of Cairo; how to know balm;
and of Joseph's Barns

The land of Egypt is long but it is narrow, for men cannot inhabit it in breadth
because of the deserts, where there is great lack of water; and therefore it is
inhabited lengthwise along the river. For they have no moisture but what the
said river furnishes; for it does not rain there, but the land is inundated by the
river at certain times of the year, as I said before. And because there is no
disturbance of the air through any rains, and the air is always fair and clear,
without clouds, there used to be the best astronomers in the world there. The
aforesaid city of Cairo, in which the Sultan dwells, is next to the city of Babylon,
as I explained before, only a little way from the River Nile in the direction of the
deserts of Syria. Egypt is divided into two parts: the one part is between the Nile
and Ethiopia, and the other between the Nile and Arabia. In Egypt is the
country of Rameses and the country of Gesen [Goshen], where Jacob the
Patriarch and his offspring dwelt. Egypt is a very strong country; and in it are
many perilous harbours, for in each harbour there lie many great reefs of stone
in the entrance. Egypt has on the east side the Red Sea, which stretches as far as
the city of Couston [Kus]. And on the west side is the land of Libya, which

because of excessive heat is barren and brings forth no kind of fruit. On the south side is Ethiopia, and on the north are great deserts which extend as far as Syria. And so Egypt is strong on every side. The land of Egypt is, in length, fifteen days' journey, and in breadth but three, not counting the deserts. Between Egypt and the land that is called Numid [Nubia] is twelve days' journey through the deserts. The folk who dwell in that country are called Numidians [Nubians] and they are Christian. But they are black in colour, and they consider that a great beauty, and the blacker they are the fairer they seem to each other. And they say that if they were to paint an angel and a devil, they would paint the angel black and the devil white. And if they do not seem black enough when they are born, they use certain medicines to make them black. That country is marvellously hot, which makes its folk so black.

In Egypt are five districts, one that is called Sahit [Saîd], another Demeser [Damanhûr], the third Resich [Rosetta] (it is an island in the river Nile), the fourth Alexandria, and the fifth is Damietta. The city of Damietta was once very strong; but it was taken twice by Christian men, and after that the Saracens cast down the walls thereof, and of all the castles in that district. And they built another city and called it New Damietta. At this city of Damietta is one of the harbours of Egypt, and another is at Alexandria, which is a strong city, well walled. But they have no water except that which comes in conduits from the River Nile. And therefore, if men cut off the water from them, they could not hold out long. In Egypt are but few castles, for the country is strong enough of itself.

In the desert of the land of Egypt a holy hermit met, once upon a time, a monstrously shaped beast; for it had the shape of a man from the navel upward, and from there downward the form of a goat, with two horns standing up on its head. The hermit asked him, in God's name, what he was; and the beast answered and said, 'I am a mortal creature, as God has made me, and in this desert I dwell, and go about to seek my sustenance. Therefore I pray thee, hermit, to pray to God for me, that He who came from Heaven to earth for the salvation of man's soul, and who was born of a maiden, and suffered bitter Passion, through whom we all live and move and have our being, may have mercy on me.' The head of that beast, with the horns, is still kept at Alexandria as a marvellous thing.

In Egypt also is a city that is called Eliople [Heliopolis] – which means 'the city of the sun'. In this city is a temple round like the Temple of Jerusalem. The priest of that temple has a book in which is written the birthdate of a bird that is called the Phoenix; and there is only one in all the world. And this bird lives five hundred years, and at the end of the five hundredth year it comes to the temple and burns himself all to powder on the altar. And the priest of the temple, who from his book knew the time of the bird's coming, makes the altar ready and lays on it divers spices and sulphur uiuum [*virgin sulphur*] *and twigs of the juniper tree, and other things that burn quickly. And then the bird comes and alights on the altar, and fans with his wings until the things mentioned be alight; and there he burns himself to ashes. On the morrow they find in the ashes as it were a worm; on the second day that worm has turned into a perfectly formed bird; and on the third day it flies away from that place to where it normally lives. And so there is never more than one. This same bird is a symbol of Our Lord Jesus Christ, in as much as there is but one God, who rose on the third day from death to life. This bird is often seen soaring about, when the weather is fair and clear; and men say there, when they see the bird soaring in the air, that they will afterwards have good, happy years, for it is a bird of Heaven. This bird is no greater than an eagle in body; he has on his head a crest like a peacock, but it is much greater than a peacock's. His neck is yellow, his back indigo; his wings are red and his tail is barred across with green and yellow and red. And in the sunlight he seems marvellously beautiful, for these are the colours that shine most fairly.*

In Egypt are places where the earth bears fruit eight times in the year. And there the finest emeralds that ever were are found in the ground; and that is the reason they are so cheap there, unlike in other places. Also, if it should happen to rain once in the summer, all the land of Egypt is full of mice. In the city of Cairo men and women who have been born in other countries are brought to market frequently and sold, just as men sell beasts in other countries. There is also, in the city of Cairo, a public building full of holes – as it were, hen's nests; and the women of the country bring thither hen and duck and goose eggs, and put them in the nests. And certain persons are employed to look after that building and to cover the eggs with warm horse dung. And through the heat of the horse dung the eggs hatch birds without the brooding of a hen or any other bird. And at the end of three or four weeks the women who brought the eggs come and take away the birds and rear them according to the custom of the country. And in this way is all the country stocked with these kinds of birds. And they do this in winter as well as in summer.

In that country at a certain time of year long apples [bananas] are sold, which men of that country call apples of Paradise. They are sweet and delicious in the mouth. And when they are cut open, always in the middle of them is found the figure of the Cross. But they will rot within eight days, and so they cannot be taken to distant lands. The trees that bear them have leaves a foot and a half broad; commonly men find a hundred of these apples in a bunch. There are also other apples that are called Adam's apples [melons], and each one has in its side the mark as it were of teeth, just as if a man had bitten them. There are also fig trees that never bear leaves, but bear fruit on their bare branches. And they are called Pharaoh's figs. A little way outside the city of Cairo is a field where balm grows on small bushes, about a foot high, and they are like wild vines. In this field too are seven wells, where Christ in His youth used to play with other children; and there He showed several marvels. This field is not so well enclosed that people who want to cannot get in, except for the time when the balm is growing – at that time the balm is looked after very carefully. For it grows nowhere else in that country or anywhere but there. For if plants or cuttings are taken and planted elsewhere, they may well grow but they will never fruit. The leaves of the balm do not smell as good as the balm itself does. The dead branches are cut away with a tool made for that job, but not out of iron; [men cut with a sharp stone or a sharp bone]. If the tool were of iron, it would vitiate the virtue and the nature of the trees, as has often been proved by experience. The people of that country get Christian men to till that field and harvest it when the time comes to do so; otherwise the trees bear no fruit, as the Saracens say themselves, and as has often been proved. The Saracens call the trees that bear the balm enochbalse, *and the fruit, which is like cubebs, they call* abebissam. *But the sap that seeps out of the branches they call* oxbalse, *that is to say* opobalsamum. *Some men say that balm grows in Greater India, in the desert where the Trees of the Sun and Moon spoke to Alexander the Great. But I have not seen that place because of the dangerous ways to it, and so I cannot tell the truth of this. And you should understand that men can easily be deceived in buying balm unless they have good understanding of the matter. For some sell a kind of gum called turpentine and put in it a little balm to make it smell good. Some also mix with it the oil of the tree or of the berries of the balm and say it is good balm. Some distil cloves, spikenard and other sweet smelling spices, and the liquor that is distilled they sell instead of balm; and in this way are many men tricked, both lords and humbler folk. For the Saracens make such adulterations to deceive Christian men, as I have often realized by experience. Merchants and apothecaries too add other adulterations afterwards, and then it is of less value. But, if it pleases you, I shall show you how you may test what is true balm and not be deceived. You must know that balm which is natural and good is a clear yellow and has a strong sweet smell. If it is thick, red, or black it is adulterated. Or take a little balm and put it on the palm of your hand and hold it in the sun; and if you cannot hold it there for long because of the heat, it is good balm. Take also a little balm on the point of your knife and touch it with a flame; if it burns, it is a good sign. Or take a drop of balm and put it in a dish or cup and add to it goat's milk; if the balm is good, immediately the milk will curdle. Put also a drop of it in clear water in a goblet or in a clean basin and stir the water and the balm together; and if the water is clear after the stirring, the balm is good, and if it be thick and cloudy it is impure. The true balm is much stronger than that which is impure. Now have I briefly told you something about balm; and now I shall tell you about Joseph's Barns, which still exist in Egypt beyond the River Nile towards* *the desert that is between Egypt and Africa.* There are Joseph's Barns which were made to keep corn in for the seven lean years which were foretold in the seven dead ears of wheat which King Pharaoh saw in a dream, as the first book of the Bible says. And they are made wonderfully cleverly of well-hewn stone. Two of them are marvellously high, and broad too; the remainder are not so big. Each one of them has a porch at the entrance. These same Barns are now full of snakes; and outside many writings in divers languages are to be seen. Some men say that they are the tombs of some great men in ancient times; but the common opinion is that they are the Barns of Joseph, and they find that in their chronicles. And truly, it is not likely that they are tombs, since they are empty inside and have porches and gates in front of them. And tombs ought not, in reason, to be so high.*

In Egypt there are different languages and different letters of other shapes than in other places; and so I here set down the letters, their sounds, and their names, so that you know the difference between those letters and the letters of other languages.

athomanus	*binchi*	*chinok*	*dynam*	*em*	*fiu*
gomor	*heket*	*janiu*	*karacta*	*liuzamu*	*miche*
narme	*oldach*	*pilon*	*qyny*	*rou*	*sicheu*
thela	*vr*	*xyron*	*ypha*	*zarum*	*thou*

8

Of the isle of Sicily;
of the way from Babylon to Mount Sinai;
of the church of Saint Katherine, and the wonders there

Before I go any further, I want to go back and tell you of other routes men may take to Babylon where the Sultan dwells, which is at the entrance to Egypt. For

* These are of course the Pyramids, and Mandeville contradicts his source, Boldensele, who correctly saw they were tombs. The legend of Joseph's Barns was current for many years after this date – it may, indeed, have been supported by this very passage.

many pilgrims go there first, and then to Mount Sinai, and then return via Jerusalem, as I said before. For first they perform their most distant pilgrimage and then come back to the holy places that are nearer, even if they are not of the same importance as is Jerusalem, to which no other pilgrimage can be compared. But to perform all their journeys most effectively and with the least labour, some men go first to the further places and then to places that are nearer. Now he who wants to go first to Babylon by another route, more direct than I have told of before from this country or others near to it, may go through France and Burgoyne [Burgundy]. It is not necessary to note all the names of the cities and towns by which men must travel, for the route is common enough and well known to all men who are accustomed to travelling. But there are many ports to take ship at; some embark at the city of Geen [Genoa], some at Venice and sail through the Adriatic Sea, which is called the Gulf of Venice and which separates Italy from Greece, and some go to Naples, some to Rome, and some to Brunduse [Brindisi] and take ship there – or indeed in other places where they find a harbour and available shipping. Also some go through Tuscany and Campagna and Calabria and Apulia and the Isles of Italy by way of Choos [Corsica], Sardinia and Sicily, which is a beautiful and large island. In that island there is a garden with different kinds of fruits, and it is always green and full of flowers, both in winter and summer. This island is three hundred and fifty leagues round; and between Sicily and Italy is only a small arm of the sea, which is called Fare [Strait of Messina]. This island of Sicily is between the Adriatic and the Sea of Lombardy. In Sicily is a kind of snake with which men of that land are accustomed to test whether their children have been begotten in lawful wedlock or not. For, if they are so begotten, the snake will go round them and do them no harm. But if they were begotten in adultery, the snake will sting and poison them. In this way men of that country who suspect evil of their wives test whether their children are theirs or not. In this island too is the mount of Etna, which by another name is called Gebel. There are vents in the earth which are always burning; seven places especially, out of which come different coloured flames of fire. By the changing of the colours men of that land know – or guess – whether there will be a shortage of corn, or whether corn will be cheap, whether the weather will be cold or hot, rainy or fine. And many other things they divine and forecast by the colours of the flames. From Italy to these vents is only twenty-five miles; and it is said that they are the entrance gates of Hell.

He who goes via the city of Pisane [Pisa], as some do, where there is an inlet of the sea and two harbours, will travel by way of the island of Greff [Corfu] which belongs to the Genoese. Afterwards men land in Greece at the town of Mirrok [Mavrovo], or at Valon [Valona], or at Duraz [Durazzo], which belong to the Duke of Durazzo, or at some other haven on the shore of that sea; and then to Constantinople, then by sea to the Isles of Greece, and to the isles of Rhodes and Cyprus. And so, following the direct route by sea, from Venice to Constantinople is 1,880 Lombardy miles. From the kingdom of Cyprus one can travel by sea to the port of Jaffa, and then, leaving all that land to port, to the city of Alexandria, which stands beside the sea. Saint Katherine was beheaded in that city; and in that city was Saint Mark martyred and buried. But afterwards the Emperor Leo had his bones brought to Venice, and there they lie still. And there is at Alexandria a fine church, whitened all over; and so are all the churches of Christian folk there, for the pagans and the Saracens make them whitewash them all over to hide the frescoes and the images that were decorating the walls. This city of Alexandria is thirty furlongs in length and ten broad; it is a very fair and noble city. At this city the River Nile enters the sea, as I said before. In that river precious stones are often found, and the wood that is called lignum aloes, which comes from Paradise. It is medicinal for many ills, and it is sold very dearly. From Alexandria men go to Babylon where the Sultan resides; it is on the Nile. This is the shortest and easiest way men can go to Babylon.

Now I shall describe the route that must be followed from Babylon to Mount Sinai, where lies the body of Saint Katherine. One must pass through the deserts of Arabia, where Moses and Aaron led the Children of Israel. On that route there is a well to which Moses led them and gave them to drink of, when they murmured against him because they were thirsty. Further on the way there is another well, called Marrac [Marah], where they found the water brackish when they went to drink; Moses put therein some kind of wood, and immediately the waters were made sweet. Thence men go through this desert to the Vale of Elim, where there are twelve wells and seventy-two palm trees bearing dates, where Moses encamped the Children. From this vale to Mount Sinai is only a day's journey.

Anyone who wants to go another way from Babylon to Mount Sinai must pass through the Red Sea, which is an arm of the West Sea; through it the Children of Israel passed dryshod, when King Pharaoh pursued them, and he and all his host were drowned in it. And it is there about six miles wide. The water of that sea is no redder than other sea-water anywhere else; but because there is much red gravel on the shore of that sea, it is called the Red Sea. And it runs up to the borders of Arabia and Palestine. By this sea men spend more than four days' travel, and then they will come to the deserts and the Vale of Elim already mentioned and so to Mount Sinai. And you must know that no man can travel through the desert with horses, for there are no stables or provender or water for horses. And so that pilgrimage is made by camel, for they can find anywhere on the route branches of trees to eat, for they like that food well, and they can do without water for two or three days, which horses cannot. From Babylon to Mount Sinai is twelve days' journey. However, some make so much *speed in their travelling that they do it in less time. On this part of the journey it is necessary to have with them latimers [interpreters] until they understand the language of the country; this is also necessary in other countries in those parts. Men also have to take all their food with them through these deserts.*

Mount Sinai is called the Desert of Sin – which is to say, the Burning Bush; for there Moses saw Our Lord God speaking to him in a burning bush. At the foot of Mount Sinai there is an abbey of monks, well surrounded with high walls and iron gates for fear of the terrible and cruel wild beasts that dwell in those deserts. The monks who live there are Arabians and Greeks, and they are dressed like hermits; there is a large convent of them. They live on dates and roots and herbs; they drink no wine usually – only on days of high festival. They are devout men and lead a pure life, and live in great abstinence and great penance. There is the church of Saint Katherine, in which are many lamps burning. They use olive oil both for food and lighting, and that oil comes to them as if by a miracle. For every year rooks and crows and other birds come flying to that place in a great flock, as if they were in their way making a pilgrimage; and each one brings in its beak instead of an offering a branch of olive, which it leaves there; and in that way there is great plenty of olive oil for the sustenance of the house. Now since birds, which have no reason, do such reverence to that glorious virgin, we Christian men certainly ought to visit that holy place with great devotion. Behind the High Altar of that church is the place where Moses saw Our Lord in the Burning Bush. And when the monks come to that place, they take off their socks and shoes because God said to Moses 'Take your shoes off your feet, for the place where you stand is holy ground.'* That place is called the Shadow of God. And beside the High Altar are four steps leading up to the tomb of alabaster wherein the body of the holy virgin Saint Katherine lies. And the prelate of the monks shows the relics of this virgin to pilgrims; with an instrument of silver he moves the bones of the virgin on an altar. Then there comes out a little oil, like sweat; but it is like neither oil nor balm, for it is blacker. Of this liquid they give a little to pilgrims – for only a little comes out. After, they show you the head of Saint Katherine, and the cloth that it was wrapped in when the angels brought the body up to Mount Sinai. And there, with that cloth, they buried it; and the cloth is still bloody, and always will be. And they show also the bush that Moses saw burning, when Our Lord spoke to him. They show also many other relics. Each monk of that house has a lamp burning, and, so I was told, when an abbot dies, his lamp goes out. And in the choosing of another abbot, the lamp of him who by the grace of God is most worthy to be the next abbot lights by itself. Each of them has his lamp, as I said; and they know by the lamp when any of them will soon die, for at that time the lamp of him who is to die gives little light. It was also told me that when a

* Exodus iii, 5.

prelate is dead and is to be buried, he who sings High Mass will find in a scroll before him on the altar the name of him who will be chosen to be their prelate; and I asked the monks if this was so. But they would not tell me, but some said that sometimes it happened so. Even so, they would not say even so much until I said to them that it was not fitting to keep close counsel and conceal God's grace and His miracle, and that they should publish it abroad and openly reveal it to excite men to devotion. And I said moreover that they sinned greatly in concealing it, as it seemed to me, for the miracles God shows are tokens of His great might, as David says in the Psalter. When I spoke thus to them, then for the first time they told me what I have just told you; further answer to the questions I asked they would not give. Into that abbey neither fleas nor flies, or any other kind of vermin of corruption, ever come, by the miracle of God and His Mother Saint Mary and of the holy virgin Saint Katherine. For once there was so great a multitude of such unclean vermin there that the monks of the abbey were so tormented with them that they left the place, and went, escaping them, up into the hills. And then the Blessed Virgin came and met them and told them to return to their abbey, and that they would never again be grieved or annoyed by them. They did as she told them and returned, and after that day they never saw flea nor fly, nor any such kind of corruption to annoy them. In front of the gate of that abbey is the well where Moses struck the rock with his staff, and it ran with water and shall do evermore.

From this abbey men go up by many steps to the Mount of Moses. And there there is a church of Our Lady, where she met the monks, as I told you. And further up the mountain is the chapel of Moses, and the rocks Moses fled into when he saw Our Lord. In these rocks is the impression of his body; for so fast did he in flight thrust his body behind them that by the miracle of God the impression of his body was left on them. And fast by is the place where Our Lord gave Moses the Ten Commandments of the Law written on two tablets of stone by God's own hands. Under a rock there is a cave, where Moses dwelled when he fasted for forty days and forty nights. But he died in the Holy Land, and no man knew where he was buried. From this mountain men go across a great valley to another high mountain, where the angels buried the body of Saint Katherine. In that valley is a church of the Forty Martyrs, where the monks of the previous abbey hold services often; that valley is very cold. Then men go on up the Mountain of Saint Katherine; and it is much higher than the Mount of Moses. Where Saint Katherine was buried is no church, no chapel, nor other dwelling; but there is a pile of stones gathered together on the spot where she was buried. Once there was a chapel, but now it is all fallen, and the stones are still there. And although the collect for Saint Katherine says that it was in one and the same place that Our Lord gave the Law to Moses and Saint Katherine was buried, you should understand that one country is meant, or else two places bear the same name. For they are both called Mount Sinai, but they are a long way apart, separated by a big deep valley.

9

Of the desert between the church of Saint Katherine
and Jerusalem; of the Dry Tree;
and how roses first came into the world

When men have visited the holy place of Saint Katherine and want to continue to Jerusalem, first they take their leave of the monks and recommend themselves to their prayers. Those monks with a good will give victuals to pilgrims to cross the deserts to Surry [Syria]. The desert lasts for thirteen or fourteen days' journey. In those deserts dwell many people, who are called Arabians, Bedouin and Ascopardes [Sudanese?]. They are people of evil condition, full of all kinds of wickedness and malice. Houses have they none, only tents, which they make of skins of camels and other wild beasts that they eat, and they drink water when they can get it. They live in places where they can get water, for example on the Red Sea and other places where they find water. Often it happens that where water is found at one time of year, at another there is none; so they build no houses in fixed places, but sometimes here, sometimes there, as they find water. This folk I speak of do not work in tilling the land, for commonly they eat no bread, except some who are living near a good town which they can go to to get bread. They roast all their meat, and the fish that they eat, on stones in the heat of the sun. Nevertheless they are strong men, good fighters; and there is a great multitude of them. They do nothing else but hunt wild beasts, to catch them for their food. And they care not for their lives, and therefore they do not fear the Sultan nor any other prince of the world, and will fight with them if they do them any annoyance. They have often fought with the Sultan, for example, at the same time I was living with him. They have no armour to defend themselves with, only a shield and a spear. They wind a white linen cloth about their heads and necks. They are a very foul and cruel folk, and of evil nature.

After men have crossed this desert on the way to Jerusalem, they come to a city which is called Bersabee [Beersheba], which was once a fine city inhabited by Christian men, and still there are some of their churches standing. In that city Abraham the Patriarch lived. Bersabee

72

[Bathsheba] the wife of Ury [Uriah] founded that city, and called it Bersabee after herself. In that city King David begat on her Solomon the Wise, who was King of Jerusalem for forty years. Thence men go to the Vale of Ebron [Hebron], which is twelve miles from there; some call it the Vale of Mamre, that is to say the Vale of Greeting [Weeping], because our first father Adam lamented there for a hundred years for the death of his son Abel, whom Cain slew. In Hebron was once the chief city of the Philistines, and giants dwelled there. Afterwards it was also the city of priests of the tribe of Judah, son of the Patriarch Jacob. And it had the privilege that when a man fled there on account of manslaughter or any other serious crime, he could live securely in that city without being challenged by any man or taking any harm. To Hebron Iosue [Joshua] and Caleph [Caleb] and their company came first to spy out how they might win the Promised Land. In Hebron King David reigned first for seven and a half years; and in Jerusalem he reigned for thirty-three and a half years. In the city of Hebron are the graves of the Patriarchs Adam, Abraham, Ysaach [Isaac] and Jacob, and of their wives Eve, Sarah and Rebecca, and they are on the slope of the hill. Over them is a beautiful church, well walled about, like a castle, which the Saracens look after very well. They hold that place in great honour because of the Patriarchs who lie there. They allow no Christian men or Jews to enter there unless they have special leave of the Sultan; for they regard Christians and Jews as dogs, who should enter no holy place. That place is called *Spelunca Duplex*, or 'double cave', or 'double grave', for one lies above the other. The Saracens call it in their language Cariatharbe, which is to say 'the place of the Patriarchs'. The Jews call it Arboth. In that same place Abraham was sitting in his doorway, when he saw the three men and worshipped one, as Holy Writ witnesses, saying *tres uidit et unum adorauit*, that is to say, 'He saw three and worshipped one.'* And there Abraham took angels into his house as guests. And a little beside there is a cave in a rock, where Adam and Eve dwelled when they were driven out of Paradise; there they had their children. And, so some say, Adam was made there. Once that place was called the field of Damascus for it was in the lordship of Damascus. Thence he was translated into Paradise, as men say; afterwards he was driven out of Paradise and put back in this place once more. The same day that he was put into Paradise he was driven out, for as soon as he had sinned, he was expelled from that blissful place. The Vale of Hebron begins there, and stretches to Jerusalem. There the angel told Adam he was to live with his wife; there he

* A garbled version of Genesis xviii, 2.

begat Seth, of whose line Our Lord Jesus Christ was born. In that vale there is a field where men extract from the earth a substance called *cambille*,* and they eat it instead of spices; they often carry it away to sell in the country round about. The pit where it is dug up cannot be made so deep or broad that it is not full up again, by the grace of God, right to the brim by the end of a year.

Two miles from Hebron is the grave of Lot, the nephew of Abraham; and a little way from Hebron is the Mount of Mamre, from which the valley took its name. And there is a tree of oak that the Saracens call *dirpe*, and it dates from Abraham's time. This is that tree which men call the Dry Tree; and they say that it has been there since the beginning of the world, and that it was always green and in leaf until the time that Our Lord died on the Cross, and then it dried. And so did all the trees in the world, as some say, or else their heart-wood died and they became hollow within; many of them are yet standing in divers places. Some prophecies say that a great lord from the western part of the world shall conquer the Holy Land with the help of Christian folk, and he shall have a Mass sung under that Dry Tree, and then it will grow green again and bear leaves and fruit. Through the power of that miracle Saracens and Jews shall be converted to the Christian faith. And therefore that tree is held in great reverence, and the people of that country do it great honour and look after it very carefully. And although it is called, and is indeed, a Dry Tree, nevertheless there is great power in it; for whoever carries a piece of it on him will never be troubled by epilepsy, nor shall his horse founder while he carries it. The Dry Tree has many other virtues and so it is regarded as truly precious.

From Hebron men go to Bethlehem in half a day, for it is only five miles. The way is pleasant and good, through a plain and a wood. Bethlehem is only a little city, long and narrow, and well walled and moated. It was called in ancient times Effrata, as Holy Writ says: *Ecce, audiuimus eum in Effrata*,† that is to say, 'Behold, we have heard of it in Effrata.' Towards the east end of that city is a fine church with many ramparts and towers, well walled on all sides. Within that church are forty-four beautiful big pillars of marble. Between this church and the city is the Field *Floridus*; it is called the 'Field of Flowers' because a young maiden was falsely accused of fornication, for which cause she was to have been burnt in that place. She was led thither and bound to

---

* Editors usually gloss this as Arabic *kinbíl*, an orange powder made of the glandular hairs of the fruit capsules of a tree *Mallotus philippinensis*, used for dyeing silk and as a vermifuge. I can offer no more convincing explanation.

† Psalm cxxxii, 6.

the stake and faggots of thorns and other wood were laid round her. When she saw the wood begin to burn, she prayed to Our Lord that as she was not guilty of that crime He would help and save her, so that all men might know it. When she had thus prayed, she entered into the fire – and immediately it went out, and those branches that were alight became red rose-trees, and those that had not caught became white ones, full of blooms. And those were the first roses and rose-bushes that were ever seen. And thus was the maiden saved by the grace of God. Also, beside the choir of that church, on the right as men descend sixteen steps, is the place where Our Lord was born. It is now very beautifully decorated, and is richly coloured with gold and silver and azure and other colours. A little thence – some three paces – is the manger of the ox and the ass. And beside that is the spot where the star fell which led the Three Kings to Our Lord; and their names were Iasper [Caspar], Melchior and Balthazar. But the Greeks call them Galgalath, Malgalath and Seraphy. These Three Kings offered to Our Lord incense, gold and myrrh. And they came hither through a miracle of God's, for they met together in a city of India which is called Chasak [Kashan]; it is fifty-three days' journey from Bethlehem, yet they were at Bethlehem the fourth day after they saw the star. Also, in the cloister of this church, eighteen steps on the right side, is the Charnel of the Holy Innocents, where their bones lie. And in front of that place where Christ was born is the tomb of Saint Jerome, who was priest and Cardinal, and who translated the Bible into Latin out of Hebrew. Outside the church is his chair, which he sat in when he was translating the Bible. A little way from this church is another church, of Saint Nicholas, where Our Lady rested when she had given birth to her Child. And because she had too much milk in her breasts, which sore hurt her, she milked it out on the red slabs of marble that were there. The spots of white milk are still to be seen on the stone. You must know that nearly all who dwell in Bethlehem are Christian. And there are fine vineyards around the city, and great plenty of wine because of the work and organization of Christian men – for the Saracens do not cultivate the vine, nor do they drink any wine. For their Book of the Law which Muhammad gave them, which they call *Alkaron* [the Koran] – some call it *Massap* [Arabic *mashaf*, holy], others *Harme* [*horme*, holy] – forbids them to drink wine. For in that book Muhammad curses all those who drink wine and all those who sell it. For some men say that once he killed a good hermit, whom he loved much, in his drunkenness, and that therefore he cursed wine and those who drink it. But his curse be on his own head, as Holy Writ says, *Et in uerticem ipsius iniquitas eius*

75

descendet, that is to say, 'And his wickedness shall fall on his own head.'* The Saracens also raise no pigs, nor eat pork; for they say it is a brother to man and that it was forbidden in the Old Law. Also in the land of Palestine and in the land of Egypt they eat but little veal or beef unless it is so old that it can work and labour no more – not because it is forbidden, for they keep these animals for tilling the land. In this city of Bethlehem was King David born; and he had six wives, of which the first was called Michal, the daughter of King Saul. He had also many concubines.

From Bethlehem to Jerusalem is only two miles. On the road to Jerusalem, half a mile from Bethlehem, is a church, where the angels told the shepherds of the birth of Christ. And on that road is the tomb of Rachel, mother of Joseph the Patriarch; and she died as soon as she had borne Benjamin. There was she buried; and Jacob her husband set twelve great stones over her, betokening the twelve Patriarchs. Half a mile from Jerusalem the star appeared again to the Three Kings. And on this road to Jerusalem are many churches, by which pilgrims go to Jerusalem.

10

Of the pilgrimages in Jerusalem,
and of the holy places thereabout

To speak of Jerusalem: you must understand that it stands well set among the hills. There is neither river nor well, but water comes thither by conduit from Hebron. And I must tell you that this city was first called Jebus, down to the time of Melchisedek, and then it was called Salem to the time of King David. And he put these two names together and called it Jebusalem; and then came Solomon and called it Jerusalem, and it is still so called. And round about Jerusalem is the kingdom of Syria; beside is the land of Palestine, and Ascalon. But Jerusalem is in the land of Judea; and it is called Judea because Judas Maccabeus was King of that land. And to the east it marches with the kingdom of Arabia, on the south with Egypt, on the west it is bordered by the Great Sea [Mediterranean], and on the north by the kingdom of Syria and the Sea of Cyprus. There used to be a patriarch in Jerusalem, and archbishops and bishops in the country round. Round Jerusalem are these cities: Hebron seven miles away, Beersheba eight miles, Jericho six miles, Ascalon eighteen miles, Jaffa twenty-seven, Rames

* cf. I Samuel xxv, 39; I Kings ii, 44.

[Rama in Ephraim] three miles, and Bethlehem two miles distant. And two miles from Bethlehem to the south is the church of Saint Markaritot [Chariton], who was once abbot there, for whom the monks made great mourning when he died. There is still a painting which portrays the great grief and mourning they made for him, and it is a piteous thing to look on.

This land of Jerusalem has been in many different peoples' hands – Jews, Cananez [Canaanites], Assirienes [Assyrians], men of Persia, Medaynes [Medians]; Macedonians, Greeks, Romans, Christians, Saracens, Barbarenes [Barbarians], Turks and many other nations. For Christ desires not that it should long remain in the hands of traitors or sinners, Christian or otherwise. And now unbelievers have held that land seven score years and more – but by the grace of God they shall not keep it for long.

You must understand that when men arrive in Jerusalem they make their first pilgrimage to the church where is the Sepulchre of Our Lord, which was once outside the city on the north; but it is now enclosed within the town wall. There is a very fine church, circular in plan, well-roofed with lead. On its west side is a fine strong ⟨tower for the bells. In the middle of that church is a tabernacle, like a little house, built in a semicircle, decorated very handsomely and richly with gold and silver and azure* and other colours. On the right side of it is the Sepulchre of Our Lord. This tabernacle is eight feet long, five wide, and eleven high. Not long ago the Sepulchre was quite open, so that men could kiss it and touch it. But because some men who went there used to try to break bits of the stone off to take away with them, the Sultan had a wall built round the Tomb so that nobody could touch it except on the left side. The tabernacle has no windows, but inside there are many lamps burning. Among the other lights there is one which is always burning before the Sepulchre, and every Good Friday it goes out by itself, and on Easter Day it lights again by itself at that very hour when Our Lord rose from the dead to life. Also inside that church, on the right side, is the hill of Calvary, where Our Lord was crucified. The Cross was set in a mortice in the rock, which is white, streaked with red, in colour. Upon the rock blood dropped from the wounds of Our Lord when He suffered on the Cross. It is now called Golgotha; people go up steps to it. And in that mortice Adam's head was found after Noah's flood, as a token that the sins of Adam should be redeemed in that place. And higher on that rock Abraham made sacrifice to Our

* As above, in the description of the church of the Nativity, probably lapis lazuli.

Lord. There is an altar there, and before it lie Godfray de Boloon [Godfrey of Bouillon] and Baudewyne [Baldwin] his brother, and other Christian Kings of Jerusalem. Where Our Lord was crucified is a Greek inscription, which reads: *Otheos basileon ysmon presemas ergaste sothias oys* – some books say, *Otheos basileon ymon proseonas ergasa sothias emesotis gis* – which means in Latin *Hic deus, rex noster, ante saecula operatus est salutem in medio terre*, which is to say, 'Here God our King before all worlds has wrought salvation in the midst of the earth.'*
Upon the rock where the Cross was set is written thus: *Gros guist rasis thou pestes thoy thesmoysi*, or, *Oyos iustiys basis thou pesteos thoy themosi*,† which means in Latin, *Quod vides, est fundamentum totius fidei mundi huius*, which means, 'This that you see is the foundation of all the faith in the world.' You must understand that when Our Lord died he was thirty-three years and three months of age. But the prophecy of David said that He would be forty years old when he died, where he says this: *Quadraginta annis proximus fui generacioni huic*, which means, 'Forty years was I neighbour to this kindred.'‡ By this it might seem that Holy Writ was not true; but indeed it is true enough, for in the old times men counted their years as of ten months, of which the month of March was the first and December last. But Julius Caesar, who was Emperor of Rome, had the two months of Januere [January] and Feuerere [February] inserted, and decided the year of twelve months, that is to say of 365 days (excepting leap years) according to the proper course of the sun. And therefore, if we work on ten months to the year, He died in the fortieth year; but according to our years of twelve months he was thirty-three years and three months old. Close by the Mount of Calvary, on the right side, is an altar where lies the pillar to which Our Lord was bound while He was scourged. Four feet away are four stones, which continually drop water; some men say those stones mourn for Our Lord's death. Near to this altar, in a place forty-two steps underground, Saint Helena found the Cross of Our Lord Jesus Christ, under a rock where the Jews had hidden it. Two other crosses were also found, on which the two thieves who hung on either side of Christ were crucified. Saint Helena did not know for certain which was the cross Christ was killed on; so she took each one in turn and laid it on a dead man, and as soon as the True Cross was laid on the dead body, the corpse rose from death to life. By there in the wall is the place where the

---

* The 'Greek' seems to be a garbled version of Ὁ θεὸς βασιλεὺς ἡμῶν πρὸ αἰώνων εἰργάσατο σωτηρίαν ἐν μέσῳ τῆς γῆς. A reminiscence of Psalm lxxiv, 12.

† Ὁ ὁρᾶς ἐστὶ βάσις τῆς πίστεως ὅλης τοῦ κόσμου τούτου.

‡ This looks like a misreading of Psalm xcv, 10.

four nails which Christ was nailed with through foot and hand were hidden; He had two nails in His hands and two in His feet. The Emperor Constantine had one of these nails made into a bit for his bridle, which he used whenever he went into battle; through its virtue he overcame his enemies and conquered many different kingdoms – that is to say, Asia Minor, Turkey, Armenia the Lesser and the Greater, Syria, Jerusalem, Arabia, Persia, Mesopotamia, the kingdom of Aleppo and of Egypt Upper and Lower, and many other lands way off into Ethiopia and India the Lesser, which was then for the most part Christian. At that time there were many good holy men and holy hermits in those countries, of whom the book *Vitae Patrum* ['Lives of the Fathers'] speaks. And now for the most part those lands are in the hands of pagans and Saracens. But, when God wills, just as those lands were lost through the sins of Christian men, even so shall they be won again by Christians, with the help of God. In the middle of the choir of this church is a circle, in which Joseph of Arimathea laid the body of Our Lord when he had taken Him off the Cross; and men say that that circle is at the mid-point of the world. In that place Joseph washed Our Lord's wounds. Also in the church of the Sepulchre, on the north side, is a place where Our Lord was imprisoned – for he was imprisoned in many places. There is yet a piece of the chain with which He was bound. It was there He first appeared to Mary Magdalene when He rose from death to life, and she thought He was a gardener. In the church of the Sepulchre there used to be canons of the order of Saint Austyne [Augustine], and they had a prior; but their lord was the Patriarch. Outside the door of the church, on the right, as you go up twenty-eight steps, Our Lord spoke to His mother, as He hung on the Cross, thus: *Mulier, ecce, filius tuus*, that is to say, 'Woman, behold thy son' – He was referring to Saint John who stood there on one side. And to him He said, 'Behold thy mother.'* And up these steps went Our Lord with the Cross on His back to the place where He was crucified. Below these steps is a chapel, where priests hold services, but according to their rite, not ours. They always make the sacrament at the altar of bread, saying the *Pater Noster* and the words of the sacrament and little more; for they do not know the additions of the popes, which our priests are accustomed to use at Mass. Nevertheless they sing their Mass with great devotion. Near there is the place where Our Lord rested when He was weary with carrying the Cross. You ought to know that the city is weakest by the church of the Sepulchre, because of the great plain between the city and the church on the east. Eastward,

* John xix, 26.

outside the walls, is the Vale of Iosaphat [Jehosaphat], which comes right up to the walls. Outside the walls, overlooking that vale, is the church of Saint Stephen, where he was stoned to death. Beside there is the gate which is called *Porta Aurea* [Golden Gate] which may not be opened. Our Lord Jesus came riding in at that gate on an ass on Palm Sunday; and the gate opened before him when he came to the Temple. The hoof-prints of the ass are still to be seen in three places on the paving-stones. Two hundred paces in front of the church of Saint Stephen is a great Hospice of Saint John, where the Hospitallers had their first foundation. Going east from the hospice is a very fine church which is called Notre Dame la Grande. A little way away is another church, Notre Dame des Latins. There stood Mary Magdalene and Mary Cleophas, sorrowing for Our Lord when He was killed, and tearing their hair. In the Hospice of Saint John just mentioned is a great house set aside for sick people, and in it there are six score and four stone pillars supporting it.

11

Of the Temple of Our Lord; of the cruelty of Herod; of Mount Sion; of the Probatica Piscina and the Pool of Siloam

Eight score paces to the east of the church of the Sepulchre is the Temple of Our Lord, which is a very beautiful building. It is circular, and very high, and roofed with lead, and paved with white marble. But the Saracens will not allow Christians or Jews to enter it, for they say that such foul men should not enter so holy a place. Nevertheless I went in, and in other places where I would; for I had letters under the great seal of the Sultan, in which he strictly commanded his subjects to let me see all the places I wanted, and to show me the relics and the holy places as I wished; and they were to conduct me from city to city if there were need, and to welcome me and my companions kindly, and obey my requests in all reasonable matters unless they were against the royal dignity of the Sultan or against their law. To other folk who ask leave and permission of the Sultan to visit the places I have mentioned he usually gives only his signet; pilgrims carry this before them through the country hanging on a spear or pole, and folk of that land do great honour to it. But to me he did a special favour, because I was a long time in his service in his court. Men do such reverence to his signet that when they see it passing before them they kneel down as we do when the priest passes by us with the pyx. To his letters as well they do great reverence; for when they are brought to any lord or any other man, as soon as he sees them he bows reverently, takes them and touches them to his head, then kisses them and reads them on his knees; then he offers to do all things that the bringer of them wants, according to the tenor of them. In this Temple of Our Lord there used to be canons regular; and they had an abbot to whom they were obedient. Charlemagne was in this Temple when the angel brought him the foreskin of Our Lord when He was circumcised; afterwards King Charles had it taken to Paris. You must realize that this is not the Temple that Solomon built; that Temple lasted only a thousand one hundred and two years. For Titus, son of Vespasian, who was Emperor of Rome, laid siege to Jerusalem to destroy the Jews, because they put Christ to death without the assent and leave of the Emperor. When he had taken the city, he had the Temple burnt and cast it down and destroyed it; he took all the Jews and slew eleven hundred thousand of them, putting the remnant in prison. He sold them thirty for a penny, because he had heard that they had sold Christ for thirty pennies. Long after this, the Emperor Julian the Apostate, who denied and forsook the Christian faith, gave the Jews leave to build the Temple again at Jerusalem, for although he had before been a Christian, he hated Christian men. And when they had built the Temple, as God willed there came an earthquake which threw down everything they had done. Then the Emperor Adrian [Hadrian], who was of the lineage of Troy, repaired the city of Jerusalem, and restored the Temple and made it again as Solomon had built it, royal and noble. But he would allow no Jew to enter, only Christians; for even if he was not a Christian himself, he loved Christians more than any other men except those of his own faith. This Emperor had the church of the Sepulchre enclosed with a wall and brought within the city – it was outside before. And he changed the name of the city and called it Helyam [Aelia], but that name did not last long. The Saracens do great honour to the Temple of Our Lord, saying it is a very holy place. When they enter it, they take off their shoes and kneel often with great reverence. When my companions and I saw them do so, we too took off our shoes and thought it was the more reasonable that we Christians should do as much worship and honour to God as unbelievers did. This Temple is sixty-four cubits wide, as many long, and six score and five high. And within, on all sides, there are pillars of marble. In the middle of the Temple is a platform twenty-three steps high, with goodly pillars round it. This place the Jews call *Sancta Sanctorum* [Holy of Holies]. Into that place none came except the

Bishop of their Law when he made sacrifice. The people stood round about on different levels according to their) dignity and worship. There are four entrances to this Temple; the doors are of cypress, well and skilfully made. Just inside the east door, Our Lord said, 'Here is Jerusalem'. On the north side, inside the door, is a well, but no water flows from it – Holy Writ speaks of this well thus: *Vidi aquam egredientem de templo* etc.* On the other side is a rock that was once called Moriac [Moriah]; but afterwards it was called Luza [Bethel], where the Ark of God stood, and other holy things of the Jews. Titus had this Ark, with the holy things, taken to Rome when he had defeated the Jews. In that Ark were the Tablets of Moses, on which the Ten Commandments were written, and the rod of Aaron, and the staff of Moses with which he divided the Red Sea when the Children of Israel passed through it dryshod, and King Pharaoh followed them. With that same staff Moses struck the dry rock, and then great plenty of water ran forth. He did many miracles with that staff. In the Ark was also a gold vessel full of manna, which men call angels' food, with many other ornaments and clothing, of Aaron and of the Tabernacle. There was a table of gold, square, with twelve precious stones, and a casket of green jasper with four figures on it, and eight names of Our Lord therein; there were seven gold candlesticks, twelve phials of gold, and four censers of gold; there were an altar of gold and four lions of gold, upon which were golden cherubim twelve spans long; there were a circle with the twelve signs of Heaven, a tabernacle of gold, twelve trumpets of silver, a table of silver, seven holy loaves, and many other holy and precious things belonging to the service of God before the Incarnation of Christ. And on this rock Jacob slept, when he saw the angels going up and down by a stair; and he said, *Vere locus iste sanctus est, et ego nesciebam*, which is to say, 'Surely, this place is holy, and I knew it not.'* And there Jacob held the angel still, which changed his name and called him Israel. And in that place David saw the angel smiting the people with a sword, and then putting it all bloody in the sheath. And on this rock Our Lord stood when the Jews wanted to stone Him to death; and the rock split apart and He hid Himself in the cleft, and a star descended and gave Him light. On this rock Our Lady sat and learned her Psalter. There Our Lord forgave the sins of the woman who was taken in adultery. There was Christ circumcised. There Melchisedek offered bread and

* 'I saw water flowing from the Temple', Ezekiel xlvii, 1.
† Vulgate, Genesis xxviii, 16: *Vere Dominus est in loco isto et nesciebam*. A number of the supposedly biblical quotations in this text are not wholly accurate (like the reminiscence of Ezekiel just above).

wine to Our Lord, as a token of the sacrament that was to come. There David knelt, praying to Our Lord so that He would have mercy on him and his people, and Our Lord heard his prayer. And there he would have built the Temple, but Our Lord forbade him through an angel, because he had done wickedness when he slew Uriah, a good knight, for the sake of his wife. And so all that he had set aside for the building of the Temple he entrusted to Solomon his son, and he built it. And he prayed Our Lord that He would hear the prayer of all those who prayed devoutly in that place, and grant their righteous requests; Our Lord granted it. And so Solomon called it the Temple of Counsel, the Help of God and the Grace of God. Outside the door of the Temple is an altar where the Jews used to offer doves and pigeons. And in that Temple was Zachary [Zechariah] the prophet slain. From a pinnacle of the Temple the Jews cast down Saint James, who was the first Bishop of Jerusalem. At the entrance to the Temple is the gate called *Speciosa* [the Beautiful] where Saint Peter healed the crippled man and made him walk. A little way from the Temple, on the right, is a lead-roofed church, which is called the School of Solomon. And towards the south is the Temple of Solomon, which is a very beautiful place; it stands in a fine large plain. In that place knights – called Templars – lived, and that was the mother house of the Templars and their Order. And just as knights lived there, so canons used to live in the Temple of the Lord. Six score paces east of this Temple in a corner of the city is the bath of Our Lord, and water used to come into it from Paradise. A little way from it is Our Lady's bed, and nearby is the tomb of Saint Simeon. To the north, outside the Temple, is a fine church of Saint Anne, mother of Our Lady; there was Our Lady conceived. In front of that church is a tree that began to grow that same night. And as you descend twenty-two steps from that church, Joachim, Our Lady's father, lies in a stone tomb. Once Saint Anne lay beside him, but Saint Helena had her translated to Constantinople. In this church is a well, like a cistern, which is called *Probatica Piscina* [the Pool of Bethesda], and it once had five entrances. In that cistern the angels used to come and bathe and disturb the water, and the man who first bathed therein after the disturbing of the water was made whole of whatever sickness he had. There was the man healed who had been sick for thirty-eight years. There Our Lord said to him *Tolle grabatum tuum et ambula*, which is to say, 'Take up thy bed and walk.'* A little thence was the house of Pilate, and also the house of Herod, the King who had the Innocents slaughtered. The same Herod was a wicked and cruel man. For first he

* Matthew ix, 6.

made away with his wife, whom he loved above all other creatures; and because of the great love he had for her, when he saw her dead he went out of his mind and stayed that way a long time. Afterwards, when in course of time he had come to his right mind, he had the children he had of her slain. And then he had his other wife killed, and a son he had by her, and his own mother. So he would have done to his brother, but he died before he could achieve his purpose. And when he saw he was dying, he sent for his sister and all the great lords of the land, and when they had come he had all the lords put in a tower; he said to his sister that he well knew that the people of his country would not mourn for him when he was dead, and so he made her swear that she would put all those lords to death as soon as he was dead, 'for so all the country will sorrow when I die'. He made his will thus, and died soon after. But his sister did not do his will; for as soon as he was dead she released the lords from the tower and told them what her brother had wanted, and let them go where they would. You ought to know that there were three Herods, which were wicked and cruel men. The one I have just been speaking of was called Herod Ascalonyte [Herod the Great]; he who cut off the head of John the Baptist was called Herod Antipater [Antipas]; and Herod Agrippa had Saint James killed, the brother of the Evangelist Saint John, and put Saint Peter in prison.

Furthermore, in the city of Jerusalem is a church of Saint Saviour, and there there is the left arm of Saint John Chrysostom, and the greater part of the head of Saint Stephen. A little south from there is a church of Saint James, where he was beheaded. And then Mount Sion: there is a fair church of Our Lady, on the spot where she lived and died. There used to be an abbot there, with canons regular. Thence Our Lady was carried by the angels to the Vale of Jehosaphat. There is also a stone brought to Our Lady by angels from Mount Sinai, and in every respect it is like the rock of Mount Saint Katherine. Near there is the gate through which Our Lady went to Bethlehem. At the beginning of Mount Sion, too, there is a chapel in which is the huge stone with which the Sepulchre of Christ was covered when He was laid in it. The three Marys saw this stone overturned and cast off the grave when they came to the Sepulchre. There is also a little piece of the pillar to which Our Lord was bound when He was scourged. Annas's house was there – he was Bishop of the Jews at that time. There too is a piece of the table on which Christ instituted the Eucharist and gave His body in the forms of bread and wine. There Peter denied Our Lord three times before cockcrow. Going down thirty-two steps below this chapel is the place where Our Lord washed His disciples' feet – the vessel the water was in is still there. Near there is the place where Saint Stephen was buried. There is an altar where Our Lady heard the angels singing Mass. At that spot Christ appeared first to his disciples after His Resurrection, when the doors were locked, and said to them, *Pax uobis* ['Peace be unto you'].* And on Mount Sion Christ appeared to Saint Thomas and told him to feel his wounds; then he believed for the first time and said, *Dominus meus et Deus meus* ['My lord and my God'].† Behind the high altar in this chapel all the Apostles were gathered together on Whit Sunday, when the Holy Ghost descended on them in the likeness of fire. There Christ kept His Easter with His disciples, and there Saint John the Evangelist slept on Our Lord's knee and in his sleep saw many of the mysteries of Heaven.

Mount Sion is inside the city, and it is somewhat higher than other places in the city. The city is stronger on that side than on others; for at the foot of Mount Sion is a good strong castle which the Sultan had built. On Mount Sion King David and Solomon and others were buried. There is the place where Saint Peter wept grievously when he had forsaken Christ. A little thence – about a stone's throw away – is another chapel, where Our Lord was condemned to death. Caiaphas's house was there. East from this chapel, at seven score paces' distance, is a deep cave under a rock, which is called *Galilea Domini*; Saint Peter hid there after he had denied Christ three times. Between the Temple of Solomon and Mount Sion is the place where Our Lord raised the girl from the dead. Below Mount Sion, towards the Vale of Jehosaphat, is a well that is called *Natatorium Siloa* [the Pool of Siloam]. Our Lord was washed there after He was baptized; there He made the blind see. There too was the prophet Ysai [Isaiah] buried. A little way off, but over against the pool, is a sculpture in stone, ancient work; it is called Absalom's hand, and Absalom had it made. A little way away is the tree on which Judas hanged himself when he had betrayed Christ. Then there is the synagogue where the Bishop of the Jews and the Pharisees came together to take counsel together against Jesus. And there Judas threw the thirty pieces of silver from him and said, *Peccaui, tradens sanguinem iustum*, that is to say, 'I have sinned in betraying righteous blood.'‡ And on the other side of Mount Sion, to the south, a stone's throw away is the field that was bought with those thirty pennies; and it is called Acheldemak, which means 'the Field of Blood'. In this field are the graves of many Christian pilgrims, for it is the custom to bury pilgrims there. There are also many churches and chapels and

* John xx, 19, 21, 26.   † John xx, 28.   ‡ Matthew xxvii, 4.

hermitages, where hermits dwell. A hundred paces thence, to the east, is the charnel-house of the Hospice of Saint John.

A mile west of Jerusalem is a fine church where the tree grew of which the Holy Cross was made. Two miles thence is a church where Our Lady met Elizabeth when they were both with child, and Saint John moved in his mother's womb and worshipped Our Lord his maker. Under the altar there is the place where Saint John the Baptist was born. Only a mile from there is the castle of Emaus [Emmaus] whither two of Christ's disciples went after the Resurrection, and they recognized Our Lord there in the breaking of bread. Also two miles from Jerusalem is the Mount Joy, which is a beautiful pleasant place; Samuel the prophet lies there in a fine tomb. It is called Mount Joy because from it pilgrims can get their first view of Jerusalem, and after their great journey they have great joy and comfort in that sight. Between Jerusalem, and the Mount of Olivet is the Vale of Jehosaphat below the walls of the city, as I said earlier; and in the middle of the valley is a little brook, called the *Torrens Cedron* [Kedron]. Over this brook the tree of which the Cross was made used to lie as a plank bridge so that men could cross it. Not far away is a pit in the ground, in which is the base of the pillar to which Christ was bound when He was scourged. In the middle of the valley is a church of Our Lady, where her grave is. You must know that when Our Lady died she was seventy-two years old. Near her grave is the place where Our Lord forgave Saint Peter all his sins. Only a little way away, to the west, under an altar, is a spring that comes from one of the rivers of Paradise. Though this church now seems lower that the ground round about it, you should know that it was not like that when it was first built; but because of the crumbling of the walls of the city, which have fallen there, the ground-level round the church has risen, and so it is now higher than the church even though the church was on level ground when it was built. Yet the common opinion is that the earth has risen by itself since the time Our Lady was buried there, and that it rises day by day. There used to be black monks [Benedictines] there, who had an abbot over them. Beside this church is a chapel, near the rock that is called Gethsemane, where Judas kissed Our Lord when He was arrested by the Jews. There Christ left His disciples before His Passion, when He went apart to pray and said, *Pater, si fieri potest, transeat a me calix iste*, which means 'Father, if it may be done, let this passion pass from me.'* In the rock the impressions of Our Lord's hands may still be seen, where He pushed the rock when the Jews took Him. A stone's throw from there,

* Luke xxii, 42.

86

to the south, is another chapel, where Our Lord sweated blood. Near there is the tomb of King Jehosaphat, from whom that valley takes its name, for he was King of that country. A bow shot thence, to the south, is a church where Saint James and Zechariah the prophet were buried. On one side of the Valley of Jehosaphat is the Mount of Olivet; it is so called because many olives grow there. It is higher than the city of Jerusalem, and therefore from it men can see into all the streets of Jerusalem. Between that hill and the city there is only the Valley of Jehosaphat, which is not very wide. Upon that hill Our Lord stood when He mounted into Heaven; men can still see the footprint of His left foot in a stone He stood on. Once there was there an abbey of black canons [Augustinian] but now there is only the church. A little thence – twenty-eight paces – is a chapel, and in it is the stone whereon Our Lord sat and preached to the people, saying, *Beati pauperes spiritu, quoniam ipsorum est regnum celorum*, etc., which is to say, 'Blessed are the poor in spirit, for theirs is the kingdom of Heaven.'* There He taught the disciples the *Pater Noster*, writing there on a stone; the writing is still visible today. Nearby is a church, where [Saint] Mary the Egyptian lies in a tomb. A little thence, to the east, is Bethphage, where Our Lord commissioned two of the disciples to fetch Him the ass on Palm Sunday. A little way to the east of the Mount of Olivet is a castle that men call Bethany. There dwelt Simon the leper, who lodged Our Lord and His disciples. This Simon was later baptized by the Apostles and called Julian, and was later made a bishop. This is the Julian men pray to for good lodging. In that same place Our Lord forgave Mary Magdalene's sins, and she washed His feet with tears and dried them with her hair. There Lazarus was raised to life from the dead, when he had lain four days stinking in his grave. There was the house of Lazarus and of Martha his sister. There Mary Cleophas also dwelt. This castle is only a mile from Jerusalem. A little way away is the place where Our Lord wept over Jerusalem. Near there is the place where Our Lady gave Saint Thomas her girdle after her Assumption. A little thence is a stone on which Our Lord sat and preached, and He will appear in the same spot on the Day of Judgement. A little way from the Mount of Olivet is the Mount of Galile, where the Apostles were all gathered together when Mary Magdalene told them of Christ's rising from the dead to life. Midway between Mount Olivet and Mount Galile is a church where the angel warned Our Lady of her death.

It is five miles from Bethany to Jericho. Jericho was once a fine city, but it is destroyed, and there is now only a little village. This city Joshua

* Matthew v, 3ff.

captured through a miracle of God, and razed it level with the earth, commanding that it should never be rebuilt; also he cursed all who built it up again. Zacchaeus, whom the Gospel tells of, who climbed up into a sycamore tree in order to be able to see Our Lord, was from this city. So too was Raab [Rahab] the harlot, who welcomed the messengers of Israel who came to spy out that land; she hid them in her house among the stalks of flax and said they had left the city before the gates were shut. Afterwards, at night, she let them down by a rope from the walls of the city and saved them from death. And so when the city was taken she was well rewarded, as she deserved to be. For Holy Writ says, *Qui recipit prophetam in nomine prophete, mercedem prophete accipiet*, which means, 'He that receiveth a prophet in the name [of a prophet]* shall receive a prophet's reward.' And so she had a special gift from God, for she foretold to the messengers that they would win all that land, and so it turned out. Afterwards Salomon [Salmon] who was Prince of the tribe of Judah wedded her; and of their line in due time came Our Lady Saint Mary, the mother of Our Lord Jesus Christ.

From Bethany men go through the desert to the River Jordan – it is nearly a day's journey. From Bethany also to a hill where Our Lord fasted for forty days and forty nights is six miles; that hill is called Quarentane. There the Devil came to tempt Our Lord and said to Him, *Dic, ut lapides isti panes fiant*, which is to say, 'Command that these stones become bread.'† On that hill in that place was once a fine church, but now there is nothing left but a hermitage, where live a sort of Christian folk called Georgians, for Saint George converted them. Abraham lived on that hill a long time. Between this hill and the River Jordan runs a little stream, whose water was once marvellously bitter; but from the time when the prophet Helizeus [Elisha] blessed it, it was sweet enough and quite drinkable. At the foot of this hill, towards the plain, is a large spring, which empties into the Jordan. From this hill to Jericho is only a mile, as one descends to the River Jordan. On the road to Jericho the blind man sat, who cried out, *Ihesu, fili Dauid, miserere mei*, which is to say, 'Jesus, son of David, have mercy on me.'‡

* Egerton and Cotton both say 'in *my* name'. Cf. Matthew x, 41.
† Luke iv, 3.
‡ Matthew ix, 27.

12

Of the Dead Sea; of the River Jordan;
of the head of John the Baptist,
and of the customs in the country of the Samaritans

Three miles from Jericho is the Dead Sea. Between Jericho and that sea
is the country of Engeddi. Once balm grew there, but it was trans-
planted from there to Egypt, where the bushes the balm grows on are
still called vines of Engeddi. On the side of this sea that you come to as
you come from Arabia is a hill of the Moabites, which is called Arnon.
Balach [Balak], son of Beor [Zippor], took Balahaam [Balaam] the
prophet up on this hill to curse the Children of Israel. This same Dead
Sea separates the lands of Judea and Arabia; it stretches from Zorea
[Zoar] to Arabia. The water of this sea is very bitter and salt, and if the
earth is watered with it it becomes barren and never bears crops. This
water often changes colour. This sea casts up from itself a substance
which is called asphalt. Each day on each side of this sea great lumps of
it, as big as a horse, can be found washed up on the shore; it is like
pitch. And so some call the sea the Lake Asfaltit [Asphaltis], which
means the Lake of Pitch. It is called a sea because of its size; for it is
seven hundred and four score furlongs in length and 150 in breadth. It
is called the Dead Sea because it neither ebbs nor flows, but always
stands still, and it neither brings forth nor fosters any living thing. It
will receive no manner of living thing into itself, man nor beast, fish nor
fowl. That has often been proved; for men have often thrown criminals
into it who have been condemned to death for their crimes, and it has
immediately cast them out again. Ships cannot sail on it unless they are
well dressed with pitch; for nothing dead can go into it without
immediately sinking, unless it is well painted with pitch. If a lighted
lantern is thrown in, it floats; if an unlit one is thrown in, immediately it
sinks. And if iron is thrown into it, it rises again and floats on top; but if
a feather is thrown in, it sinks. And that is against nature. And just so
for sins against nature were the five cities which once stood there
destroyed and drowned – that is, Sodom and Gomorrah, Aldama
[Admah], Sobeym [Zeboiim], and Segor [Zoar]. But Zoar for the most
part was saved by the prayer of Lot, for it stood on a hill. In clear
weather men can still see the walls of it above the water. No man dares
live near this sea, nor drink of its water. Some men, as I said, call it the

Lake Asphaltis, and some the Devil's Lake, some the Stinking River, for its water does stink. By the side of this sea grow trees that bear apples fine of colour and delightful to look at; but when they are broken or cut, only ashes and dust and cinders are found inside, as a token of the vengeance that God took on those five cities and the countryside round about, burning them with the fires of Hell. On the right side of this sea Lot's wife was turned into a block of salt because she looked behind her against the orders of the angel at the time when God destroyed the cities. You know that Lot was Aram's [Haran] son, and Aram was Abraham's brother; and Sarah, Abraham's wife, and Melcha [Milcah], Nachor's [Nahor] wife, were Lot's sisters. When Sarah bore Isaac she was ninety years old. Abraham also had another son, who was called Ishmael, and he was circumcised when he was fourteen years old. But Isaac was circumcised when he was eight days old.

The River Jordan runs into the Dead Sea, and ends there, for it runs no further. It is only a mile to the west from a church of Saint John the Baptist where Saint John baptized Our Lord. Christian men commonly wash themselves there. And a mile from the Jordan is another stream, which is called Iaboth [Jabbok] which Jacob crossed when he came back from Mesopotamia. The River Jordan is not very big, but is full of fish; it flows down from Liban [Lebanon], rising there in two springs, one of which is called Ior and the other Dan; it takes its name from the two springs. It flows through a country called Maran [Lake Merom], then through the Sea of Tiberias and below the hills of Gelboe [Gilboa]; there is a rich plain on each side of the river. The mountains of Lebanon stretch to the desert of Pharan, separating the kingdom of Syria and the country of Fenice [Phoenicia]. On those hills very tall cedars grow, and they bear long apples which are as big as a man's head. The River Jordan separates Galilee and the land of Idumea and the land of Betron [Bosra]; in some parts it runs below the earth, as far as a fair plain which is called Meldan* and the Jordan is very wide there. In that plain is the tomb of Job. In this river Christ was baptized by Saint John, and there the voice of His Father was heard saying, *Hic est filius meus dilectus, in quo michi bene complacui*, which is to say, 'Here is my beloved son, in whom I am well pleased. Hear Him.'† And there the Holy Ghost descended on Him in the form of a dove, and thus at His Baptism all the Trinity was present. Through that River Jordan the Children of Israel passed dryshod; they set great stones in the midst of the water as a

* MS Harley 4383 has 'qu homme appelle Meldan en Sarazinois, ceo est a dire Foire ou Marchee.' 'Meldan' is clearly the Arabic *maidan*, square or market place.

† Matthew iii, 17.

token of the miracle. Naaman of Syria bathed himself in that river seven times, and he was healed of his leprosy and made as sound as a fish. There are many churches near the River Jordan with Christian men dwelling in them. A little way from it is a city called Hayla [Ai] which Joshua besieged and took. Beyond the Jordan is the Vale of Mamre, which is a very beautiful valley. Two miles from the hill – which I mentioned before – where Our Lord fasted forty days and nights, towards Galilee, there is a high mountain to which the Devil led Our Lord and showed Him all the kingdoms of the earth and said to Him, 'All these I shall give Thee, if Thou wilt fall down and worship me.'*

You ought to know that as one makes one's way east from the Dead Sea out of the borders of the Land of Promise there is a fine strong castle, standing on a hill called Carras, which means Mount Real [Krak]. Baldwin, who was King of Jerusalem, and who conquered all that land, had that castle built and garrisoned by Christians. Below that castle is a good town, called Soboach [Shobek], where many Christians live securely enough under tribute [to the Saracens]. Thence men go to Nazareth, from which Our Lord had His surname. From there to Jerusalem is three days' journey. One travels through the country of Galilee, through Ramathaim Sophim [Ramah in Ephraim] and the hills of Ephraim, where lived Helchama and Anna [Elkanah and Hannah] the father and mother of Samuel the prophet. Samuel was born there, but he was buried on the Mount of Joy, as I said above. Then one reaches Sylo [Shiloh], where the Ark of the Lord was kept by Hely [Eli] the priest of the Law. The people of Hebron sacrificed there to Our Lord. There Our Lord first spoke to Samuel. Near there, at the left side, is Gabaon [Shobek] and Rama Beniamyn [Ramah in Benjamin] of which Holy Writ speaks. Thence one goes to Sychem [Shechem], which by another name is called Sychar, in the country of Samaria, ten miles from Jerusalem. Some call it Neopolis, which means 'new city'. Very close to it is Jacob's Well, where Our Lord spoke to the Samaritan woman. There was once a church there; it is now destroyed. Beside that well Jeroboam King of Israel had two golden calves made, and sent one of them to Dan and the other to Bethel, commanding the people that they should worship them as gods. A mile from Shechem is a city called Bethel where Abraham dwelled for a time. A little way from there is the sepulchre of Joseph the son of Jacob, who ruled Egypt; his bones were brought from Egypt and buried there. In the city of Shechem Dinah the daughter of Jacob was ravished, on whose account her brothers slew many of the people of that city. A little way from that city is the Mount

* Luke iv, 7.

Garisym [Gerizim] where the Samaritans perform their sacrifices. On
that hill Abraham was to have offered his son Isaac to Our Lord. Near
there is the Vale of Dothaym [Dothan]. In that vale is the cistern into
which Joseph was cast by his brothers before they sold him to the
Ishmaelites – it is two miles from Shechem. Thence men go to a city of
Samaria that is called Sebaste [Sebastiyeh], the chief city of that country,
set among the hills like Jerusalem. But that city is not as large as it once
was. Saint John the Baptist was buried there between two prophets,
Elisha and Abdias [Obadiah?]. But he was beheaded in the castle of
Macheron [Machaerus] by the Dead Sea, and his disciples carried him to
Sebastiyeh. There Julian the Apostate, when he was Emperor, had his
bones exhumed and burnt, and the ashes were scattered in the wind. But
the finger with which Saint John indicated Our Lord, saying, *Ecce Agnus
Dei* etc. [Behold the Lamb of God], could not be burnt. This finger Saint
Tecle [Thecla] the Virgin had taken to the mountains [of Sebastiyeh], and
there great honour is done to it. Once there was in that place a fine
church, but it is now destroyed with all the other churches that were
there. There the head of Saint John was enclosed in the wall; but the
Emperor Theodosius had it taken out, and he found it wrapped in a
bloody cloth. So he had it taken to Constantinople, and half of it is still
there; the other half is in Rome in the church of Saint Silvester. The vessel
in which the head was put when it was struck off is at Genoa, and men do
it great honour. Some say that Saint John's head is at Amyas [Amiens] in
Pykardy [Picardie]; and some say that that one is the head of Saint John
the Bishop. I do not know; God knows.

From Sebastiyeh to Jerusalem is twelve miles. Among the hills of this
land is a well which changes colour four times in the year. Sometimes it
is green, sometimes red, sometimes turbid and sometimes clear; men
call that well Iol.* The people of that land are called Samaritans, and
they were converted and baptized by the Apostles. But they did not
keep to the Apostles' teachings, and so they have fallen into errors and
follow a sect of their own, keeping a law different from the laws of the
Christians, Jews, Saracens and pagans. Nevertheless they believe in
one God, and say there is none beside him, who made all and will judge
all. They follow the Five Books of the Bible [the Pentateuch] to the
letter, and use the Psalter as the Jews do. They say they are the true
children of God, and better loved by Him than other men. Their
manner of dress also differs from other mens,' and they wind their
heads with a red linen cloth so that they shall be known apart. For the
Saracens wrap their heads in white, Christian men who dwell there

* The Bath of Job.

wrap theirs in blue, and the Jews in yellow cloth. Many Jews live there, paying tribute as the Christians do. And if you would know what kind of letters the Jews use, here you may see them set out with their names: Aleph, Beth, Gymel, Deleth [Daleth], He, Vau, Zai [Zain], Heth [Cheth], Theth [Teth], Ioth [Jod], Caph, Lameth [Lamed], Mem, Nun, Sameth [Samech], Ain, Fe [Pe], Sade [Tzaddi], Coph, Res [Resh], Sen [Schin], Tau. Now will I set out the shapes of the letters:

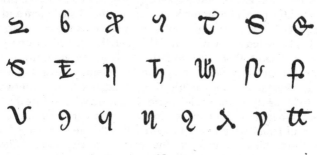

13

Of the province of Galilee, and where Antichrist will be born; of the age of Our Lady; of the Day of Judgement; and of the customs of the Syrian Jacobites

From this country I have spoken of men go to the plains of Galilee, leaving the hills on one side. Galilee is a country in the Promised Land, and in it are the cities of Naym and Capharnaum [Capernaum], Corozaim [Chorozin] and Betsayda [Bethsaida] where Saint Peter and Saint Andrew were born. At Chorozin Antichrist will be born. But some say he will be born in Babylon, and therefore the prophecy says, *De Babilonia exiet coluber, qui totum [mundum] deuorabit,** which means, 'Out of Babylon shall a serpent come which shall devour all the world.' This Antichrist will be brought up in Bethsaida, and he will reign in Chorozin; and so Holy Writ says of them, *Ve tibi, Corozaym! Ve tibi Bethsaida! Ve tibi Capharnaum!* which is to say, 'Woe unto you, Chorozin! Woe to you, Bethsaida! Woe to you, Capernaum!'† Cana of Galilee is there, four miles from Nazareth; Saint Simon was born there. There too Our Lord did His first miracle, at the wedding of

* Source unknown: there is something like it in the Apocryphal Epistle of the Apostles.
· † cf. Matthew xi, 21–23; Luke x, 13–15.

Architriclyne*, when he turned water into wine. In the marches of Galilee, among the mountains, was the Ark of God taken. On the other side is the hill of Endor in Hermon. A little way from there Barach [Barak], son of Abymalech [Abinoam] and the prophetess Debbora [Deborah], overcame the hosts of Idumea, when Cisara [Sisera] the King was killed by Iabel [Jael] the wife of Aber [Heber], as the Bible relates. In that same place Gideon and three hundred men defeated three kings, Zeb, Zebee and Salmana [Zebah, Zeeb and Zalmunna], and carried the pursuit over the River Jordan; they killed them and the largest part of their army. Five miles from Naym is the city of Iesrael [Jezreel], also called Zaraym. Iesabel [Jezebel] the wicked queen was of that city; she had Naboth slain unrighteously for his vineyard. A little way from this city is the field of Mageddo [the plain of Megiddo], where the King of Samaria slew Josias† the King of Judah, who was afterwards carried to Mount Sion and buried there. A mile from Jezreel are the hills of Gilboa, where King Saul, his son Jonathan and a great number of the Children of Israel were killed in battle. For this reason King David cursed those hills. A mile to the east is a city called Citople [Scythopolis], or Bethsaym [Bethshan]. The Philistines hung the head of King Saul on the walls of that city.

Thence men go through the plain of Galilee to Nazareth, which was once a big city; but now there is only a little unwalled village. In Nazareth was Our Lady born, but she was conceived at Jerusalem. Our Lord took His surname from Nazareth. There Joseph wedded Our Lady, when she was fourteen years old. There the angel Gabriel greeted Our Lady, saying, *Aue, gratia plena! Dominus tecum*, that is, 'Hail Mary, full of grace! The Lord is with thee.'‡ In that same place is a chapel, built beside a pillar of a church that was there in the old days; Christian pilgrims make great offerings there. The Saracens look after this chapel very strictly because of the profitability of the alms-giving. The Saracens there are very evil, much crueller than in other places; for they have destroyed all the churches that used to be there. There is the Well of Gabriel, where Our Lord used to bathe when He was young. And from that well He used to fetch water for His mother, and she used to wash His clothes there. From Jerusalem to Nazareth is three days' journey. Our Lord was brought up there. Nazareth means 'flower of the garden'; and well may it be called so, for there the Flower of Life

* Latin *architriclinus*, 'ruler of the feast'. Cana is confused with Canaan, the home of Simon.

† Probably Jehoram, killed by Jehu: II Kings ix, 24.

‡ cf. Luke i, 28.

was nourished, Our Lord Jesus Christ. Two miles from Nazareth, on the road men follow to the city of Acre is the city of Seffûrich. Half a mile outside Nazareth is Our Lord's Leap; for the Jews took Him up to a high rock to cast Him down and kill Him, but Our Lord passed through them and leapt to another rock, where the prints of His feet are yet to be seen. And therefore some men, when they fear thieves, say the verse that is written here, *Ihesus autem transiens per medium illorum ibat*, that is, 'Jesus passing through the midst of them went His way.'* And they also say these verses of the Psalter, *Irruat super eos formido et pauor in magnitudine brachii tui, Domine. Fiant immobiles quasi lapis, donec pertransiat populus tuus, Domine, donec pertransiat populus tuus iste, quem possedisti*, that is to say, 'Let dread in the greatness of thine arm fall on them, O Lord. Be they as still as stone until your people pass, O Lord, until your people pass over, whom you have brought.'† When this has been said, a man may go boldly forward without hesitation. You should know that Our Lady Saint Mary, when she bore Christ, was fifteen years old, and she was with Him on earth thirty-three years and three months.

From Nazareth to Mount Tabor is three miles; it is a high and beautiful hill. Once there was a town and many churches, but all are now destroyed. There is however still a place called the School of Our Lord where He instructed His disciples in the secrets of Heaven. At the foot of that mountain Melchisedek, who was God's priest and King of Jerusalem, met Abraham as he came down that mountain, after the defeat of his enemies. On that hill Our Lord transfigured Himself before Peter, James and John; they saw Him talking with Moses and Elijah. And so Saint Peter said, *Bonum est nos hic esse. Faciamus hic tria tabernacula*, which means 'It is good to be here. Let us make three tabernacles.'‡ And Christ told them to tell no man of that vision until He had risen from the dead. On that same hill, in that very place, on the Day of Judgement will the four angels blow their trumpets and raise all who are dead to life. And they shall come, body and soul together, before God the Sovereign Judge in the Vale of Jehosaphat, to hear judgement upon themselves; it will be on Easter Day, at the hour of Christ's Resurrection. For, as the learned say, in the same space of time that He went and harrowed Hell He will destroy the world and take His friends and lead them to joy without end, and damn the wicked to everlasting pain.

Also a mile from Mount Tabor is Mount Hermon; there was the city of Naym before whose gates Our Lord raised the widow's son to life

* Luke iv, 30.　　　† Exodus xv, 16, not the Psalms.　　　‡ Matthew xvii, 4.

from the dead. Three miles from Nazareth is the castle of Seffûrich, where the sons of Zebedeus [Zebedee] and Alpheus were born. Seven miles from Nazareth is Mount Cain; at its foot is a well where Lamech slew Cain with an arrow, taking him for a wild beast. From Seffûrich men go to a city called Tiberias, standing on the Sea of Galilee. Although it is called a sea, it is not a sea or arm of the sea, but a lake of fresh water; it is nearly a hundred furlongs long and forty wide. There are many good fish in it, [and the River Jordan runs through it]. It is of great value to the country. Where the River Jordan leaves the Sea of Galilee there is a great bridge, over which men leave the Promised Land for the land of Basan and the land of Gerassen [Gennesaret], which border the Jordan.

From there one can get to Damascus in three days, through the country of Traconye [Gaulonitis], which stretches from Hermon to the Sea of Galilee, which is also called the Sea of Tiberias or the Lake of Gennesaret. It has these different names after the cities that stand on its shores. Upon this sea Our Lord walked when He said to Peter, *Modice fidei, quare dubitasti?*, which means, 'You man of little faith, why were you afraid?'* And that was when Peter went towards Christ on the water, and was on the point of drowning; but Christ took him by the hand and said the words I have just quoted. Also Christ appeared after His Resurrection to His disciples when they were fishing in this sea, and filled their nets full of fish. They gave Him part of a broiled fish and a honeycomb. Peter and Andrew also fished in this sea, and James and John, when Christ called them and told them to follow Him. They immediately left their nets and followed Him. In this city of Tiberias is the table at which Our Lord ate with His disciples after His Resurrection, about which meal Holy Writ says, *Cognouerunt Dominum in fractione panis*, that is to say, 'They knew Our Lord in the breaking of the bread.'† Next to this city is a hill where Our Lord fed five thousand men with five loaves and two fish. In this city, too, a wicked man once threw a burning firebrand at Our Lord to rouse Him to anger; he hit Him on the head, and the brand fell to the ground and stuck there and grew, and in due time it became a great tree. It still grows there. At the head of the Sea of Galilee, to the north, is a castle called Sephor [Safed] near Capernaum, and there is no stronger castle in all the Holy Land. By that castle there is a good little town, of the same name as the castle. Saint Anne, Our Lady's mother, was born in that castle, and there was the house of Centurio.‡ That region is called *Galilea Gentium*, and it fell to

* Matthew xiv, 31.   † Luke xxiv, 35.
‡ The centurion of Matthew viii, 5.

the lot of Zebulon and Neptalim [Naphtali]. Thirty miles from that castle is the city of Dan, also called Caesarea Philippi; it stands at the foot of Lebanon, where the River Jordan rises. That is another boundary of the Land of Promise, which stretches from north to south as far as Beersheba – nearly nine score miles. In breadth it reaches from Jericho to Jaffa, and that is forty Lombardy miles – or indeed forty of our own miles, for the measure is the same. But I am not talking about the league used in France, Gascoyne [Gascony], Provence, or Germany, where they use 'great miles'.

The Holy Land is in Syria. For Syria lasts from the deserts of Arabia to Cicil [Cilicia], that is to say, Armenia the Greater – going from south to north; east to west it reaches from the great deserts of Arabia to the West Sea [Mediterranean]. But many kingdoms are comprised in this realm of Syria – Judea, Palestine, Galilee, Sem Cecil [Little Cilicia] and many others. It is the custom in that country and many of its neighbours that when two countries are at war and either party besieges a city, town or castle, they use doves instead of messengers to bear letters between the parts of the realm. They bind the letters to the necks of the doves, and then let them fly away. The doves, through habit and use, fly to the other part, and when the letters are taken from their necks they fly again to where they were reared.

Know that among the Saracens, in several places, many Christian men dwell under tribute; they follow different laws and customs according to the constitution of the realm they dwell in. Nevertheless they are all baptized and believe in God as Father, Son and Holy Ghost. Still, they differ in some articles of our belief. There are some Christian men called Iacobynes [Jacobites], whom Saint James the Apostle converted, and Saint John the Evangelist baptized them. They maintain that confession should only be made to God and not to men. For they say that God never ordained that one man should confess to another, and therefore David says in the Psalter, *Confitebor tibi, Domine, in toto corde meo*, that is to say, 'Lord, I shall confess myself to Thee in my whole heart.'* And in another place he says, *Delictum meum tibi cognitum feci*, which means, 'Lord to Thee shall I make my trespass known.'† And again he says, *Deus meus es tu, et confitebor tibi* – 'Thou art my God, and to Thee shall I confess.'‡ And still again he says, *Quoniam cogitacio hominis confitebitur tibi*, that is, 'For the thought of man shall confess to Thee'.§ The Jacobites also say that a man should ask forgiveness only of him whom he has injured. But God never ordained – nor did any of His prophets, so they say – that a man should reveal his sins to anyone

* Psalm cxi, 1.   † Psalm xxxii, 5.   ‡ Psalm cxviii, 28.   § cf. Job xlii, 2.

except God. And to support this they allege the authority of the Psalter, as I have told you. They also say that Saint Augustine and Saint Gregory and other Doctors of the Church affirm the same thing. For Saint Augustine says, *Qui scelera sua cogitat et conuersus fuerit, ueniam sibi credat*, which is to say, 'Whoever knows his own sin and is converted from it, may believe he has pardon.' And Saint Gregory says this: *Dominus potius mentem quam uerba considerat*, which means, 'Our Lord takes more notice of thoughts than of words.' Saint Hilary also says, *Longorum temporum crimina in ictu oculi perient, si corde nata fuerit contemp- cio* – 'Sins done over a long time shall perish in the twinkling of an eye, if scorn for them be born in a man's heart.' They adduce such authorities in their own language and not in Latin; and because of their authorities they say that men should make confession to God and not to men. And so when they want to make confession, they make a fire beside themselves, throw incense on it, and, as the smoke goes up, they say, 'I make my confession to God and ask forgiveness for my sin.' And although this was the manner of confession in former times, Saint Peter and other Apostles who have come since have ordained in their wisdom that men should make confession to priests, who are men like themselves. For they considered that no good medicine can be given to a sick man unless the nature of the sickness is known, and just so a man can give no suitable penance unless he knows the quality and number of the sins. For one type of sin is more serious than another, and in some places more so than others, and at some times more than others; therefore it is necessary that the man who shall impose penance knows the sin and its circumstances.

There are other Christians called Surrianes [Syrians]. They follow a law midway between us and the Greeks. They let their beards grow as the Greeks do, and make their sacrament at the altar of unleavened bread like the Greeks, and use the Greek alphabet; they confess as the Jacobites do. There are others, too, Georgienes [Georgians], whom Saint George converted. Him they honour and reverence before all other Saints. They all shave their heads, the clergy in a round tonsure and laymen in a square one. They follow the law of the Greeks. There is yet another group, who are called Christian men 'Of Girdles',* for they are girdled as are the Franciscans. There are also some called Nestorians, some Arrianes [Arians], some Nubians, some Gregorienes [Greeks], some Indians, which last are of Prester John's land. They are

* The origin of this odd phrase is in the sumptuary laws passed at various times by the Muslim authorities compelling Jews and Christians to wear distinctive dress – including leather girdles.

all called Christian men, and they keep and follow many articles of our faith, but in many points they vary from us and our faith. All their differences would be too much to relate.

14

Of the city of Damascus; of three routes to Jerusalem,
one by land and by sea, and the next more
by land than by sea, and the third all by land

Now that I have told you of the many kinds of people who live in these countries, I will once more turn to my theme and tell you how one can return from those countries to these Whoever wants to come back from the land of Galilee that I mentioned before will go by Damascus, which is a lovely city full of good merchandise. It is three days' march from the sea, and from Jerusalem five. They transport their merchandise on camels, mules, dromedaries and horses, and other kinds of beasts; their goods are brought by sea from India, from Persia, from Chaldea, from Armenia, and from many other regions. This city was founded by Eleazar of Damascus, who was the son of the steward of Abraham the Patriarch, and the city was called after his surname. He hoped to be lord of all that country after Abraham, for Abraham had not yet fathered Isaac. In that place Cain slew his brother Abel. Besides Damascus is Mount Seyr [Seir]. In Damascus there are many wells, both inside and outside the city; there are also many fair gardens, giving great plenty of fruit. Nowhere else is a city like it for gardens of fruit. There is a very large population in that city, and it is well walled, with a double rampart. Many physicians dwell in that city, and once Saint Paul followed the profession of medicine there, before he was converted; Saint Luc [Luke] was his pupil in learning medicine, and many others were as well. For in that city he kept a school in that science, but afterwards he was a physician of souls. He was converted in Damascus, and stayed there three days and three nights, and neither ate nor drank, nor saw anything with his bodily eyes; but in the spirit he was taken up into Heaven, where he saw heavenly secrets. A little way from Damascus is a castle called Arkes [Arqa] – a good strong castle. From Damascus men come past a place called *Nostre Dame de Sardenake* [Saidenaya], five miles this side of Damascus. It is on a rock. It is a beautiful and delightful place, somewhat resembling a castle – there was one there once. There is a fine church where live Christian monks and nuns. They have excellent wine there. In this church, behind the High Altar on the wall, is a wooden panel on which a portrait of Our Lady was once painted, which often became flesh; but that picture is now seen but little. Nevertheless that panel constantly oozes oil, like olive oil; there is a marble vessel under the panel to catch it. They give some to pilgrims, for it heals many of their illnesses; and it is said that if it is kept well for seven years, it afterwards turns into flesh and blood.

From Saidenaya men come through the Vale of Bochar [Bekaa], which is a fine fertile valley, producing all kinds of fruit. It is surrounded by hills. There are in it lovely rivers and broad meadows and noble grazing for cattle. Men travel past the mountains of Lebanon, which stretch from Armenia the Greater in the north to Dan, which is the northern end of the Promised Land, as I said before. Those hills are very fruitful, and there are many fine wells, cedars and cypresses, and many other different kinds of trees. There are also many well-peopled towns near the borders of these mountains.

Between the city of Arqa and the city of Raphane [Rafineh] is a river, called the Sabatory. On Saturdays it runs fast, and for the rest of the week it either stands still and does not run at all, or runs only slowly. Among these hills I mentioned there is another stream too which at night freezes solid and during the day no frost at all is seen. As one comes back from these hills, there is a hill higher than any other; they call it the High Hill. There is a fair great city, called Tripoli, in which many good Christian men live, following the same rites and customs as us. Thence men come to a city called Beirut, where Saint George slew the dragon. It is a good town, with a fine castle inside it, and it is three days' journey from Saidenaya. Sixteen miles on this side of Beirut is the city of Sidon. At Beirut pilgrims who want to go via Cyprus embark, and they arrive at the port of Surry or Tyer [Sûr and Tyre are the same], and so in a short while they reach Cyprus. Or men can sail from the port of Tyre and, without touching at Cyprus, land at some port in Greece, and so get back to this part of the world.

I have now told you about the longest and furthest route that men follow to Jerusalem, via Babylon and Mount Sinai and many other places you have heard me speak of, and I have also indicated the ways by which men can turn back to the Land of Promise. I shall now tell you about the shortest and quickest way to Jerusalem. For some folk do not want to use the other route – some because they have not enough money, some because they have not enough people to go with, some because they cannot stand a long journey, some because they fear the dangers of the deserts, some because they want to hurry home to see their wives and children, or for some other reasonable cause they have to get home quickly. And so I will show how men can travel fastest and make their pilgrimage to Jerusalem in the shortest time. A man coming from the lands of the West will go through France, Burgundy and Lombardy, and so to Venice or Genoa, or some other port, and will embark there and sail to the isle of Corfu, which belongs to the Genoese. Then he arrives in Greece at the port of Mavrovo, or Valona, or Durazzo, or some other port in Greece; he has a rest, buys his supplies, and then takes ship again and sails to Cyprus. He will arrive at Famagusta, not touching at the isle of Rhodes. Famagusta is the chief port of Cyprus, and there he will take a rest, buy his food, and then embark; he will land no more, if he so wishes, until he gets to the port of Jaffa, which is the harbour nearest to Jerusalem. It is only a day and a half's journey from Jerusalem – say thirty-six miles. From Jaffa you go to the city of Rames [Ramleh], only a little thence; it is a fine city, with many good folk in it. Outside that city, to the south, is a church of Our Lady, where Our Lord showed Himself to her in three clouds, betokening the Trinity. A little way away is another city, called Dispolis, but it was once called Lidda [Lûdd]; a well-inhabited town; there is a church of Saint George there, where he was beheaded. Thence men go to the castle of Emmaus, and so to Mount Joy; there many pilgrims first see Jerusalem. Samuel the prophet lies at Mount Joy. Thence men go to Jerusalem. To one side of that route is the city of Ramatha [Ramah in Ephraim] and Mount Modyn [Latron]; Matathias, father of Judas Maccabeus, came from there, and the graves of the Maccabees are there. Beyond Ramah is the town of Techue [Tekoa], where Amos the prophet came from; his grave is there.

I have already told you about the holy places at Jerusalem and in the places round about, and so I shall say no more of them now. But I will go back and tell you of other routes that can be followed, keeping more to dry land – useful for those who cannot endure travelling by sea, but prefer to go by land even if it is more trouble. [You make your way] to one of the ports of Lombardy, for there is the best place to buy provisions; or you can go to Venice or Genoa or some other port. A man then crosses the sea to Greece, to the port of Mavrovo, Valona, or Durazzo, or some other port. From there he goes by land to Constantinople, and crosses the stretch of water called the Arm of Saint George, which is an inlet of the sea. Thence he goes by land to Ruffynell where there is a good strong castle; thence to Pulueral [Bafira?] and the castle of Sinople [Sinope]; then he goes to Capadoce [Cappadocia] which is a great country, with many high mountains. He will pass through

Turkey to the port of Chiutok and to the city of Nicaea which is only seven miles thence. The Turks won this city from the Emperor of Constantinople; it is a fine city, well walled on one side, and on the other is a great lake and a great river, called Lay. Thence men go through the hills of Nairmount [the Phrygian Black Mountains], the vales of Mailbrins, the open moors; one passes the town of Ormanx or the towns that stand on the great and noble rivers Riclay [Heraclea] and Stancon [Kunya] and so to Antioch the Lesser which is on the River Heraclea. There are many fine hills in those parts, many fair woods and great plenty of wild game to hunt.

He who wants to go a different way will go through the plains of Romany [the Greek Empire in Asia Minor] bordering the Roman Sea. On that coast is a castle called Florach and it is a very strong place. Further up into the mountains is a fine city called Toursout [Tarsus], and also the cities of Longemaath, Assere [Adana] and Marmistre [Mopsuestia]. When a man has crossed these mountains and moors, he goes through the city of Marioch [Marash] and Artoise [Artah], where there is a great bridge over the River Ferne, or Farfar [Pharphar or Orontes] – a great river, which is navigable; it runs fast from the mountains to Damascus. Near the city of Damascus is another river that comes from the Lebanon, which is called the Abbana [Abana]. At the crossing of this river Saint Eustace, once called Placidas, lost his wife and two children. This river runs through the plain of Archades and then to the Red Sea. Thence men go to the city of Phenice [Philomelium], where there are hot springs and hot baths. Then men go to the city of Ferne [possibly Ilgun], and from Philomelium to Ilgun is ten miles. There are many fine woods. Then men arrive in Antioch [the Greater], ten miles thence. It is a fair city, well walled with many towers and turrets; it is still a great city, but it was once greater than it is now. It was once two miles long and half a mile wide. Through the middle of the city ran the river Farfar [Orontes], with a great bridge over it. Once on the city walls there were 350 towers, and each pier of the bridge was a tower. This is the chief city of the kingdom of Syria. Ten miles from it is the port of Saint Symeon where the river debouches into the sea. From Antioch you go to a city called Lacuth [Latakia], then to Gebel [Gebal], and then to Tortouse [Tortosa]. Near there is the land of Channel [Edessa, Homs] where there is a strong castle called Maubek [Baalbek]. From Tortosa men travel to Tripoli by sea, or else by land through the mountain passes. There is a city called Gibilet [Djebeil]. From Tripoli men go to Acre; and from there there are two ways to Jerusalem, one to the left and the other to the right. The left hand route takes you by Damascus and the River Jordan. The right hand route takes you by Maryn [the sea shore?] and through the land of Flagramy, and close to the mountains to the city of Haifa which some men call the Castle of Pilgrims. Thence to Jerusalem is a three days' journey, during which men go through Caesarea Philippi, then to Jaffa, Ramleh, the castle of Emmaus, and so to Jerusalem.

Now I have told you some of the ways by land and sea by which men can go to the Holy Land, according to the countries they are starting from. They all come to one goal. There is still another way to Jerusalem, totally by land, and, from France or Flanders, no sea is to be crossed. But that route is very long and dangerous and full of difficulty, and so few go that way. But if a man wants to, he goes through Germany and Prussia and so to Tartary. This Tartary is under the suzerainty of the Great Khan of Cathay, whom I intend to talk about later. It is a hard land, sandy and infertile. There grows no corn, no wine, no beans, no peas, nor any other fruit fit to keep a man alive. But there are beasts in plenty, and so they eat meat only, without bread, and sup the broth, and they drink the milk of all kinds of beasts. They eat cats and dogs, rats and mice, and all other kinds of beasts; and since they have little wood, they cook their meat on fires of animal dung dried in the sun. They eat but once in the day, prince or anyone, and even at that one meal they eat very little. They are a very foul folk, cruel and full of ill will. That land is seldom without great storms. And in summer there are great thunderstorms, which kill a lot of animals and people. The air temperature changes, too, very quickly – now great heat, then great cold – and so it is a bad place to live. The prince who governs that land is called Baco [Batu] and he dwells in a city called Orda.* Certainly, no good man will live in that land, for it is fit for growing hemlock and nettles and other such weeds; it is good for nothing else, as I heard (for I have not myself been there). I have, however, been in other lands that border it, for example Russia, Nyfland [Livonia], the kingdom of Crakow and Lettow [Lithuania] and in the kingdom of Graften [Silistria] and many other places. But I never followed that route to Jerusalem, and so I cannot talk about it. I have heard that people cannot easily go that way in winter because of the rivers and the marshes that are there which cannot be crossed unless there is a good hard frost with snow. If there were no snow, no one could make progress over the ice. Three days' journeying like this might take a man from Prussia to a habitable Saracen land. And, as Christian men each year do go that way, they carry their supplies with them on the ice on sledges and carts

* The chief camp of the Khan of the Golden Horde, near the Volga.

without wheels; for they shall find no provender except what they bring with them. They can stay there just as long as their food lasts, and no more. When spies of that land see Christian men coming to make war on them, they run to the towns and cry loudly, 'Kera, Kera, Kera'* and immediately arm to defend themselves. You ought to know that the frost and snow there is much harder than here; and so each man has a stove in his house, where he eats and drinks. For it is outrageously cold there, since it is the north side of the world, where the cold is usually more intense than in other places because the sun shines little there. And on the south side of the world in some places it is so hot that no man can live there for the appalling heat.

15

Of the customs of the Saracens and of their law;
how the Sultan talked with the author of this book;
and of the beginning of Muhammad, etc.

Now, because I have talked of the Saracens and their lands, I will tell you something of their laws and their creed, as it is contained in the book of their law, the Koran. Some call it *Messaph* [Arabic *mashaf*, 'holy'] and some *Harme* [*horme*, 'holy'] according to the language of different countries. Muhammad gave them this book. Amongst other things in that book is contained the statement, and I have often read and seen it there, that good men, when they are dead, will go to Paradise, and the wicked shall go to the pains of Hell. All Saracens believe this firmly. And if they are asked what paradise they are talking about, they say it is a place of delights, where a man shall find all kinds of fruit at all seasons of the year, and rivers running with wine, and milk, and honey, and clear water; they say they will have beautiful palaces and fine great mansions, according to their deserts, and that those palaces and mansions are made of precious stones, gold and silver. Every man shall have four score wives, who will be beautiful damsels, and he shall lie with them whenever he wishes, and he will always find them virgins. They all believe they will have all this in Paradise, and this is against our creed. The Saracens accept the Incarnation, and they will willingly speak of the Virgin Mary; they say that she was taught by an angel, and that the angel Gabriel told her that she had

* Compare the Arabic verb *karra*, meaning 'regroup and return to battle'.

been chosen by God before the world's beginning to conceive Jesus Christ and bear Him; they say she bore Him and yet was a virgin afterwards as she was before. And the Koran agrees with this. They also say that Christ spoke as soon as He was born, and that He was (and is) a holy and a true prophet in word and deed, and merciful and just to all, and without sin. They also affirm that when the angel saluted Our Lady and told her of the Incarnation, she was greatly ashamed and astonished at his words; they say this was principally because there was at that time in the district an evil man, called Takyna, who dabbled in sorcery, through his enchantments pretending to be an angel and deceiving young maidens often to seduce them. Therefore Mary was afraid, and conjured the angel to say whether or not he was Takyna. And the angel answered her and told her to have no fear, for he was God's true messenger. Their book, the Koran, also says that when Mary was delivered of her Child, in the shade of a palm tree, she was greatly ashamed and wept, saying she wished she was dead. And immediately the Child spoke and comforted her, saying, 'Be not afraid, for in you has God made His covenant for the salvation of the world.' And their Koran witnesses in many other places that Jesus Christ spoke as soon as He was born. That book says that Christ was sent by God Almighty into the world as an example and mirror for all men. It also speaks of the Day of Judgement, how God will come and judge all men; the good He will draw to His side and give them everlasting joy and glory, and the wicked He will damn to the unending torments of Hell. They say that Christ is the best among all the prophets, the most worthy, the nearest to God, and that He made the Gospels, in which are healthy doctrine, truth, and exhortation for those who believe in God; they say he was greater than a prophet, in that he lived without sin, gave sight to the blind, healed lepers and raised men to life again from the dead – and went to Heaven in His body. When they can get hold of written copies of the Gospels, they honour them greatly, especially the gospel of *Missus est**; that gospel those who are literate kiss with great devotion, and say it often in their prayers. Each year they fast for a whole month, eating only in the evening, and they keep them from their wives all that month. Those who are sick, though, are not obliged to perform this fast. The book, the Koran, also speaks of the Jews, saying they are wicked and accursed, because they will not believe that Jesus was sent from God; it also says they lie about Mary and her Son Jesus Christ, when they say they crucified Him. The Koran says they did not crucify Jesus, for God took Him up to Himself without

· * Luke i, 26.

death and transferred the form and appearance of His body to Judas
Iscariot, and it was him the Jews crucified, thinking it was Jesus. But
Jesus, they say, was taken all alive into Heaven, and in His flesh will He
come to judge the world. This Christians do not believe, and therefore
they say that they do not believe correctly when Christians maintain
Christ was killed on the Cross. All their chief ideas are in the Koran. The
Saracens also say that if Jesus had been crucified, God would have
acted contrary to His justice in allowing such a guiltless innocent to die;
they say we are wrong about this. But it is they who are wrong. They
freely admit that all the deeds of Christ, His sayings, His teaching and
His gospels are good, and true; and His miracles also are true. They
freely confess that the Virgin Mary was a good and holy maiden, pure
and unspotted, both before and after the birth of Christ; and that those
who believe perfectly in God shall be saved. And because they come so
near to our faith in these points – and many others – it seems to me that
they could be much more quickly and easily converted to our creed by
the preaching and instruction of Christian men. They say they well
know from their prophecies that the law of Muhammad shall fail as the
law of the Jews failed, and that the Christian law shall endure to the end
of the world. If a man ask them what their creed is, they answer, 'We
believe in God, who made Heaven and everything else from nothing,
and nothing was made except by Him. We believe the Day of Judgement will come, when each man will be rewarded according to his
deserts. We also truly believe that all that God spoke through His holy
prophets while they were on earth is the truth.' They also say that
Muhammad in the Koran ordained that every man should have three or
four wives. But now they take more, for some of them have nine; and
each man takes as many concubines as he can maintain on his wealth. If
any of their wives should sin against her husband and let another man
sleep with her, it is then lawful for her husband to divorce her and take
another wife in her stead; but he has to give her a portion of his
property. When men speak of the Trinity to them they say that there are
three Persons, but not one God. For their Koran does not talk of the
Trinity. Nevertheless they grant that God has a Word, for otherwise He
would be dumb; and a Spirit, or else He would be without life. When
men speak to them of Christ's Incarnation, of how by the word of the
angel God sent wisdom to earth and [shrouded Himself] in the Virgin
Mary, they say all this is true and they believe it, and that God's Word
has great power, and the man who does not know God's Word does
not know God. They also say that Christ was God's Word; so says the
Koran, where it says that the angel spoke to Mary saying, 'Mary, God

shall send to thee the Word of His mouth, and His name shall be called Jesus Christ.' Also they say that Abraham was God's friend, Moses God's spokesman, and Jesus Christ the Word and Spirit of God, and that Muhammad was the true messenger of God; of all these four Jesus was the worthiest and most excellent. Thus it seems that the Saracens have many articles of our faith, if not perfectly; so it would be the easier to convert them and bring them to our truth – especially those who are literate and know the Scriptures. For among them they have the Gospels and the Prophets and all the Bible, written in the Saracen language. But they do not understand Holy Writ spiritually, but according to the letter, as do the Jews; and so Saint Paul says, *Litera occidit, spiritus autem uiuificat*, which is to say, 'The letter kills, but the spirit giveth life.'* Therefore some Saracens say that the Jews are wicked men, and cursed, because they have broken the Law that God gave them through Moses; and they say Christian men are wicked and evil because they do not keep the Commandment of the Gospel, which Jesus Christ ordained for them.

Now I shall tell you what the Sultan told me one day in his chamber. He made everyone else leave his chamber, lords as well as others who were there, for he wanted to have a private talk between ourselves alone. And when they had all gone out, he asked me how Christians governed themselves in our countries. And I said, 'Lord, well enough – thanks be to God.' And he answered and said, 'Truly, no. It is not so. For your priests do not serve God properly by righteous living, as they should do. For they ought to give less learned men an example of how to live well, and they do the very opposite, giving examples of all manner of wickedness. And as a result, on holy days, when people should go to church to serve God, they go to the tavern and spend all the day – and perhaps all the night – in drinking and gluttony, like beasts without reason which do not know when they have had enough. And afterwards through drunkenness they fall to proud speeches, fighting and quarrelling, till someone kills somebody. Christian men commonly deceive one another, and swear the most important oaths falsely. And they are, moreover, so swollen with pride and vainglory that they never know how to dress themselves – sometimes they wear short fashions of clothing, sometimes long, sometimes cut full, sometimes figure-fitting. You ought to be simple, meek and truthful, and ready to give charity and alms, as Christ was, in whom you say you believe. But it is quite otherwise. For Christians are so proud, so envious, such great gluttons, so lecherous, and moreover so full of

* II Corinthians iii, 6.

covetousness, that for a little silver they will sell their daughters, their sisters, even their own wives to men who want to lie with them. And everyone takes another's wife, and no one keeps his faith to another: and you so wickedly and evilly despite and break the Law that Christ gave you. Certainly it is because of your sinfulness that you have lost all this land which we hold and keep. Because of your evil living and your sin and not because of our strength God has given it into our hands. And we well know that when you serve your God properly and well, and serve Him with good works, no man shall be able to stand against you. We know too by our prophecies that the Christians shall recover this land again in the time to come, when you serve your God well and devoutly. But as long as you live as you do in wickedness and sin, we have no fear of you; for your God will not help you.' When I had heard the Sultan speak these words – and many more which I will not repeat now – I asked him, with great respect, how he came by so full a knowledge of the state of Christendom. And then he had all the great lords and worthies that he had previously sent out called in; and he detailed four of them – great lords – to talk to me. These described to me all the manners of my country, and of other countries in Christendom as fully and as truly as if they had always lived in them. These lords and the Sultan spoke French wonderfully well, and I was astonished by that. Finally I understood that the Sultan sends some of his lords to different kingdoms and lands in the guise of merchants – some with precious stones, some with cloths of gold, some with other jewels – and that these visit all realms in order to size up the manners of us Christian men and spot our weaknesses. It seemed to me then a cause for great shame that Saracens, who have neither a correct faith nor a perfect law, should in this way reprove us for our failings, keeping their false law better than we do that of Jesus Christ; and those who ought by our good example to be turned to the faith and Law of Jesus Christ are driven away by our wicked ways of living. And so it is no wonder that they call us sinful and wicked, for it is true. But they are very devout and honest in their law, keeping well the commandments of the Koran, which God sent them by His messenger Muhammad, to whom, so they say, the angel Gabriel spoke often, telling him the will of God.

You ought to know that Muhammad was born in Arabia, and at first was a poor fellow, looking after horses and camels and travelling with merchants to Egypt, which at that time was inhabited by Christians. In the deserts of Arabia, on the highroad to Egypt, there was a chapel, and a hermit living in it. And Muhammad went into this chapel to speak with the hermit. And when he entered the chapel, the doorway, which was very low, suddenly grew as tall as the gate of a great palace. This, as they say, was the first miracle he did, when he was young. After that Muhammad began to be wise, and rich, and a great astronomer. The prince of the land of Corodan [Khorasan] made him ruler and governor of his land; and he governed it wisely and graciously, so that, when the prince was dead, he married the princess, who was called Cadrige [Khadija]. This Muhammad had epilepsy, and often fell through the violence of that illness; and the lady sorrowed much that she had married him. But he made her believe that each time he fell the angel Gabriel appeared and spoke to him, and that he fell down because of the dazzling brightness of the angel. And therefore the Saracens say that the angel Gabriel often spoke to him. This Muhammad reigned in Arabia in the year of Our Lord 620; he was of the race of Ishmael, who was Abraham's son, whom he begot on Agar [Hagar] his handmaiden. And for this reason some Saracens are called Ishmaelites, some Agarrenes after Hagar, and some Ammonites after two sons of Loth [Lot], which he begot on his two daughters. Some, quite properly, are called Saracens, after the city of Sarras [Shiraz?]. Also Muhammad once well loved a good hermit who lived in the wilderness a mile from Mount Sinai on the road as one goes from Arabia to Chaldea and India – a day's journey from the sea, where Venetian merchants often come to buy merchandise. And Muhammad went so often to this hermit to hear him preach that his servants grew angry and disgruntled about it. For he went thither so often, and so eagerly listened to this hermit preaching that many a time he made his men stay awake all night long; and it seemed that his men dearly wished that this hermit were dead. So it happened one night that Muhammad was drunk with wine, and fell asleep; and while he slept, his men drew his own sword from its sheath and slew the hermit with it; when they had done this, they sheathed the sword again, all bloody. In the morning, when Muhammad woke and found the hermit dead, he was very angry and would have slain all his men, for he said they had murdered him among themselves. But with one accord and one voice they all said that he himself had slain him in his sleep, when he was drunk, and they showed him the sword all bloody; and then he believed that they were telling the truth. Then he cursed wine and all those who drink it; and therefore devout Saracens will not touch it. But they do have another kind of drink which is good and delicious and very fortifying, which is made of different spices; especially calamus, of which good sugar is made. Nevertheless some Saracens will gladly drink wine in private, but not publicly – for if they drink wine openly they will be censured for it. It sometimes happens that Christian men become Saracens, out of poverty, or foolishness, or through wickedness; and the man who is chief master and judge of their law, when he receives them into their faith, says *La elles ella sila Machomet rores alla hec*, which means, 'There is no God but one, and Muhammad his messenger.'

Since I have told you something of the Saracens' law, of their manners and customs, I will tell you of the letters they use, with their names and shapes:

almoy, betach, cathi, delphoi, ephoti, fothi, garophi, hethim, iocchi, kacchi, lothyn, malach, nahalet, orthi, porizeth, qutholath, routhi, salathi, totinthus, uzazot, yrtim, theth.

These are the names of the letters, and this is what they look like:

And here I will set down their letters in another way as I have seen them in other books; this form I like better than the other:

almoy, bethath, cathi, delphoi, ephothi, fothi, garophi, hechim, iocchi, kaythi, lothim, malach, nahalot, orthi, corizi, 3och, rutolath, routhi, salathi, thatimus, yrthom, azazoth, arotthi, 3otipin, ichet.

These are the letters:

They have these four letters more than we do because their language is so different; they speak very gutturally. Just so, we in England have two other letters in our language that are not in their alphabet, that is, þand 3, which are called 'thorn' and 'yogh'.

16

Of the lands of Albania and Libya; of the desires in the Watching of the Sparrowhawk; and of the Ark of Noah

Now I have told you about the Holy Land and the countries around, the ways thither, and to Mount Sinai, to Babylon and other places, which I spoke of above. Now I shall pass on and speak of different lands and countries that are beyond the Holy Land. For there are many diverse kingdoms, countries, and isles in the eastern part of the world, where live different kinds of men and animals, and many other marvellous things. Those countries are divided by the four rivers that flow out of the Terrestrial Paradise. Mesopotamia and the kingdom of Chaldea and Arabia are between two rivers, that is to say the Tygre [Tigris] and the Euphrates; the kingdoms of Media and Persia are between the Tigris and the Nile; and the kingdoms of Syria, of Palestine, and Phoenicia are between the Euphrates and the Mediterranean Sea, which stretches from the city of Marrok [Morocco] on the Spanish Sea to the Great Sea [the Black Sea]. So it stretches three thousand and forty Lombardy miles beyond Constantinople. Towards the sea which is called Occiane [Ocean] is the kingdom of Scithy [Scythia] which is quite surrounded by hills. Below Scythia, from the sea of Caspy [Caspian] to the River Thanay [Don] is the land of Amazonia, which is the Land of Women, where women live by themselves with no man among them. Then there is the realm of Albania, a great land; it is called Albania because the people of that land are whiter than the people of the lands round about. In that land are marvellously big powerful dogs, which fight with lions and kill them. Then there is the land of Hircany [Hircania], of Bactrice [Bactria] and many others. Between the Red Sea and the Great Sea Ocean to the south is Ethiopia and Upper Libya. For Libya the Lower begins at the Spanish Sea, where are the Pillars of Hercules, and reaches to Egypt and Ethiopia. In Libya the sea seems much higher than the land, as if it would overflow the land, and yet it does not pass its bounds. In that land is a great hill, which can be seen from far off, but men cannot get near it. In Libya, when a man turns to the east, his shadow is on his right side, as it is on his left in this country. In the sea of Libya no fishes are found; for none may live there because of the dreadful heat of the sun. Because of the great heat the water there is always as if it were boiling. And you should know that there are many more countries and isles in those parts of the world – it would be too much to tell of all of them; but of some I shall speak more fully later.

A man who wants to travel to Tartary, or Persia, or Chaldea, or India, will take ship at Genoa, or Venice, or at some other port mentioned before, and so cross the sea and arrive at the port of Trapazonde [Trebizond], which is a good city, once called *Le Porte de Pounce* [The gate of Pontus]. In this city lies Saint Athanase [Athanasius], who was Bishop of Alexandria, and who made the psalm *Quicunque uult*. This Athanasius was a great doctor of divinity, for he preached more profoundly of Holy Writ than others did; and so he was accused of heresy before the Pope. The Pope sent for him and had him imprisoned. And while he was in prison he made that psalm and sent it to the Pope and said, 'If I am a heretic, then everything written here is heresy, for this is what I believe.' And when the Pope saw that, he said it was exactly our belief and had him released, commanding that psalm to be said each day at Prime; he considered Athanasius a good and holy man. But Athanasius would never afterwards return to his bishopric, because wicked men had through hatred accused him before the Pope. Trebizond was once an appanage of the Emperor of Constantinople, but a mighty and rich man, sent by the Emperor to hold it against the Turks, kept it himself and had himself called Emperor of Trebizond.

From the city of Trebizond one goes to Lesser Armenia. In that country there is an old castle set on a rock, which in French is called *'le Chastel Despuere'*, that is, in English, the castle of the Sparrowhawk. It is between the city of Larrais [Laiazzo, now Ayas] and the city of Percipre [Perschembre?], belonging to the Lord of Croke [Corycus]; he is a rich man and a good Christian. In that castle a sparrowhawk is to be found sitting on a perch, and a fair lady of Faerye sitting by it looking after it. And whoever will come and guard that sparrowhawk, keeping it awake continuously for seven days and seven nights (or, as some men say, three days and three nights) without company and without sleeping, will have this fair lady come to him at the end of the seventh day (or the third) and grant him whatever earthly thing he asks for; it has been tried many times. There came once a King of Armenia, a mighty lord and a worthy, and kept this hawk awake to the end of the appointed days. Then the lady came to him and told him to ask whatever earthly thing he wished, as he had done his task well. The King answered and said, 'I am a lord rich enough; therefore I ask nothing else but your body, to have at my desire.' And she answered and said, 'Foolishly and unwisely have you asked. For my body you may not have, because I am not an earthly but a spiritual creature.'

'Truly,' said the King, 'I will ask for nothing else.' 'Now I cannot draw you away from your folly,' said the lady, 'but I shall give you unasked what is righteous; for you and all who come of you shall have war and no lasting peace unto the ninth generation, and shall always be in subjection to your enemies and lack all kinds of goods.' Just so has it turned out, for the King of Armenia never had peace, but always war, since that time, and he and all that are his are poor and needy and live under the tribute of their enemies. At another time a humble man's son came and watched the sparrowhawk. He asked of that lady that he might be rich and fortunate in trade, to get worldly wealth; she granted it. He became the richest merchant of all that land, so that he could not count the thousandth part of his goods. So he was wiser than the King before him. After this there came a knight of the Templars and watched this sparrowhawk well; he asked that he might always have his purse full of gold, and the lady granted him his request. But she said that he was asking for the undoing and the destruction of his Order, because of the great pride in his riches and the great trust he put in his purse. So it turned out. It is good for him who is to watch this hawk that he be very careful not to sleep; for if he sleeps, he is lost forever, and shall never come again where men are. This castle is not on the direct route to those countries just named; but it behoves a man who wants to see wonders sometimes to go out of his way.

The direct route from Trebizond to Greater Armenia is to a city called Artiron [Erzerum], which used to be a fine, rich city; but the Turks have destroyed it. In the neighbourhood little wine is grown or any other fruits, for the land is high and cold; but there are many rivers and good springs which come underground from the Euphrates, which is a day's journey from that city. This River Euphrates comes under the earth from the direction of India and comes up again in the land of Allazar. Men go through Greater Armenia to the Sea of Persia. From the city of Erzerum you can go to a mountain called Sabissebella or Sabissacolle. Near it is another hill called Ararat (the Jews call it Thano) where Noah's ship rested after the Flood. It is still there, and can be seen from far off in clear weather. That mountain is seven miles high. Some men say they have been there and put their fingers into the hole where the Devil came out when Noah said *Benedicite*; but they are not telling the truth.* No man can climb that hill because of the snow, which is always there, winter and summer. And never a man went there since Noah's time except for one monk, who, through the grace of God, went there

* The story of the Devil has not been traced, though traditionally he was on board. There may be a reminiscence of a mystery play here.

and brought back a timber of the ship, which is still in an abbey at the foot of the mountain. This monk greatly desired to climb that hill, and so one day he set about it. By the time he had climbed a third of the way up, he was so weary that he could not go further, and he rested there and fell asleep. When he awoke he found himself once more back at the foot of the hill. Then he beseeched God to allow him to go up; and an angel came to him and told him go up. He did so, and brought the plank down. Since then no man went there, and so those who say they have been are lying.

A little way from there is the city of Dayne [Ani], which Noah founded; and also the city of Anye [Ani], in which there used to be a thousand churches. From that mountain one goes to a city called Taurizo [Tabriz], a beautiful and noble place. By that city is a hill of salt, and every man may take what he wants. Many Christian men dwell there, paying tribute to the Saracens. The city of Tabriz was once called Faxis; it is one of the most important trade-centres in the world, and merchants come thither from many lands. There they manage to trade all kinds of merchandise that they seek. This city is in the land of the Emperor of Persia, and it is said that the Emperor takes more in that city in customs dues on merchandise than the richest Christian king in the world has to spend.

From this city men go via many towns and castles for many days in the direction of India, and then come to a city called Sodonie [Sultaniyeh], ten days' journey from Tabriz, and a fine and noble city. The Emperor of Persia lives there in the summer because the land is cool. There are many great rivers, which bear big ships. Then one travels for many days through many countries, and comes to a city called Cassach [Kashan], a good rich city, with plenty of corn and other victuals. Some men say that it was at that city the Three Kings met, who went to make offerings to Christ in Bethlehem; it is fifty-three days' journey from Bethlehem. From this city men go to another, called Beth [Yezd], a day's march from the Gravelly Sea. This is the noblest city in the Persian Empire; some call it Cardabago [Persian *Chau bagh*: 'royal gardens']* and others Vapa. The Saracens say that no Christian man

* This name is a result of a complicated corruption. The original possibly reproduced the Persian phonetically with some accuracy; it may then have been misread as 'chardabag', and then misunderstood as (in French) 'char Dabago'. A copyist, unable to understand this sudden reference to flesh (*char*) assumes 'appellent' has been omitted and supplies it, and adds a supporting detail; so that M S Harley 4383, for example, reads 'et lappellent ils la char Dabago et le vin Vapa' (And they call flesh Dabago and wine Vapa – *vappa*, Latin 'flat wine'). It is

can dwell in that city for long and not die – no man knows the cause. Thence men make many days' marches through many cities, which would be too tedious to detail, until they come to a city called Carnaa [Persepolis], which used to be so big that its walls were twenty-five miles round. There the empire of Persia ends. And if you would like to know what kind of letters they use, here you can hear them:

Alma, Bem, Cem, Dem, Ethyn, Folthin, Gith, Hith, Iothyn, Kynyn, Lathyn, Moin, Nichoin, Ozeph, Phisan, Quinth, Yr, Seth, Toith, Vith, Xith, Ya, Zofin.

17

Of the land of Job and of his age; of the clothing
of the people of Chaldea; of the land where women live
without the company of men; and of the knowledge
of and the properties of the true diamond

When men leave Persepolis they enter the land of Job, a fair and good country, with great plenty of fruits and other riches. That land is called Sweze [Susiana?]. In that land is the city of Theman [Carmana?]. You should know that Job was the son of Are of Gosra [Zerah of Bosra], and was prince and ruler of that country. He was so rich he could not reckon the hundredth part of his goods. And although he was a pagan, nevertheless he served God very devoutly according to the custom of his creed, and his service was acceptable to God. Afterwards, through God's sufferance, he fell into great misfortune and poverty, when he was three score and ten years old. But God, mindful of his great patience and great humbleness, restored to him more riches and honour than he ever had before. Afterwards, when the King of Idumea died, he was made King, and, as some men say, his name was changed to Jobab. He lived there 170 years; when he died he was 248 years old. In that land of Job there is no lack of anything necessary to man's life. There are hills where a man finds manna more plentiful – and better – than anywhere else. Manna is called the bread of angels; it is a very white, sweet substance, sweeter than sugar or honey. It comes from the dew of Heaven falling on the herbage, where it coagulates and grows white.

---

to the credit of some scribe in Egerton's descent that he recognized the garble and saw that place names were at issue and not gastronomy. But his chances of a full restoration were slim.

Men make it into medicines for rich men, for constipation and the cleansing of too rich blood.

The land of Job borders the land of Chaldea, which is a big country. Their language is richer and fuller than that of any land on that side of the sea. The way there is by the Tower of Babel, as I said before, where the confusion of tongues was first made; it is four days' journey from Chaldea. In the realm of Chaldea there are very handsome men, well dressed in cloth of gold and precious stones. But the women are very ugly and ill-dressed, and they go barefoot.* They wear a nasty garment, baggy and knee-length, with long voluminous sleeves (like those of Benedictine monks) hanging to their feet. The hair of their heads is thick and black, and hangs to their shoulders. Their women are very swarthy and ugly to look at, and of evil behaviour. In the kingdom of Chaldea is a city called Ur, where Thare [Terah], Abraham's father, once dwelt. That was in the time of Ninus who was King of Babylon, Arabia and Egypt. This Ninus built the city of Niniue [Nineveh], but Noah started on it before; since however Ninus finished it, it is called Nineveh. In Nineveh was Thoby [Tobit] buried, of whom Holy Writ speaks. Abraham left Ur at the command of God, after his father died, taking with him Sarah his wife and his nephew Lot – at that time he had no children himself – and came to the land of Canaan and lived in a place called Shechem. This Lot was the one who was saved at the overwhelming of Sodom and Gomorrah. The folk of Chaldea have their own language, letters and figures; this is what they look like:

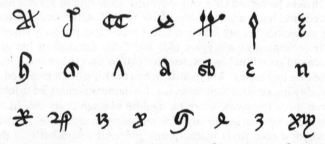

Next to Chaldea is the land of Amazoun [the Amazons], which we call the Maiden Land or the Land of Women; no man lives there, only women. This is not because, as some say, no man can live there, but because the women will not allow men to rule the kingdom. There was once a king in that land called Colopheus, and there were once men living there as they do elsewhere. It so happened that this king went to

* From here to the end of the alphabet is omitted in Defective.

war with the King of Scythia, and was slain with all his great men in battle with his enemy. And when the Queen and the other ladies of that land heard the news that the King and the lords were slain, they marshalled themselves with one accord and armed themselves well. They took a great army of women and slaughtered all the men left among them. And since that time they will never let a man live with them more than seven days, nor will they allow a boy child to be brought up among them. But when they want to have the company of man, they go to that side of their country where their lovers live, stay with them eight or nine days and then go home again. If any of them bears a child and it is a son, they keep it until it can speak and walk and eat by itself and then they send it to the father – or they kill it. If they have a girl child, they cut off one of her breasts and cauterize it; in the case of a woman of great estate, the left one, so that she can carry her shield better, and, in one of low degree, they cut off the right, so that it will not hinder them shooting – for they know very well the skill of archery. There is always a queen to rule that land, and they all obey her. This queen is always chosen by election, for they choose the woman who is the best fighter. These women are noble and wise warriors; and therefore kings of neighbouring realms hire them to help them in their wars. This land of the Amazons is an island, surrounded by water, except at two points where there are two ways in. Beyond the water live their lovers to whom they go when it pleases them to have bodily pleasure with them. Next to the land of the Amazons is a country called Termegutte [Terra Margine, east of the Caspian], a fair and pleasant country; because of the great beauty and richness of this land King Alexander wanted to build there his first city of Alexandria. For in that land he built twelve Alexandrias, of which this was the first; but it is now called Celsite [Seleucia, now Merv].

On the other side of Chaldea, to the south, is the land of Ethiopia, which is a great country, reaching as far as Egypt. Ethiopia is divided into two main parts, that is, the southern and the eastern parts. The southern is called Mauritayne [Mauretania], and the people of this part are blacker than those in the eastern part. In this part there is a well which during the day is so cold that no man can drink from it, and at night too hot to put a hand in. Beyond Mauretania, going by sea to the south, is a vast country, but it is uninhabitable because of the terrible heat of the sun. In Ethiopia all the rivers are so turbid and so salt because of the excessive heat of the sun that no one dare use them. The people of that country very easily get drunk; they have little appetite for their food, and commonly have diarrhoea. They live only a short time.

In that land, too, there are people of different shapes. There are some who have only one foot, and yet they run so fast on that one foot that it is a marvel to see them. That foot is so big that it will cover and shade all the body from the sun. In Ethiopia are young children whose hair is white, and as they grow old, their hair gets black. In this land of Ethiopia is the city of Saba, of which one of the Three Kings who gave gifts to Our Lord was King.

From Ethiopia you go to India through many different countries. You should know that India is divided into three parts, that is to say, India the Greater, which is a mountainous and hot land; India the Lesser, to the south, a temperate land; and the third part, to the north, so cold that, because of the great cold and continual frost, water congeals into crystal. On the rocks of crystal good diamonds grow, which are of the colour of crystal; but they are dimmer than crystal and as brown as oil. They are so hard that no metal can polish or split them. Other diamonds are found in Arabia, which are not so good, and softer. Some are found in Cyprus, which are still softer; and so they can be polished more easily. Also they are found in Macedonia; but those of India are the best. And some are often found in a mass, in the mines where men find gold, and those are as hard as those of India. And just as good diamonds are found in India on the rocks of crystal, men find good hard diamonds on the rocks of adamant in the sea, and on the mountains too – about as big as hazel nuts. They naturally grow in cube shapes. They grow together, male and female, and are fed with the dew of Heaven. And according to their nature they engender and conceive small children, and so they constantly grow and multiply. I have many times tested and seen that if a man takes with them a little of the rock they grew on, provided they are taken up by the roots and watered with the dew of May, each year they grow visibly, so that the small ones become bigger. A man should carry a diamond on his left side; then it is of more virtue than when on the right, for the natural bent of its growth is to the north, which is the left side of the world and the left side of a man when he turns to face the east.

And if you wish to know the virtues of the diamond, I will tell you them according to Ysidre [Isidore of Seville] *libro 16 Ethicorum, capitulo de cristallo*, and Bertilmew [Bartholomaeus Anglicus] *De Proprietatibus rerum, capitulo de adamante.* * The diamond gives to the man who carries it boldness (if it is freely given to him) and keeps his limbs healthy. It

* Isidore of Seville, *Etymologiae* xvi, 13.2; and see *John of Trevisa's translation of Bartholomew's On the Properties of Things*, ed. M. C. Seymour et al. (Oxford, 1975), Book xvi, cap. 8.

gives him grace to overcome his enemies, if his cause is righteous, in both war and law. It keeps him in his right mind. It protects him from quarrels, fights, debauchery, and from evil dreams and fantasies, and from wicked spirits. And if any man who meddles in sorcery or enchantments wants to hurt one who carries a diamond, he will not worry him. No wild or poisonous animal will hurt one who carries it. You ought to understand that the diamond must be freely given as a present, not coveted or bought, and then it is of greater power and makes a man more stalwart against his enemies. It heals the man who is lunatic; and if poison should be brought to the place where the diamond is, the stone immediately grows moist and begins to sweat, and men can easily polish it. But some craftsmen out of deceitfulness will not polish the stone, in order that it should be believed that the stone cannot be polished. In India too diamonds can be found of a violet colour, and somewhat brown, which are very good and very precious. But some do not like them as well as these others I have spoken of. Nevertheless they seem to me as good and as precious as the others; for truly, I have often seen them tested. They have others too which are as white as crystal, but they are dimmer and cloudy; still, they are very good and of great virtue. And they are nearly all quadrangular and pointed; but there are some that of their own nature are three cornered, and some six.

I shall say a little more about this stone, especially on account of those who export this stone to different countries to sell it. A man who wants to buy this stone must be able to recognize it with certainty because of the deceitfulness of those who sell them. Often to those who have no great knowledge of gems they sell pale crystals and other kinds of stones instead of diamonds, which are not so hard as diamonds; usually their points are broken off and they can easily be polished. But some jewellers will not polish them completely, to make men think that they cannot be polished. But the diamond can be tested in this way. Take the diamond and rub it on a sapphire, or on crystal, or on another precious stone, or on polished burnished steel. Then take the adamant, that attracts the compass needle, by which seamen are guided in the sea, and put the diamond on the adamant, laying a needle in front of it. If the diamond is good and full of power, the adamant will not attract the needle while the diamond is there. This is the test which they use overseas. But it often happens that the good diamond loses its powers because of the failings and dissoluteness of the man who carries it. Then it is necessary to make it win its powers again, or it will be of little value.

18

Of the customs in the isles around India;
of the distinction between idols and simulacres;
of three types of pepper growing on one tree;
and of the well that changes colour each hour of the day

In India there are very many different countries. It is called India because of a river that runs through that land, which is called Inde [Indus]. Eels of thirty feet long are found in that river. The people who dwell near the river are an ugly colour, yellow and green. In India there are more than five thousand good large isles that people live in, not counting those that are uninhabited. Each of these isles has many cities and towns, and many people. The people of India are not naturally disposed to travelling beyond their own country, for they live under [the influence of] the planet called Saturn. That planet performs his circle through the twelve signs [of the Zodiac] in thirty years; the moon, which is our planet, passes through the twelve signs in a month. Because Saturn is so slow-moving, men who live under him in that climate have no great desire to move about much, but stay in their own lands and desire no other. It is quite the opposite in our country. We are in a climate under the rule of the moon, which is a planet that moves quickly – the traveller's planet. So it gives us the desire to travel and visit different countries of the world, for it moves round the world more quickly than other planets.

Men travel through India by way of many countries to the Great Sea Ocean. Then they come to the isle of Chermes [Ormuz], whither merchants of Venice, Genoa and many other countries come to buy merchandise. But it is so hot there that the men have their testicles hanging down to their thighs because of the violent heat, which weakens their bodies. Men of that country who know what to do bind them up and use certain cooling astringent ointments to hold them up – otherwise they could not live. In this land and in Ethiopia and many other lands men and women frequently go to the rivers and lie in them all naked from undern [mid-morning] of the day until it be past noon, because of the great heat of the sun. They lie totally under water, except for their heads. Women there are not ashamed if men see them naked. Much ugliness can be seen there. In this isle there are ships made without nails or strappings of iron, because of the rocks of adamant in

the sea, which would attract ships to themselves. There are so many of
these rocks in those parts that if any ship in which there was any kind
of iron passed that way, it would be drawn to the rocks by the power of
the adamant, and would never get away again.

From this island men go by sea to the isle of Cana [Thana], where
there is great plenty of wine and corn. Once it was a very big island,
with a good harbour; but the largest part of it has been washed away by
the sea. The King of that isle was once so great and powerful that he
fought against Alexander the Great. The people of that isle have a
variety of religions: some worship the sun instead of God, some fire,
some snakes, some trees, some the first thing they come across in the
morning, and some worship simulacres and some idols. Now between
simulacres and idols there is a great difference. For simulacres are
images made in the likeness of something that occurs in nature, while
idols are images made in the likeness of whatever a man wishes, that is
not natural. Amongst all the varieties of animals you will not find one
that has three heads – one a man's, one a horse's, another of an ox or of
some other beast – as they make their idols. You must understand that
those who worship simulacres honour them for the sake of worthy
men, perhaps those who were doughty men in battle, like Hercules,
Achilles and others like them, who performed many marvels in their lives.
For they say they know well that they are not the God of nature, who
made everything, but that they are beloved of God because of the marvels they performed. So they say of the sun; for it often alters the
weather during the year, and gives heat to nourish the creatures of the
earth. Because it is of such value, they say they are sure it performs
God's will and that God loves it before any other thing; and therefore
they worship it. They say the same about the other planets and about
fire, because of the great good that comes from them. About idols, they
say that the ox is the holiest animal, and most useful, on earth, for it
does much good and no evil. They say they are sure that it cannot be
without the special grace of God, and therefore they represent their
God as half man and half ox, for man is the loveliest and best creature
God made and the ox the holiest. They worship snakes too, and other
beasts they meet first thing in the morning, especially those beasts
which it is good luck to meet and after seeing which they are fortunate
all the rest of the day, as they allege from long experience. So they say
this lucky encounter comes from God, and therefore they have had
images made like these creatures for their houses, so that they can
worship them before they meet anything else. In this isle of Thana there
are many wild beasts, like lions, leopards, bears, and others. There are

rats there as big as dogs are here; the men catch them with great mastiffs, for cats are too small. In this country, as in many others, when men are dead, they do not bury them; for the heat is so great that immediately the flesh is consumed, even to the bone.

From there men go to a city called Sarchie [Baroch?], a fine and good city. Many Christians of good faith live there, and there are many men of religion, especially friars. Thence one goes to the land of Lombe [Polumbum; Quilon] by sea. In that land pepper grows in a forest called Combar, and it grows nowhere else in the world but there. The forest is twenty-three days' journey in length. ⟨There are two good cities, of which the one is called Flabryne [Bandinanah] and the other Zinglauns [Cranganur]. In both cities Christian men and Jews live in great numbers, for the country is fertile and good. But it is very hot, and so there is a great abundance of different sorts of snakes and serpents. You must know that the pepper grows in the manner of wild vines beside the trees of the forest, so that it can rely on them for support. Its fruit hangs in great clusters, like bunches of grapes; they hang so thick that unless they were supported by other trees, the vines could not carry their fruit. When the fruit is ripe, it is all green like the berries of ivy. They gather the fruit and dry it in the sun, then lay it on a drying floor until it is black and wrinkled. They have three types of pepper growing on the one tree: first, the 'long' pepper which ripens according to its own nature, then white pepper, which is not burnt or toasted with fire or heat of the sun, and the black pepper dried by a fire or the sun. They call long pepper *spotyn*, the black *fulphul*, the white *bonoile*. The long pepper comes first, when the leaves begin to grow; it is like the flower of the hazel, which comes before the leaves. Then comes white pepper, with the leaves, in great clusters, like green grapes. When it is gathered, it is white, and somewhat smaller than the black pepper. Finally the black pepper comes in great abundance. They sell only a little – or none at all – of the white pepper to other countries, but keep it for their own use, because it is better and more beneficial and more temperate in its operation than the others, and it will also keep its power longer. Understand that the heavier the pepper is, the better and fresher it is. Still, it often happens that merchants adulterate pepper when it is old, as Isidore says. For they take old pepper and soak it, scattering over it frothy matter of silver or lead, and then dry it again. Because of the increased weight it seems fresh and new. Of their three kinds of pepper, they have most abundance of the black. In that land, as I said, there are many different kinds of snakes and serpents because of the heat – and also because of the pepper. Some say that at certain times of the year when they go to gather the pepper, they make fires here and there to burn the snakes or make them run away. But, with all respect, it is not so. For if they built fires round the pepper, they would burn the pepper and the trees it grows on, or shrivel them so that they would bear no more fruit; that is not true. On the contrary, they anoint their hands and feet and other places of the body with an ointment made of the juice of a fruit they call lemons, mingled with other things, and then they go boldly to get the pepper. The snakes and poisonous serpents run away when they perceive the smell of the ointment; in this way, truly, they get the pepper.

At the head of this forest is the city of Polumbum. Beside it is a mountain,) from which the city takes its name, for the mountain is called Polumbum. At the foot of this mountain is a noble and beautiful well, whose water has a sweet taste and smell, as if of different kinds of spices. Each hour of the day the water changes its smell and taste. And whoever drinks three times of that well on an empty stomach will be healed of whatever malady he has. And therefore those who live near that well drink of it very often, and so they are never ill, but always seem young. I, John Mandeville, saw this well, and drank of it three times, and so did all my companions. Ever since that time I have felt the better and healthier, and I think I shall do until such time as God in his grace causes me to pass out of this mortal life. Some men call that well the *fons iuuentutis*, that is, the Well of Youth; for he who drinks of it seems always young. They say this water comes from the Earthly Paradise, it is so full of goodness. Throughout this country there grows the best ginger there is anywhere; merchants come thither from distant countries to buy it.

And in this country the people worship the ox, in place of God, because of the simple goodness of the animal. They say there that the ox is the holiest beast in the world and has many virtues. For six or seven years the ox will draw the plough and help to work for man's sustenance, and after that one can eat him. The King of that land always has an ox with him, wherever he may be, and honours it as his god. And the man who looks after this ox gathers the dung in one golden vessel and the urine in another. What he collects each night he takes on the morrow to their prelate, who is called Archiprothopapaton, and he carries it to the King and says many blessings over it. And the King puts his hands in the urine of the ox, which they call gall, and rubs his brow and his breast with it. Then, with great reverence, he takes some of the dung and rubs it on his face and breast, as he did with the urine, to the intent that he may be filled with the virtues of the holy ox and that he may be blessed by that holy thing. Following the King, other lords and princes act in the same manner; and after them, servants and others, each in their degree, as long as any of the stuff is left. In that land their idols, their false gods, have the shape half of a man and half of an ox; and in those idols a devil speaks to them and answers their questions. In front of these idols they often kill their children instead of a sacrifice, taking their blood and sprinkling it upon the images; this is how they sacrifice to them. And when any man dies in that country they burn his body so that he should suffer no pain by being eaten by worms when in the grave. If he has no children, they burn his wife with him. For they say it is reasonable that she should bear him company in the next world as she did in this. And if she has children, they let her live to bring them up if she wants to. And if she chooses to live with her children rather than to be burned with her husband, she will be deemed untrustworthy and unnatural, and she will never again be praised nor will any man thenceforth trust her. And if the wife die before her husband, he will not be burnt with her against his will; if it pleases him he can take another wife. Good vines grow in that country; there the women drink wine and not men. And women shave their beards, and not men.

19

Of the judgements given by the hand of Saint Thomas the Apostle in the city of Calamy; of the devotion and sacrifice offered to idols there; and of the procession round the city

From this land one goes through many different places to a country called Mabaron [Coromandel]; it is ten days' journey from the land I have just spoken of. It is a great kingdom, with many good cities and towns. In that land of Coromandel lies Saint Thomas the Apostle, his body uncorrupted, in a beautiful tomb in the city of Calamy [Mailapur], for he was martyred and buried there. Afterwards, though, the Assirienes [Syrians] took his body and transported it to a city in Mesopotamia that is called Edisse [Edessa]. But soon after it was translated again to the aforesaid city and laid in its tomb; and his arm, with the hand which he put into Our Lord's side after the Resurrection, when he said, *Noli esse incredulus, sed fidelis,** lies outside in a reliquary. Men of that country judge who is right by that hand. For if there be a quarrel between two parties and each affirms right is on his side, they

* 'Be not faithless, but believing', John xx, 27.

· cause the case of each party to be written in a scroll and put these scrolls in the hand of Saint Thomas; quickly the hand casts away the scroll that contains the false case, and keeps the other. So men often come thither from far lands, to settle the right of a doubtful case between two parties. The church where Saint Thomas lies is large and beautiful and full of statues of their idols; these images are each the size of two men at least.

But there is one image which surpasses all the others in size, and it is richly adorned with gold and precious stones on all sides, and sits in a nobly decorated chair. It has round its neck as it were broad sashes of silk, embroidered with gold and precious stones. To that image people often come on pilgrimage with great devotion, as frequently as Christian folk come to Saint James [at Compostella]. And some of them, out of the great devotion they have for that idol, will constantly look at the earth as they walk, not looking about them, lest they should see anything that would hinder their devotion. Others come in pilgrimage carrying sharp knives in their hands, with which, as they go along, they wound themselves in the arms and legs and other places, so that the blood runs from their wounds in great profusion. This they do for love of that idol, and say that he who dies for love of that idol will be blessed indeed. Some of them bring with them their children and slay them, sacrificing them to that idol. They take their children's blood and sprinkle it upon the image. Some, too, from the time they leave their homes until they arrive at their idol, kneel on the earth with great devotion at every third step. And they bring with them incense and other sweet-smelling things to cense that image, as here we do the Host. In front of that image, there is as it were a pool or fishpond full of water; into it pilgrims cast gold and silver and precious stones without number as offerings. Therefore the priests who look after that idol, when they have need of any money to repair the church, or for any other thing pertaining to that idol, go to that pool and take out as much as they need. You must know that when there are great festivals of that idol – the dedication of a church, or the enthroning of the idol – all the country assembles there. They set this idol with great reverence in a chariot, arrayed in cloth of gold and silk, and lead it about the city with great solemnity. In front of the chariot there go first in procession the maidens of that land, two by two; and then all the pilgrims that have come from far countries, some of whom out of great devotion to that idol fall down in front of the chariot and let it roll over them. And so some of them are slain, some have their arms and legs broken; and they believe that the more pain they suffer here for the love of that idol, the more joy they will have in the other world and the nearer God they will be. And truly they suffer so much pain and mortification of their bodies for love of that idol that hardly would any Christian man suffer the half – nay, not a tenth – for love of Our Lord Jesus Christ. For sometimes two or three hundred in a single day will kill themselves for love of that idol, and their bodies are brought before that idol and accounted saints. And just as among us a man would think it honourable if among his kindred a confessor or holy martyr was canonized, and his virtues and miracles written in books, even so it seems to them a great honour when any of their cousins or friends kill themselves for love of that idol, and they write their deeds and their names in books and in their prayers. And the more of their kindred who kill themselves in this way, the gladder they are, and every man of them says to his fellow, 'We have more saints in our family than you have.' When anyone intends to kill himself for love of the idol, he calls all his friends together and makes many minstrels go before them with great solemnity; and thus they come before the idol. He who is to kill himself stands in front of the idol with a sharp drawn knife in his hand, and with that knife he cuts off a piece of his flesh and throws it up to the face of the idol and then says devout prayers and commends himself to his god. Then he strikes himself with the knife in different places until he falls down dead. Then his friends offer his body to the idol, singing and saying, 'Behold what thy loyal servant has done for thee! He has forsaken wife and children and all the riches and pleasures of this world, and his own life, for love of thee. He has made sacrifice unto thee of his own flesh and blood. Wherefore, we pray thee, set him beside thee among thy dear friends in the joy of Paradise, for he has well deserved it.' And when they have done thus, they burn his body and everyone takes a portion of the ashes and keeps them as relics. They say it is a holy thing, and through the virtue of these ashes they shall be saved, and kept from all kinds of danger. And when they lead their idol around the city in procession, as I told you, next in front of the chariot go all the minstrels of the country with all kinds of musical instruments, and make melody. And when they have in this manner led the idol all round the city with great solemnity, they lead it again to the temple and set it again in its usual place. And then in honour of that idol and its feast many people kill themselves with sharp knives in great numbers, as I said before.*

* The account of the Juggernaut, though essentially the same, is considerably shorter in Defective.

20

*Of the foul customs followed in the isle of Lamory;
and how the earth and sea are of round shape,
proved by means of the Star Antarctic*

From this country men go through the Great Sea Ocean by way of many isles and different countries, which would be tedious to relate. At last, after fifty-two days' journey, men come to a large country called Lamory [Sumatra]. In that land it is extremely hot; the custom there is for men and women to go completely naked and they are not ashamed to show themselves as God made them. They scorn other folk who go clothed; for they say that God made Adam and Eve naked, and men ought not to be ashamed of what God has made, for nothing natural is ugly. They say also that men who wear clothes are of another world, or else believe not in God who made all the world. In that land there is no marriage between man and woman; all the women of that land are common to every man. They say that if they were to do otherwise they would sin greatly, because God said to Adam and Eve, *Crescite et multiplicamini et replete terram*, that is to say, 'Increase and multiply and fill the earth.'* And therefore no man says, 'This is my wife,' nor any woman, 'This is my husband.' When women are delivered of a child, they give it to whom they want of the men who have slept with them. And in the same way the land is common property. So one year a man has one house, another year another; each man takes what pleases him, now here, now there. For all things are common, as I said, corn and other goods too; nothing is locked up, and every man is as rich as another. But they have an evil custom among them, for they will eat human flesh more gladly than any other. Nevertheless the land is abundant enough in meat and fish and corn, and also gold and silver and other goods. Merchants bring children there to sell, and the people of the country buy them. Those that are plump they eat; those that are not plump they feed up and fatten, and then kill and eat them. And they say it is the best and sweetest flesh in the world.

And you must understand that in this land, and many others thereabouts, the star called *Polus Arcticus* [Pole star], cannot be seen; it stands ever in the north and never moves, and by it seamen are guided. It is not seen in the south. But there is another star, which is called

* Genesis i, 22.

Antarctic, which is exactly opposite the first star; and seamen steer by that star there as here they do by the Pole star. Just as their star cannot be seen here, so our star cannot be seen there. It can be seen from this that the world is quite round; for the parts of the firmament which can be seen in one country cannot be seen in another. It can be proved thus. If a man had adequate shipping and good company, and had moreover his health, and wanted to go and see the world, he could traverse the whole world, above and below. I prove that thus, according to what I have seen. For I have been in Braban [Brabant] and seen by the astrolabe that the Pole star is there sixty-three degrees in elevation, and in Germany near Boem [Bohemia] it is sixty-eight degrees, and further to the north it is seventy-two degrees and some minutes. All this I saw with the astrolabe. Understand that in the south, opposite this star, is the star called Pole Antarctic. These two stars never move; and around them moves the firmament, like a wheel on an axle-tree. So the line between these two stars divides the whole firmament into two equal parts. Afterwards I went to the south, and found that it was in Libya one first sees the Antarctic star; as I went further, I found that in Upper Libya it is eighteen degrees and some minutes in elevation (sixty minutes make a degree). And so, passing by land and sea to the country I speak of, and other lands and isles beyond, I found this Antarctic star to be thirty-three degrees in elevation. And had I had company and shipping that would have gone further, I do believe we should have seen all the roundness of the firmament, that is to say both the hemispheres, upper and lower. For as I told you before, half the firmament is between these two stars, which I have seen. Of the one half I saw a part to the north as far as sixty-two degrees ten minutes, under the Arctic Pole; and of the other to the south I saw thirty-three degrees and sixteen minutes, under the Antarctic Pole. Half the firmament contains only 180 degrees, of which I have seen sixty-two degrees ten minutes of Arctic, and of Antarctic I have seen thirty-three degrees sixteen minutes. This adds up to four score and fifteen degrees and a half. So there wants only four score and four and a half degrees, for me to have seen all the firmament. The quarter of it contains four score and ten degrees. And so I have seen three parts of it, and nearly five and a half degrees more. So I say truly that a man could go all round the world, above and below, and return to his own country, provided he had his health, good company, and a ship, as I said above. And all along the way he would find men, lands, islands, cities and towns, such as there are in those countries. For you know well that those men who live right under the Antarctic Pole are foot against foot to those who live right below the Arctic Pole, just as we and those who live at our Antipodes are foot against foot. It is like that in all parts. Each part of the earth and sea has its opposite, which always balances it. And understand that to my way of thinking the land of Prester John, Emperor of India, is exactly below us. For if a man were to go from Scotland or England to Jerusalem, he would be going upwards all the way. For our land is in the lowest part of the West, and the land of Prester John is in the lowest part of the East. They have day when we have night, and night when we have day. And however much a man climbs when he goes from our country to Jerusalem, he must descend as much to the land of Prester John. The cause is that the earth and sea is round. For it is a commonplace that Jerusalem is in the middle of the earth; it may be proved thus. Let a man take a spear and stick it in the ground at noon at the time when day and night are of equal length, and it will cast no shadow on either side. David bears witness of this where he says, *Deus autem rex noster ante secula operatus est salutem in medio terre*, which means, 'God our King wrought salvation in the midst of the earth before the beginning of the world.'[*] Therefore those who go from our countries of the West to Jerusalem must make as many days' journey downwards to Prester John's land as they made upward to Jerusalem. So a man can travel into all those countries, girdling the roundness of the earth and sea, until he comes to a point exactly below us. I have often thought of a story I have heard, when I was young, of a worthy man of our country who went once upon a time to see the world. He passed India and many isles beyond India, where there are more than 5,000 isles, and travelled so far by land and sea, girdling the globe, that he found an isle where he heard his own language being spoken. For he heard one who was driving a plough team say such words to them as he had heard men say to oxen in his own land when they were working at the plough. He marvelled greatly, for he did not understand how this could be. But I conjecture that he had travelled so far over land and sea, circumnavigating the earth, that he had come to his own borders; if he had gone a bit further, he would have come to his own district. But after he heard that marvel, he could not get transport any further, so he turned back the way he had come; so he had a long journey! Afterwards it happened that he went to Norway, and a gale blew him off course to an island. And when he was there he knew it was the island he had been in before and heard his own language, as the beasts were being driven. That could well be, even if men of limited understanding do not believe that men can travel on the underside of

· [*] Psalm lxxiv, 12.

the globe without falling off into the firmament. For just as it seems to us that those men there are under us, so it seems to them that we are under them. For if it were possible for a man to fall off the earth to the firmament, all the more reason for the earth and the sea, which are very heavy, to fall thither too. But that cannot happen, as God Himself witnesses when He says, *Non timeas me, qui suspendi terram ex nichilo*, that is to say, 'Have no fear of me, who have hanged the earth from nothing.'*

Yet even though it is possible for a man to travel all over the globe, nevertheless only one in a thousand, perhaps, would travel a route round the earth that would bring him back to the country he started from. For there are so many routes, and countries, where a man can go wrong, except by special grace of God. For the earth is very big, and in circumference it is some 20,425 miles, according to the opinion of wise scholars in the past, whom I am not going to contradict. But it does seem to me, with my limited understanding, that, with all respect, it is a lot more. Let me make you understand why. Imagine a large circle; and let there be described round the point (which is called the centre) of that circle another smaller circle; divide it by lines into many segments and let those lines meet in the centre, so that there will be as many segments in the great circle as in the smaller, even if the area of them is less. Let the big circle stand for the firmament, which is divided by astronomers into twelve signs, each in turn divided into thirty degrees; so there are 360 degrees in all the firmament. Now let the small circle stand for the earth, and divide it into as many parts as the firmament, each part corresponding to a degree of the firmament – seven hundred and twenty divisions in all. [Understand that according to astronomical writers seven hundred furlongs of earth correspond to a degree of the firmament, that is eighty-seven miles and four furlongs.]† Multiply these by 360, and it comes to 31,005 miles [*sic*], each mile being like our mile of eight furlongs. And this is the circumference of the earth according to my opinion and understanding. And you should know that, according to the view of ancient and wise philosophers and astronomers, England, Scotland, Wales and Ireland are not counted in the height of the earth, as is apparent in books of astronomy. For the height of the earth is divided into seven parts, which are called seven climates after the seven planets; each one of the planets rules one of the climates. These countries are not in those climates, for they are down in

* A reminiscence of Job xxvi, 7. Garbled, and not the Vulgate.

† Omitted in Egerton; supplied from MS Harley 4383. The sentence is in Cotton.

the Far West. Similarly the isles of India, opposite us, are not counted in the climates for they are in the Far East. These climates surround all the world.* Nevertheless some astronomers appropriate these countries to the moon, which is the lowest planet, making its orbit most swiftly. Now I shall return to my account where I left off, and tell you of more countries and isles in India and beyond.

21

Of the palace of the King of Java; of the trees that bear flour, honey, wine and venom; and of other marvels and customs in the environing isles

Near this isle of Lamory which I spoke of is another island, called Somober [Sumatra]. This is a great and good island, with a noble and mighty King. The people of this country mark themselves on the face with a hot iron, to be distinguished from other folk by this mark of their high rank; for they account themselves the noblest people in the world. They war unceasingly against the naked folk I spoke of before. Near there is another island, which is called Boteniga, a fertile island full of all kinds of riches. And round about this isle are many others, and different countries and different sorts of men, of which it would be too much to tell in full.

But passing thence a little way by sea, men come to a great isle called Iava [Java]. The King of this land is a great and mighty lord, and has seven other kings of seven isles nearby under him. There are a marvellous number of people in Java; they grow different kinds of spices in more abundance than in other places – ginger, cloves, nutmegs, mace, and many others. You should know that mace is the husk of the nutmeg. There is great plenty of everything in this isle. The King has a beautiful and costly palace. All the steps into his hall and his chambers are alternately of gold and silver. The walls inside are covered with plates of gold and silver, and on them are engraved stories of kings and

---

* A difficult passage. Part of the problem is that Ptolemy, whose work was the basis of much medieval theoretical geography, had no knowledge of the East or of northern Europe, and so these parts must lie outside all schemes based on his ideas (like the climates). The word 'height' corresponds to 'superficie' in the French and the 'superficyalte' in Cotton; probably the sense is as in the OED, 'superficies' 2 or 4.

knights and battles, with crowns and circlets of precious stones on their heads. No man would believe the grandeur and wealth of this palace if he had not seen it. The King is so great and powerful that he has often discomfited the Great Khan, the mightiest emperor in the world, in battle. For they have often been at war because the Great Khan wanted to make this King his vassal; but the King has always withstood him and put him off manfully.

Sailing thence by sea, men come to another isle which some call Thalamass and some Pathen [Borneo?]. It is a great kingdom, with many fair towns and cities. There grow here trees that bear flour, from which men make bread, fine and white and of good taste; it resembles wheaten bread, but it is not quite of the same taste. There are also other trees that bear poison, against which there is only one antidote; that is to take the leaves of the same tree, crush them, soak them in water and drink it, or else a man will die very quickly, for neither treacle nor any other medicine will help. With this preparation the Jews once thought to have poisoned all Christendom, as one of them confessed to me; but, blessed be Almighty God, they failed in their purpose. And if you want to know how the trees bear flour, I tell you that one cuts with a hatchet round the bole of the tree near the ground in many places, so that the bark is pierced; then a thick liquid flows out, which they catch in a receptacle and set in the sun to dry. When it is dry they grind it in a mill, and it is then fine white meal. And wine, honey and poison are drawn from the trees in the same way and kept in pots. There is in that isle too a dead sea; it is like a loch, and it has no bottom. Whatever is thrown into it will never be found again. Beside that loch grow reeds of marvellous length; there they call them *thaby* [bamboo]. And of these reeds they make houses and dwellings and ships and their other necessaries, as we do here from oak and other trees. Let no man say this is a fable or an untruth, for truly I saw with my own eyes many of these reeds lying on the sea-shore, a single one of which twenty men of my company could not carry nor even comfortably lift it from the ground. There are also other reeds of less size, and under their roots men find precious stones of great virtue. For no kind of iron can harm or draw blood from a man who carries one of these stones on him. So men of that country fight very bravely both on water and on land because of their precious stones. But their enemies, who know the type and powers of the stones, make arrows and crossbow bolts without iron, and wound and kill them with these.

From this island men go by sea to another, called Calanok [Indo-China?]; it is a large country, plentiful in goods. The King of that land has as many wives as he wants. For he has all the fair ladies of that land brought before him, and he takes one of them one night, another another; and so some of the kings will have at different times a thousand or more. And she who has been with him for one night nevermore comes to him unless he sends for her. Therefore he has a great number of sons and daughters; some kings have a hundred children, some two hundred, some more. The King also has fourteen thousand tame elephants, which he keeps at a town in his kingdom. When he has a war against any lord near him, he has castles made and tied on the elephants; in these castles he puts soldiers to fight against his enemies. Their enemies do the same; for that is the fashion of warfare in those lands. These elephants they call *warkes* in their language.

In that land, too, there is a marvel that is not in other lands. For all kinds of fish in the sea come at a certain time of year, each kind in turn, and gather close to the shore – some on the shore. They lie there three days, and the men of that country come there and take what they want. And then that kind of fish goes away, and another kind comes ashore for another three days; and people take of them. And thus do all kinds of fish until all of them have done it, and men have taken as much as they wanted. No man knows the cause of this. But the folk of that land say that God shows them that grace to do honour to their King, as the most worthy earthly monarch, because he has so many wives and begets so many children on them, filling the world, as God commanded Adam and Eve, when He said, *Crescite et multiplicamini et replete terram*, which is to say, 'Increase and multiply and fill the earth, and be lords of the fishes in the sea.' This seems to me one of the greatest marvels I saw in any land, that fish who have the whole sea to swim in at their pleasure should voluntarily come and offer themselves to be killed without any compulsion by any creature. And indeed I am sure it does not happen without some great cause and meaning.

There are also in that land such great snails [tortoises and turtles] that three or four men can shelter in their shells, as if in a little house or lodge. There are also others less big, about the thickness of a man's thigh; and both sorts are all white, except the head, which is black. There is a third kind of snail, too, much smaller than the other two. Of them they make a meat for the King and other great lords. In that land it is a custom when a man dies that his wife is buried alive with him; for they say it is sensible that she should keep him company in the next world as she did in this.

Thence men go across the Great Sea Ocean to another island called

Caffilos. There they have a custom that when their friends are seriously ill, they hang them on trees, so that they can be chewed and eaten by the birds; for they say it is better for them to be eaten by birds, which are God's angels, than to be eaten by worms in the earth.

Thence one goes to another land, where the people are of evil customs. They train great dogs to worry men. And when their friends are getting near death and they believe they can live no longer, they make these dogs worry them; for they will not let them die naturally in their beds lest they suffer too much pain in dying. When they are dead, they eat their flesh instead of venison.

And from this country you go via many others in the sea to one called Melk [Malacca?]. There are wicked and cruel folk there too. For they have no delight or pleasure in anything except slaughtering people to drink their blood. And the man who can kill the greatest number of men is the most respected and worthiest among them. There is no drink they like so much as man's blood, and they call it God. If there is any quarrel among them, no full agreement can be made until each has drunk the other's blood; and in the same way relationships are sealed between them. Agreements and relationships among them are not valid unless made in this way.

From here one goes to another isle, called Tracota, where the people are like animals lacking reason. They live in caves, for they do not have the intelligence to build houses; and when they see a stranger passing through the country, they run and hide in their caves. They eat snakes, and do not speak, but hiss to one another like adders. They care nothing for gold, silver, or other worldly goods, only for one precious stone which has sixty colours. It is called traconite after the country. They love this stone very much indeed, even though they do not know its properties; they desire it simply for its beauty.

Thence one travels by sea to another land, called Natumeran [Nicobar islands]. It is a large and fair island, whose circuit is nearly a thousand miles. Men and women of that isle have heads like dogs, and they are called Cynocephales. These people, despite their shape, are fully reasonable and intelligent. They worship an ox as their god. Each one of them carries an ox made of gold or silver on his brow, as a token that they love their god well. They go quite naked except for a little cloth round their privy parts. They are big in stature and good warriors; they carry a large shield, which covers all their body, and a long spear in their hand, and dressed in this way they go boldly against their enemies. If they capture any man in battle, they eat him. The King of that land is a great and mighty lord, rich, and very devout according to his creed. He has round his neck a cord of silk on which are three hundred precious stones [orient pearls], like our rosary of amber. And just as we say our *Pater Noster* and *Aue Maria* by telling our beads, just so the King says each day on his beads three hundred prayers to his god, before he eats. He wears a splendid ruby round his neck, which is nearly a foot long and five fingers broad. They give him this ruby when they make him King, to carry in his hand, and so he rides round the city and they all make obeisance to him. After that he always wears it round his neck, for if he did not he would be King no longer. The Great Khan of Cathay has much coveted that ruby, but he could never win it in war or by any other means. This King is a very righteous man and just according to his law, for he punishes everyone who does another man wrong in his realm. Therefore men can travel safely and securely through his land, and no one is so bold as to annoy them, rob them, or take any kind of goods from them.

From here one goes to another isle called Silha [Ceylon]. The circumference of it is eight hundred miles. A great part of this country is waste and wilderness, and uninhabited; therefore there are great numbers of dragons, crocodiles and other kinds of reptiles, so that men cannot live there. The crocodile is a kind of snake, brown on top of the back, with four feet and short legs and two great eyes. The body is so long and so big that where it has travelled across the sand it is as if a great tree has been dragged there. In that wilderness there are also many other kinds of wild beast, especially elephants. And in that isle there is a high mountain, and on the very top of it is a great loch full of water. Men of that land say that Adam and Eve wept for a hundred years on that hill after they were expelled from Paradise, and that that water collected from their tears. In the bottom of that lake precious stones are found, and round it grow reeds in great profusion, among which there are crocodiles and other snakes living; in the lake there are horse eels [leeches?] of marvellous size. Once a year the King of that isle gives all the poor people leave to go into the lake and gather precious stones, out of charity and for love of Adam and Eve's God; each year enough of those precious stones are found. When these poor folk go into the lake to gather the stones, they anoint themselves all over with the juice of the fruit called lemons, and do not fear the crocodiles nor the other poisonous reptiles. The water of this lake empties down the side of the mountain. And by that river pearls and precious stones are found. Men say in that land that snakes and other venomous animals do no harm to strangers or pilgrims who pass through; they hurt only the natives and those who live there. There are also wild geese with two heads and white wolves with bodies as big as oxen, and many other kinds of animals. And understand that the sea which surrounds this island and other isles nearby seems so high above the land that it looks to men who see it as if it hung in the air on the point of falling and covering the earth; and that is a marvellous thing, as the prophet says, *Mirabiles elaciones maris*, that is, 'Wonderful are the risings of the sea.'*

22

How men know through the idol if sick men will die or not;
of the people of different shapes, and very ugly; and of the monks
who give their alms to baboons, monkeys and marmosets

From this isle men go south by sea to another which is called Dundeya, a big island [Andaman Islands]. There live here a people of evil customs, for fathers eat their sons and sons their fathers, husbands their wives and wives their husbands. For if it chance that a man's father is sick, the son goes to the priest of their religion and asks him to inquire of their god – who is an idol – whether his father will live or die of that sickness. And the devil within that idol may answer that he will not die at that time, and indicates some medicines to heal him with; then the son returns to his father and does as instructed until he is well again. But if it says he will die, the priest and the son and the wife of the sick man come to him and throw a cloth over his mouth and stop him breathing, and kill him. When he is dead they take his body and cut it in little pieces, and summon all his friends, and all the musicians they can get, and make a solemn feast and eat the dead man's body. And when they have eaten all the flesh, they collect all the bones together and bury them according to their custom with great solemnity and loud singing. And thus each friend does to another; and if it so happen that a man who is a relation of the dead man keeps away from the feast and comes not to the funeral, all the family will accuse him of a serious fault, and he will never after be counted among their friends. They say that they eat the flesh of their friend so that worms should not eat him in the earth, and to release him from the great pain that his soul would suffer if worms gnawed him in the earth. They also say, when they find his flesh lean through long illness, that it would be a great sin to allow him to live longer or suffer pain without a cause. If they find his flesh fat, they say they have done well to have killed him so quickly and sent him

* Psalm xciii, 4. This last paragraph is transposed to Chapter 22 in Defective.

to Paradise, not allowing him to be tormented too long in this world. The King of that land is a great and mighty lord, and has under his rule fifty-four large islands; in each of them is a crowned king, all obedient to him.

There are many different kinds of people in these isles. In one, there is a race of great stature, like giants, foul and horrible to look at; they have one eye only, in the middle of their foreheads. They eat raw flesh and raw fish. In another part, there are ugly folk without heads, who have eyes in each shoulder; their mouths are round, like a horseshoe, in the middle of their chest. In yet another part there are headless men whose eyes and mouths are on their backs. And there are in another place folk with flat faces, without noses or eyes; but they have two small holes instead of eyes, and a flat lipless mouth. In another isle there are ugly fellows whose upper lip is so big that when they sleep in the sun they cover all their faces with it. In another there are people of small stature, like dwarfs, a little bigger than pygmies. They have no mouth, but instead a little hole, and so when they must eat they suck their food through a reed or pipe. They have no tongues, and hiss and make signs as monks do, to each other, and each of them understands what the other means. In another isle there are people whose ears are so big that they hang down to their knees. In another, people have feet like horses, and run so swiftly on them that they overtake wild beasts and kill them for their food. In another isle there are people who walk on their hands and their feet like four-footed beasts; they are hairy and climb up trees as readily as apes. There is another isle where the people are hermaphrodite, having the parts of each sex, and each has a breast on one side. When they use the male member, they beget children; and when they use the female, they bear children. There is another isle where the folk move on their knees marvellously, and it seems as if at each step they would fall; on each foot they have eight toes. There is still another isle where the people have only one foot, which is so broad that it will cover all the body and shade it from the sun. They will run so fast on this one foot that it is a marvel to see them. There is also another isle where the people live just on the smell of a kind of apple; and if they lost that smell, they would die forthwith. Many other kinds of folk there are in other isles about there, which are too numerous to relate.

Going eastwards many days' journey from these isles one comes to a great kingdom, called Mancy [Manzi]. It is in Greater India, and it is the best and pleasantest land, and the most bountiful in good things, in the power of man. Here many Christian folk live with the Saracens, for it is a great and good land. There are more than two thousand noble cities, not to mention other good towns. The land of India is the best populated land anywhere, because of the great quantity of good things. There are no beggars or poor men there. Except that they are pale in colour, the people there are very handsome. The men have thin beards with few hairs in them – hardly will fifty hairs be found in one beard. The hairs are few, scattered here and there like the beard of a leopard or a cat, and very long. In that land there are the loveliest women of any land beyond the seas; some call that land Albany because the women are so white.

The chief city of this land is Latoryn [Canton], on the sea, and it is bigger than Paris. Through this city runs a great river, which is navigable. It runs into the sea a little way – a day's journey – from the city. There is no city in the world better planned, no city that has more ships belonging to it, no city that has a better, larger, or stronger harbour. All the people of that city and the surrounding country worship idols. There are all kinds of birds, half as big again as they are in this country. There are geese all white, as big as swans here, and they have on their heads a perfectly round red spot. There is great plenty and availability of all kinds of food, and also a lot of snakes, which they use in feasts and delicious dishes. If a man gives a great feast and gives his guests all the best foods that can be got anywhere yet gives them no snakes he will have no thanks for all his feast.

There are many other fair cities in that land, and also great abundance of food. There are also many churches and religious houses, of their religion of course. In the churches there are great idols, like giants, to which on festival days they give meat and drink in this manner. They bring before them dishes hot from the fire, and let the smell of them go up to the idols, and then they say that they have fed well enough; when they have done this, the men of religion eat the food. In this land there are white hens without feathers, but they have white wool on them like sheep do in our country. Women of that land who are married wear crowns upon their heads, so that they may be known from those who are unmarried. In this land they catch a beast called a *loyre* [otter], teach it to go in the rivers and ponds, and it catches great fish, as many and as often as they want.

From there men go by land many days' journey to another city called Cassay [Kinsay, Hangchow], which is the biggest city in the world. Its name means 'city of Heaven'. This city is fifty miles round, and there is a marvellous number of people in it. It has twelve great gates; before each gate, three or four miles off, is a good town. This city is built in the same way as Venice; there are in it twelve thousand bridges or more.

On each bridge there is at each end a strong tower, and soldiers inside to guard the city against the Great Khan, whose land borders theirs. On one side, along the city, there runs a great river. Many Christian men live there, and many merchants of different nations, for the country is bountiful and good and full of all sorts of riches. Very excellent wine grows there, which they call *bygon*; it is a very strong wine, most pleasant to drink. The King of that land used to dwell in that city, and there is there a house of Christian friars.

From this city one can take a ship or boat on the river to a monastery a little way away; they are very devout in their religion. In that monastery there is a very large, beautiful garden, where grow trees of many different kinds. There are also many different sorts of animals, such as marmosets, and apes, and others, to the number of three or four thousand. And when the convent has eaten, a monk takes the food set aside for alms and carries it to the garden; and he rings a little bell of silver that he has in his hand; then all these animals come out of their burrows to him. And he makes them sit in rows and doles out to them the food in fine dishes of gilded silver, and they eat it. When they have done, he rings the bell again and they go back to where they came from. These monks say that those beasts which are pretty and gentle are the souls of lords and gentle folk, and those beasts which are not so are the souls of other men. They maintain that the souls of men when they leave their bodies enter into those beasts; that is their firm belief, and no one can shake their opinion. The souls of great men, they say, go into gentle and beautiful animals, and the souls of men of low rank go into ugly animals; and therefore they give them meat and alms for the love of God. I asked the monk who was administering the alms if it would not have been better to have given that relief to poor men rather than to beasts, and he answered me by saying that in that country there were no poor men and, if there were, it would still be more charitable to give it to those souls who are suffering their penance there and can go no further to get their food rather than to poor men who have intelligence and who can work for their living. Those same animals they catch young and train them to come for the alms. I saw many other marvels in that land, which I shall not speak of now in order to make my book shorter.

From this city one goes six days' journey to another great city, which is called Chibense [Nanking]. The walls of this city are twenty miles round; within it are sixty fine bridges, all of well-wrought stone. In this city used to be the premier seat of the King of Manzi, for it is a fine city.

From there men cross a great river, called the Dalay [Yangtze]. It is the finest and largest river of fresh water in the world, for even at its narrowest it is four miles wide. After that one enters again the land of the Great Khan. This river, the Yangtze, runs through the middle of the land of the Pigmens [pygmies], who are men of small stature, for they are only three spans tall [two feet]. But they are very handsome and well proportioned to their size. They marry when they are a year and a half old, and beget children; they usually live seven or eight years. If they live to nine they are considered marvellously old. These small men do marvellous work in silk and cotton, and other such delicate work – much more delicately than other men. Frequently they fight with cranes, having perpetual war with them; and when they can kill one, they eat it. They do not work in tilling the land, or other heavy labour; they have among them men of our size who till the land and dress the vines and do all the other heavy work that is necessary. And these small men have great scorn for big men, and find them as much an oddity as we find giants. There is in that land a good city where a lot of these small men live. And among them live big men too, of the usual size; if they have children, they are born as small as the children of the pygmies. The nature of the country is such that nothing but small things are engendered there. The Great Khan, who is lord of it, has this city looked after very well. And understand that the pygmies, even if they are small, are perfectly sensible according to their age, and are very clever, and can judge between good and evil.

From this city one journeys through the country via many towns and cities to a city called Iamcaly [Yangchow], which is rich and fair. Merchants come there from different lands to buy all sorts of merchandise. This city gives each year to the Great Khan fifty thousand [*cumans*] of gold florins, so the citizens told me. Know that a *cuman* contains ten thousand florins; and so the sum this city gives each year comes to five hundred thousand [*sic*] florins of gold. The King of that land is a great and mighty lord, but he is subject to the Great Khan; he has twelve great princes under him. In every decent town in that country there is a good custom: if a man wants to make a feast for his friends, in each town there are certain good inns, and he who wants to give the feast goes to the innkeeper and says, 'Prepare a dinner for me for so many men in your inn.' He tells him the number, what kinds of food he wants, and how much he wants to spend. Then the innkeeper goes and organizes everything necessary, so that nothing is lacking; and therefore everything is arranged much better than if he who is giving the feast gave it in his own house.

Four miles from the city of Yangchow, towards the headwaters of the

Yangtze, is another city, called Menk [Ningpo]. There is a great fleet of
ships there, and they are all white as snow from the kind of wood they
are made of. They are built like great houses, with halls and chambers
and other conveniences.

Thence one goes by many other towns to another city called Lanteryn
[Linching]; it is eight days' journey from Ningpo. It stands on a great
river called the Caremoran or Caromosan [Hwang-ho], which runs
through the land of Cathay. Often it does great damage to the country
by overflowing when it is in spate.

23

Of the Great Khan of Cathay;
of the royalty of his palace, and how he sits at meat;
and of the great number of servants who serve him

The land of Cathay is a great country, beautiful, rich, fertile, full of good
merchandise. Every year merchants come there to get spices and other
sorts of merchandise – they go there more frequently than they do
elsewhere. You should understand that the merchants who come from
Venice or Genoa or other places in Lombardy or the Greek Empire
travel by land and sea for eleven or twelve months before they get to
Cathay, the chief realm of the Great Khan. In the east there is an old
city, near which the Tartarenes have built another, called Gaydon [the
great court of the Mongols, near Peking]. This city has twelve gates,
and each gate is a mile from the next, so the circuit of the city is
twenty-four miles [*sic*]. This city is the seat of the Great Khan; his
throne is in a very fair palace, the boundary wall of which is two miles
and more long. Within that wall there are other fine palaces too. In the
garden of the great palace is a hill on which is another beautiful and rich
palace – there is not another like it in all the world. And all round the
palace and the hill are many trees, bearing many different sorts of fruit;
beyond, there are deep broad dykes; beyond those again, there are
many fishponds and pools, whereon there are many water fowl, like
swans, cranes, herons, bitterns, mallards and others. Outside those
again are all kinds of wild game – harts and hinds, bucks and does, and
roe deer, and others. And whenever the Great Khan wants to have
sport hawking or hunting, he can kill wildfowl with hawks and kill deer
with his hounds or other means without leaving his room. This palace,
his seat, is wonderfully large and beautiful; and the hall of that palace is

richly furnished. Within the hall are twenty-four pillars of gold; and all the walls are covered with the red skins of beasts, called *panters* [pandas?]. They are very fine animals, sweet smelling, and because of the good smell of the skins no harmful air can come therein. These skins are as red as any blood, and shine so in the sun that a man can hardly look at them because of their brightness. The folk of that country honour that beast, when they see it, on account of its good properties and the sweet smell that comes from it; they praise the skin of it as much as if it had been of fine gold. In the middle of the palace a dais has been made for the Great Khan, adorned with gold and precious stones. At its four corners there are four dragons made of gold. This dais has a canopy of silken cloth, barred across with gold and silver, and there are many large precious stones hanging on it. And below the dais are conduits full of drink, which the people of the Emperor's court drink from; beside the conduits are set vessels of gold which men can drink from when they wish. This hall is nobly and gloriously set out in every way. First, up on the top of the high dais, in the very middle, the throne for the Emperor is positioned, high up from the pavement, where he sits and eats his food. The table he eats on is made of jewels set in fine gold, and is bordered with gold set full of gems. The steps up which he goes to his throne are all of precious stone set in gold. At the left side of his throne is the seat of his chief wife, one step lower than his; it is of jasper, with sides of fine gold set with precious stones, and her table is of jasper bordered with gem-inlaid gold. The seat of his second wife is a step lower than the other's; and her seat and table are adorned as magnificently as the other wife's. The table and seat of the third wife is a step lower still. For he always has three wives with him, wherever he goes far or near. Next to his third wife on the same side sit other ladies of the Emperor's kin, each one a step lower than another according to how near they are in blood-relationship to the Emperor. The women of that country who are married have on their heads something like a man's foot, made of gold and gems and peacock feathers, beautifully made and glinting in the light; this is a token that they are under the rule of a man. Those who are not wedded do not have such hats. On the right hand of the Emperor sits his eldest son, who will rule after him, a step lower than his father. His seat and table are in every way exactly like the Empress's. Then there sit other lords of the Emperor's family, everyone according to his degree, like the ladies on the other side. Each has a table to himself, like the ladies; they are either of jasper or crystal or amethyst or *lignum aloes*, which comes out of Paradise, or of ivory. And all the tables are bordered with gold set full of precious stones, so that there is not one that is not worth a great treasure. Under the Emperor's table, at his feet, sit four clerks, who write down all the words he says while he is eating, whether they be good or ill. For everything that he says really must be done, for his word must not be gainsaid for anything.

On festival days great tables of gold are brought before the Emperor on which stand peacocks and other birds, cleverly and intricately made. Those birds are so wonderfully made by man's craft that it seems as if they leapt, and danced, and flapped their wings, and disported themselves in other ways; it is wonderful to see how such things are done. By what craft they do all this I cannot say; but I do know for sure that those people are marvellously clever in anything they want to do, more than any other people in the world. They surpass all other nations in cleverness, for good or ill, and they know it themselves. Therefore they say that they see with two eyes and Christian men with one; for after themselves they consider Christian men the most wise and clever. They say that people of other nations are blind, without eyes, as far as knowledge and craft are concerned. I busied myself greatly to know and understand by what means these things I mentioned were done; but the chief craftsman told me that he was so bound by a vow to his god that he could show the method to no man except his eldest son. Above the Emperor's table and round a great part of the hall is a great vine made of fine gold; it is wonderfully delicately wrought, with many branches and grapes like the grapes of a growing vine; some are white, some yellow, some red, some black, some green. All the red ones are made of rubies or garnets or alabandine, the white are made of crystal or beryl; the yellow are made of topazes or chrysolites; the green of emeralds; the black of onyx or garnets. This vine is made of precious stones so exactly and carefully that it looks like a growing vine.

And great lords and barons stand before the Emperor's table to serve the Emperor; and none of them is so bold as to speak a word unless the Emperor speak first to them – except for minstrels who sing him songs, or tell him tales, or crack jokes or jests to please the Emperor. All the vessels which are used for serving in his hall or chamber, especially at his own table or at those where great lords sit, are of jasper or crystal or amethyst or fine gold. And all their cups are of emeralds or sapphires, of topazes or other precious stones. They make no vessels of silver, for they set no store by silver. They will neither eat nor drink of vessels made of it; they use it for steps, pillars, pavements for halls and chambers. In front of the hall door stand certain lords and other knights to ensure that none enters that door except those the Emperor wishes, unless he be of the household or a minstrel; no others dare come near.

You must know that I and my companions were living with the Great Khan for sixteen months as soldiers against the King of Manzi, for they were at war when we were there. The reason for our staying with him was that we greatly desired to see his great nobleness and the state and ceremonial of his court; also we wanted to see the extent of his riches, to know if what we had heard before was true. Truly, we found it more rich and noble than we had heard reported; and we should never have believed it if we had not seen it with our own eyes. There is no such court here in this land. For here kings and lords keep as few men in their courts as they can; but the Great Khan supports at his charge in his court each day folk without number. But you should know that food and drink are more pleasingly dressed in our country than there, and here men sit more decorously at meat than they do there. For all the common people of the court have their meat laid on their knees when they eat, without any cloth or towel, and for the most part they eat flesh, without bread, of all kinds of beasts. When they have finished eating, they wipe their hands on the skirts of their robe. They only eat once a day. This is the way the common folk in the Great Khan's court behave. But the stateliness of the Khan himself and of other lords who sit with him is noble and royal, surpassing that of all earthly men. For truly, under the firmament there is no lord so great nor so rich and powerful as the Great Khan of Tartary. Not even Prester John, Emperor of Greater and Lesser India, nor the Sultan of Babylon, nor the Emperor of Persia, nor anyone else, can be compared to him. Truly, it is a great pity he is not a Christian; nevertheless he will gladly hear men speak of God and allow Christian men to live in his empire. For in his land no man is forbidden to believe in whatever religion it pleases him to believe. And if some men perhaps will not believe me about what I have said, and say it is all a fable, what I say about the nobleness and excellence and riches of the Great Khan and his court, and the multitude of men there that I told of, I do not really care. But let the man who will, believe it; and leave him alone who will not. I shall nevertheless say something of what I saw with my own eyes, of him and his people and the government of his court, whether they will believe it or not. Nevertheless I well know that if anyone had been there (or in the countries that border his land, if he had not been to his court), he would have heard so much of his nobility and excellence that he would easily believe what I myself have said. And so I am not going to stop myself telling you things that I know are true because of those who are ignorant of them or will not believe them. So I shall now tell you more of the Great Khan and of his state and government, how he journeys from one district to another, and how he makes his great feasts.

24

Why men call him the Great Khan;
of the style of his letters; of the inscription
round his seals, the great and the little, etc.

But first I shall tell you why he is called the Great Khan. You know that all the world was lost in Noah's flood, except for a little group, that is Noah and his wife, his sons and their wives. For Noah had three sons, Sem [Shem], Cham [Ham], and Japhet. Ham was the one who saw his father's privy parts naked as he lay asleep, and went to his brothers and showed that sight in scorn; and so afterwards his father, when he knew of it, cursed him. But Japhet went backwards to his father and covered up his private parts. These three sons of Noah divided the earth between them after the Flood. Shem, because he was the eldest, chose the best and largest part, which is towards the East, and it is called Asia. Ham took Africa, and Japhet took Europe. Ham was the richest and mightiest of the brothers; and from him came many more descendants than from his other brothers. From one of his sons called Chus [Cush] came Nimrod the giant, who was the first king there ever was; and he began to build the Tower of Babel. In his time many devils came in the likeness of men and lay with the women of his race and begat on them giants and other monsters of horrible shape – some without heads, some with dog's heads, and many other misshapen and disfigured men. Of the kindred of Ham came the pagans and different kings of men in the isles of India. And because this Ham was so powerful that no one could withstand him, he had himself called God's son and Lord of the World. And therefore some men say that the Emperor of Tartary had himself called Ham [Khan], for he is considered the most excellent lord in the world and occupies the same land that Ham was lord of. And of Shem, so they say, come the Saracens; and of Japhet the people of Israel and we who live in Europe. This is the opinion of the Saracens and the Samaritans; thus they made me believe until I got to India; when I got there, I well knew it was otherwise. Nevertheless it is true that the people of Tartary and all those who live in Greater Asia come from the race of Ham. But the Emperor of Cathay is called Khan and not Ham, and for this reason.

It is not yet eight score years since all the people of Tartary were in subjection and bondage to other nations about them, and were made herdsmen and keepers of animals. But amongst them there were seven principal tribes, the chief and noblest of which was called Tartre [Tartar]. The second was called Tangut, the third Eurac, the fourth Valair, the fifth Semok, the sixth Menchy and the seventh Tobak. It happened that in the first tribe was an old man, who in his time had been strong and bold, but he was not rich; his name was Chaanguys [Genghis]. One night this man was lying in his bed, and in a vision a knight armed all in white and on a white horse came to him and said, 'Khan, are you asleep?' He answered, 'No.' The knight said, 'Almighty God has sent me to show you His will. His will is that you tell the seven tribes that you will be their Emperor. And you will conquer and win all the lands about you, and they shall be subject to you as you have been to them. This is the will of Almighty God.' In the morning he went to the seven tribes and told them of his vision, and they despised him as a fool; he left them in shame and confusion. And the next night the same White Knight appeared to the seven tribes and told them in God's name that they should make Genghis their Emperor, for he would free them from the domination of other nations and conquer and win many realms. And by common consent in the morning they made Genghis their Emperor, setting him on a throne and doing him all the honour and reverence they could, and called him Khan as the White Knight had done. And when he had been chosen Emperor in this way, he thought he would test their trustworthiness and obedience, to see whether he could trust them absolutely or not; and he made many statutes and laws, which they call Ysachan [*yasa khan*, the code of Genghis]. The first law was that they should obey God Almighty and trust that He would deliver them from all bondage, and call on Him in their need. Another law was that all men capable of bearing arms should be equipped and numbered, and that to each group of ten there should be a master, to each twenty a master, to each hundred, thousand, ten thousand, and twenty thousand, there should be a master. After this he commanded all the greatest and richest of the seven tribes to give up everything they held through inheritance of rank, and from thenceforward be pleased with what he himself of his grace gave them. They did so. He commanded too that every one of them should bring his son before him and kill him with his own hands, striking off his head; and they did so, with no delay. And when he saw that they did not hesitate to do what he told them, he told them to follow his banner. And then he conquered all the lands round about and made them subject to him.

One day afterwards it happened that the Khan was riding with a small company to see the lands he had won; and suddenly he met a great multitude of his enemies. Being a good warrior he went boldly in front of all his men against his enemies, to give his followers an example and the will to fight. He was struck from his horse and it was killed. When his men saw him on the ground, they thought he had been killed, and fled, and their enemies followed, not knowing that the King had been struck from his horse. When the Khan saw his enemies had gone, he went to a nearby wood and hid in a thick bush. When the enemy returned from the pursuit, they went to search the wood to see if anyone was hiding there, and they found many and killed them. So it happened that they came near the place where the King was hidden, and saw a bird – an owl – sitting on the tree under which the King lay concealed. When they saw that bird sitting so still, each one said that no man was in that place. So they went away; and so this King was saved from death, and rejoined his men under cover of darkness. When they saw their lord living, they were very glad and thanked Almighty God – and the bird – who had saved their lord from death and delivered him out of the hand of his enemies. Ever since that time men of that land have done great honour to that bird above all others; and they love it so much that when a man can get a feather from it, he looks after it reverently, as if it were a relic, carrying it on his head with great respect, thinking to be blessed thereby and saved from all kinds of dangers. Afterwards the Khan gathered all his men and rode against his enemies, destroying them utterly.

And when he had won all the lands about him as far as Mount Belyan [the Altai?], the White Knight appeared to him again and said, 'Khan, the will of God is that you cross the Altai, and you will conquer that land and make its people subjects of your empire. And because you will find no easy route thither, go to the Altai, which is next to the sea [Lake Balkhash?], and kneel there in worship of God Almighty nine times facing the East, and He shall show you a way to travel by.' And the Khan did as he bade; as soon as he arrived, the sea, which before beat against the mountain, drew back and revealed a good road nine feet broad between the mountain and the sea. And so he passed, with all his men, and conquered the land of Cathay, which is the biggest land in the world. And on account of the nine kneelings and the nine foot breadth of the road the Khan and the men of Tartary honour the number nine.

So when a man makes a gift of horses, or birds, or bows, or arrows, or of anything else they are accustomed to send to the Emperor, they shall be better thanked if they give nine of them; the gift will then be more acceptable to the Emperor than if he gave a hundred times as much in not so fortunate a number. They think the number nine to be the holiest number there is, because God's messenger so carefully stressed that number.

When the Great Khan had conquered the land of Cathay, and had put many other lands under his rule, he fell very ill and was sure he would not recover from that sickness, but die of it. ⟨So he had called before him his twelve sons, and told each to bring one arrow, which they did. He told them to bind them tightly together, with three thongs, and they did as they were told. When they were so tied together, he told his eldest son to break them; he tried and could not. He told another son to break them, and he could not either. He told eleven of his sons to do this, but none of them could break them tied together. At last he said to his youngest son, 'Son, go and untie those arrows from each other, and break each one on its own.' He did as he was told and broke them one after the other. Then the King asked his sons why they could not break them, and they replied that they were so tightly tied together that they could not. The Emperor answered, 'How then could your youngest brother so easily do it?' 'They were untied from each other,' they said. 'Just so,' said their father, 'will it be with you. For as long as you are knit together with the three bonds of love, loyalty and agreement, no man in this world will be able to fight you or annoy you; but as soon as the knot of these bonds is undone, that is, as soon as you are divided and struggle with one another, you will be routed and destroyed. And if you steadfastly love one another, you will be lords of all nations.' And he died soon after he had instructed his sons in this way and made arrangements about his empire on the advice of the great lords of his kingdom.⟩ After him Cichota [Ogotai] his eldest son reigned, and was called Khan as his father was. His brothers went forth and conquered many lands and kingdoms, even as far as Prussia and Russia; each had himself called Khan. But they were all subject to the eldest brother, who was therefore called the Great Khan, like his successors. ⟨After Ogotai reigned his eldest brother Guys Khan [Kuyuk]; after him, Mango [Mangu], who was baptized and became a devout and good Christian. He sent letters of perpetual peace to all Christian men who lived in his realm, and sent his brother Halaon [Hulagu] with a great army to wrest the Holy Land from the Saracens and give it to Christian men, and to destroy the law of Muhammad; and

148

also to capture the Caliph of Baghdad who was Lord and Emperor over the Saracens. Hulagu went and captured the Caliph, and found with him great plenty of treasure, so much that it seemed to him there could not be much more in the world after what was found with him. And then Hulagu said to him, 'Why would you not pay for enough men with your treasure to withstand me and defend your land?' And he said, 'I had enough men of my own.' Then said Hulagu, 'You were the God of the Saracens, and gods don't need food and drink; and so as far as we are concerned you will never have anything to eat or drink; but if you want you can eat your treasure and precious stones, which you have so eagerly gathered up and loved so much.' And he locked him up without food or drink with his treasure; he died from hunger and thirst. This Hulagu conquered all the Holy Land, and won it for Christian men. Meanwhile the Great Khan died; [and so the project was dropped]. After Mangu the Good another reigned as Khan, called Chebisa [Kubilai]; he was a good Christian too, and reigned forty-two years. He founded a great city in the kingdom of Cathay, which is called Jong [Peking]; it is bigger than Rome. Another Khan reigned after him, and he denied the Christian creed and became a Saracen. So have been all the Khans after his time.)

Realize that the realm of Cathay is bigger than any kingdom in the world; and so the man who is Great Khan is the greatest King, passing all other Kings, and the richest in gold, all kinds of treasure, and of greatest royalty. The style of his letters is this: *Caan, filius dei excelsi, omnium uniuersam terram colencium summus imperator et dominus dominancium*, that is, 'Khan, son of God Almighty, and the sovereign Emperor of all those who till the earth and lord of all lords.' And the inscription round his privy seal is this, *Dei fortitudo. Omnium hominum imperatoris sigillum*, that is, 'The strength of God. The seal of the Emperor of all men.' This Emperor and the people of that land, though they are not Christians, nevertheless believe in the Mighty God who made the heavens and the earth; and when they went to threaten anyone, they say, 'God knows I shall do you an evil turn.'

25

Of the organization of the court of the Great Khan
when he holds solemn festival; of his philosophers;
and of his arrangements when he progresses through the country

I have now told you why he is called the Great Khan. Now I shall tell you of the organization and government of his court, when he holds great festivals – that is principally four times a year. The first occasion is his birthday; the second is the date when he was presented in their temple, which is called Moseak [mosque], where he was circumcised; the other two are festivals of their idol. The first is the anniversary of the first enthronement of the idol in their temple, and the second is held at the season when the idol first began to speak, give answers, and do miracles. The Emperor does not arrange other feasts with such solemnity, except for the weddings of his sons. A marvellous multitude of people gather at each of their feasts; they are all well dressed, and organized in thousands, hundreds, and twenties, and every man knows what he must do and busily attends to his duty, so that no fault is found. First four thousand barons, rich and mighty, are commissioned to oversee the running of the feast and serve the Emperor. All these barons have golden crowns on their heads studded with precious stones and pearls; they are dressed in cloth of gold and silken camlet, and other such things, and they are as gorgeous as they can be. They may well have such clothes, for they are of less value than woollen clothes are here. Their feasts are held in tents made of cloth of gold or of camlet or of silk; they are so intricately made that no one could imagine anything more delicate. These four thousand barons are divided into four companies; each company is dressed in a uniform of their own, of a different colour to that of the other companies. The first company is of dukes, earls, marquises and emirs; they are dressed in cloth of gold and green silk; the second in red, the third in blue, and fourth in yellow. Their robes are so cleverly and delicately embroidered with gold and precious stones and pearls that if a man from our country had a comparable dress, one could safely say he was not a poor man – for gold and precious stones are of much greater value here than they are there. And each of the nobles carries before him a table of jasper, or ivory, or crystal; in front of them walk minstrels playing on different instruments. When the first thousand has passed and done their duties, they draw to one side; then comes the second thousand, then the third, and so on, and do their jobs as did the first. And none of them speaks a word; thus they go round the hall.

Beside the Emperor's table sit many philosophers and men learned in different branches of knowledge – some in astronomy, some in necromancy, some in geomancy, some in pyromancy, some in hydromancy and many other similar sciences. Some have before them astrolabes of gold, some spheres of precious stones, some the scalp of a dead man, some a vessel of gold full of hot coals, some a vessel of gold with water and wine and oil in it. Some also have clocks, wonderfully made, some golden vessels full of sand, and others different instruments appropriate to their science. At certain moments, when they see the right time, they say to men who stand near them, 'Let everyone be silent!'; and one of those men says to all the hall, with a loud voice, 'Be silent!' Then says another of the philosophers, 'Let every man do obeisance and bow to the Emperor, who is God's son and Lord of the world, for this is the right moment.' Then every man bows his head to the earth, and then says the philosopher to them, 'Lift up your heads again.' And at another instant another philosopher says, 'Every man put his little finger in his ear!'; and they do so. Again, another philosopher says, 'Every man put his hand before his mouth!'; and they do so. And so all the time these philosophers are telling them to do different things, which they say have great meaning. I asked quietly what these things did mean; and one of the philosophers said that the inclining of the head meant that all those who bowed to him would be obedient and faithful to the Emperor, so that they would be false or traitorous to him for no gifts or promises. The putting of the finger in the ear meant that none of them would hear ill spoken of the Emperor, neither by father or brother, relation or stranger, which he will not reveal to the Emperor or his council. Putting the hand before the mouth means that none of them will speak evil of the Emperor. And in the same way, all the other things they order the people to do they say have great meaning. And you must know that nothing is made or got ready for the Emperor – clothes, meat, drink or anything – except at times indicated by the philosophers, who through their science and their calculations work out and predict hours suitable for doing such things. And if a man begins war against the Emperor in any country, immediately the philosophers know it and tell the Emperor and his council, and he sends his army thither to check the malice of his enemies.

When the philosophers have given all the orders it is their job to give, the minstrels begin their playing again, one after the other. When they have made music for a long while, one of the Emperor's officers goes up on a richly and carefully made stage and shouts with a loud voice, 'Silence!', and all are quiet. Then all those who are of the Emperor's kin go and dress themselves richly in cloth of gold, and each of them comes with many white horses caparisoned as well and richly as they can be. The steward of the court then says to this lord and that, calling them by name, 'Come and honour the Emperor of the world.' So he names them all in turn, each in his rank, and each then comes one after the other before the Emperor and presents him with nine white horses. After them come the great barons and present him with a jewel or some other rich gift, each giving one appropriate to his degree. And when they have all in this way given presents to the Emperor, the prelates of their religion make theirs. Afterwards the chief prelate gives a blessing, saying one of the prayers of their cult. Then the minstrels begin their music again. And when they have made music for a while, they are told to be quiet, and then there are brought before the Emperor lions, leopards, and other kinds of beasts and birds and fishes and reptiles, to honour the Emperor, for they say that everything that has life ought to honour the Emperor and obey him. Then in come jugglers and enchanters and do many marvels; for they make it appear that the sun and moon are coming to do reverence, and these shine so brightly that they cannot be looked at. And they make such darkness that it seems night; afterwards they make it light again. Then they make it seem that damsels come in, singing and dancing. Then they make other damsels come in, bringing cups of gold full of mares' milk, offering it to lords and ladies to drink. After this they will make an appearance of knights jousting in the air, fully armed; and they strike so with their spears that the pieces from them fly about the tables in the hall. And when this is done, they make harts and wild boars come in with hounds hunting them. These and many other marvels they do, until the Emperor has finished eating.

This Emperor, the Great Khan, has many men living in his court, as I said, and minstrels to the number of thirteen *cumans* – I told you before how many made a *cuman*. But you must know that all these minstrels do not live continuously at the Emperor's court; when a minstrel comes before him, of whatever nation he be, he is received into the court and his name noted down. So wherever he goes after that time, he calls himself one of the Emperor's minstrels, and this is how there is so great a number of them. He also has fifteen *cumans* of men detailed to do nothing else but look after birds of different kinds, like gerfalcons,

falcons noble,* lanner hawks, sakers, sparrowhawks, singing night-ingales, and talking parrots. He also has a thousand elephants. He has many physicians, of whom two hundred are Christian men, and twenty Saracens; but he trusts most to the Christians. There are also in his court many barons and other officers who are christened and converts to the Christian faith through the preaching of good Christian men who live there; and there are many who will not reveal themselves openly, or let it be known that they are Christians.

This Emperor can spend as much as he wishes to, for he coins no money except from leather, or paper, or the bark of trees. When this money gets old, and the printing on it is defaced by heavy use, it is brought to the King's treasury and his treasurer gives new for old. This money is printed on both sides, like money is in other countries, and it is current throughout the Great Khan's lands. They make no money there of gold and silver, when it is brought thither by different nationalities from other lands, but the Emperor has his palace adorned with it and makes useful things of it as he pleases. In his chamber on a pillar of gold is a ruby and a carbuncle, each a foot long; and this carbuncle lights all the chamber at night. He has also many precious stones and rubies in his chamber; but those two are the greatest and most precious of all.

The Great Khan lives in summer in a city in the north called Saduz [Shangtu, Coleridge's Xanadu], where the air is very cool; and in winter he lives in the city of Camalach [Khan-balik, near Peking], where the air is very hot. But the place where he usually lives is Gaydon [Tatu, near Peking], where the air is temperate according to the climate of the country. Nevertheless men of this country would find it very hot. And when this Great Khan is to ride from one country to another, four hosts are organized for him, each of many people, of which one host goes a day's journey before him. And this host lodges one night where the Emperor will lodge the following night; and everything they need is marshalled and got ready. In that host are fifty *cumans* of men – horsemen and foot; and each *cuman* contains ten thousand as I told you before. Another host travels to his right, half a day's journey distant, and the third on his left at a similar distance. The fourth follows him about a bowshot behind; in that host there are more men than in the other three. Each of those hosts has its line of march carefully planned; and where they are to lodge at night they find everything necessary ready supplied. And if it happens that any man in

* Probably peregrines and merlins, these being the birds appropriate in hawking to those of gentle but not royal birth.

those hosts die on the march, they immediately put another in his place, so that the full number may be maintained.

You must understand that the Great Khan never rides a horse unless he is going somewhere with a private company. He rides in a chariot with four wheels, and on it is a room made of a wood called *lignum aloes*, which at certain times comes from Paradise in the rivers that flow thence. And because of the kind of wood it is made of, that room has a noble smell; it is covered all over inside with plates of gold set with jewels. Four elephants and four white warhorses caparisoned in rich clothes draw this vehicle. Five or six lords in rich apparel ride around it, so that no one except lords can come to him unless he should call any man to him. And on top of that room in a little cabin sit men with four or five gerfalcons, so that if they find any wild bird on the route as they travel, they can let them fly to make sport for the Emperor. In front of this chariot no man rides nearer than a bowshot except for the lords already mentioned. And with the same arrangement of chariots and men are the Empresses led through the country, each on her own; but they do not have anywhere near so many men in their hosts as the Emperor does. The eldest son of the Emperor travels by another route in his chariot in the same sort of arrangement, with a great multitude of folk. For there are so many people in that land it is a marvel to see. Sometimes it happens, when they are not going far, that the Empresses and the Emperor's children go together and their men are [mingled together]; yet they are even so split into four hosts, as I said.

Know that the land of the Great Khan is divided into twelve provinces, and in each province is a royal king. ⟨These kings have other lesser kings beneath them, and they are all subject to the Great Khan, whose empire is so large that a man takes seven years to make the circuit of it by land and water. For there are many great deserts through which men must pass, in which neither city nor town is found. But in certain places common hostelries are maintained, where travellers can get everything that is needful to them in their journey. And there is a very useful and marvellous system in that land, by which, when any news is heard – especially anything harmful or against the Emperor – he has word of it within a day and a night, even if it is far off, even three or four days' journey. For always there are messengers and ambassadors kept in every province, and they, as soon as any rumour that concerns the Emperor begins, take any dromedaries or horses that they can get and with all the haste they can they ride to the nearest hostelry. When they get near it, they blow a horn, and the messengers who are in the hostelry know well when they hear the horn that there is news to take to the Emperor, and make their dromedaries or horses ready to carry letters with the news on to the next hostelry. There they do the same, and so on from hostelry to hostelry until they get to the Emperor; and in this way in a very short time the Emperor has the news of all the country. Similarly with the Emperor's couriers, when there is urgent news to deliver. Every courier has a long cord with lots of bells on it, and when he comes with letters near one of these hostelries, the courier stationed there knows by the ringing of the bells that letters are coming to be taken speedily to the Emperor, and gets ready to set out. And when the other arrives, he hands over his letters to this fresh man and rests there; the fresh man runs with all haste to the third hostelry and rests there, as the first man did; and so they do from hostelry to hostelry until they reach the Emperor. These couriers are called in their language *chidibo*, which means 'messenger'.⟩

Each of the twelve provinces mentioned above has two thousand cities and more, and towns without number. And when the Emperor rides through any city or town, each man makes a fire in front of his door on the road the Emperor will come by, and throws on it incense and other things to give a good smell to the Emperor. And if men of the Christian religion live near where he will pass, as they do in many cities in that land, they go to meet him in procession with the Cross and holy water, singing in a loud voice, *Veni Creator Spiritus*. And when he sees them coming he commands the lords that ride near him to stand aside for the men of religion to come to him. As soon as he sees the Cross he doffs his hat – which is very richly made with pearls and precious stones, and they say there that this hat is worth a kingdom. Then he bows devoutly to the Cross, and the prelate of those religious men says two prayers before him and blesses him with the sign of the Cross; the Emperor bows very devoutly for the blessing. Then that same prelate gives him some kind of fruit, like apples or pears or something, nine in number on a plate of gold. For the custom there is that no man can come before the Emperor unless he give him something, after the old law that says, *Nemo apparebit in conspectu meo uacuus*, that is, 'No man come into my sight empty-handed.'* And then they go home again to their place. And men of religion living where the Empress and the Emperor's eldest son come do the same.

Do ⟨understand that all those men who are in the hosts of the Great Khan I just mentioned, and those of his wives and eldest son, do not live all the time in his court. But whenever they are told to go with him, they are ready to his command, and when the journey is done, they go

* Exodus xxiii, 15.

home again to their own houses, all except those who are of the Emperor's court. Those indeed are a great number, who are employed to serve the Emperor and his wives and children and run the court. For there are with him continually in his court fifty thousand horsemen and two hundred thousand foot, not counting different officials of the palace, and those I spoke of before who are in charge of the wild beasts and birds.) [There is beneath the heavens no lord so rich, so mighty nor so great as the Great Khan, nor above or below the earth; for Prester John who is Emperor of Upper India, the Sultan of Babylon, and the Emperor of Persia cannot be compared to him in power or nobleness of wealth, for in all these things he surpasses all earthly princes. So it is a great pity that he does not believe properly in God. Nevertheless, he very willingly hears men speak of God, and allows Christians to live in all parts of his land; for he forbids no man to believe whatever faith he wants.]*

In the land of the Great Khan every man has as many wives as he wants, for some have a hundred, some forty, some more, some less. And they marry their relatives there, all except mothers and daughters and sisters; they will wed half-sisters on their father's side but not their mother's. Also they marry the wives of their brothers, when the brothers are dead, and their stepmothers after the death of their fathers.

26

Of the faith and customs of the Tartars living in Cathay;
and what is done when the Great Khan dies;
and how he is chosen, etc.

They wear wide-fitting clothes, without fur, in those parts. They are made of purple or silk or camlet. Their clothes are slit at the side, and lace up with silken cords. Some do wear fur, with the hair turned outwards, but they wear no hoods. Women of that country are clad in the same way, so that the two sexes can hardly be told apart, except for the married women who wear those tokens on their heads I told you about before. Their wives do not live together, but each by herself; their husbands go now to this one, now to that, as it pleases him. Their houses are made of sticks, are round, and have but one window, where

* This passage, missing in Egerton and partly in Defective, is here translated from MS Royal 20B.X. It occurs in Cotton.

the light comes in and the smoke goes out. The roof-covering and the doors are of felt. And when they go to war they carry their houses with them upon carts, as men in other countries carry tents and pavilions. They make the fire in the middle of their houses. They have great plenty of all kinds of animals except pigs; and that is because they breed none. They all believe in one God who made all things; but nevertheless they have idols of gold and silver, of felt and cloth, to which they offer the first milk of their animals and the first morsels of their meat and drink before they themselves eat or drink any of it. Sometimes they offer horses and other beasts to them. The god of nature they call Yroga, and whatever name the Emperor has, they add to it Khan. When I was there the Emperor's name was Thyak [Kuyuk], and they called him Kuyuk Khan. His eldest son was called Theophue [Jochi] and when he becomes Emperor he will be called Jochi Khan. At that time the Emperor had twelve other sons besides Jochi, of which one was called Cunnyt, another Ordu [Ogodai], the third Chahadoy [Chaghatai], the fourth Burgu [Guyuk], the fifth Vengu [Qadam?], the sixth Nachaly [Kuchu?], the seventh Cadu [Batu], the eighth Syban, the ninth Creten [Orda?], the tenth Balac [Berke], the eleventh Babilan [Boal?] and the twelfth Carygan [Tuku-Timur?]. And he had three wives, of which the first and principal was the daughter of Prester John, and she was called Serioth Khan [Sorghaqtani]; the second was called Borach Khan [Ibaka Bek], and the third Charauk Khan.

The men of that country begin everything they have to do in the new moon, and reverence it much; they also worship the sun, and kneel often to it. They usually ride without spurs, but they have in their hand a whip or crop or some other thing to goad their horses with. They hold it a great sin to put a knife in the fire, to take meat out of a cauldron or pot with a knife, to hit a horse with a bridle, to break one bone with another bone, or to throw milk or any other liquid that is drunk on the earth. The greatest sin a man can do, they say, is to piss in their houses where they live; if anyone pisses there and they know about it, they kill him. The place where a man has pissed must be purified or no man is so bold as to enter it. They must confess their sins to the priests of their religion, and when they are shriven they give a great sum of money to buy off their penance. When they have bought it off in this way, they pass through a fire to cleanse them of their sins. And in the same way a messenger who brings a present to the Emperor shall pass through a fire with the present to purify it, to ensure that he brings no poison or anything else to harm the Emperor. Whatever man – or woman – is taken in adultery, they kill, and also all thieves and robbers. All the men and women of that land are good archers, and the women are as good warriors as the men and will run as fast. And the [women] do all kinds of crafts, for example tailoring and cobbling and other such trades. They commonly drive the plough, the cart and the wagon; and they are carpenters as well as men, and make houses and all other necessaries – bows and arrows and other weapons excepted, which the men alone make. Women wear breeches there as well as men. All the people of that land are marvellously obedient to their rulers, and they never fight among themselves; nor are they thieves and robbers, but each one of them loves and respects the others. They do not usually do much honour to foreigners even if they are important people. They eat dogs and lions, mares and foals, mice and rats, and other beasts both great and small, excepting pigs and other animals forbidden in the Old Law. And they eat every bit of the animals except the dung. They eat very little bread except in the courts of lords. And in many places they have neither peas nor cabbages, nor other things for pottages; they use boiled meat and broth for their pottages. For they hardly eat anything else but meat and the broth from it. And when they have eaten, they wipe their hands disgustingly on their clothes; for they use neither table-cloths nor napkins except in lords' houses. And when they have eaten they put their dishes and bowls unwashed in the pots and cauldrons with the meat that they leave, until they eat later. And rich men drink mares' milk, and that of camels and asses and other beasts; and they easily get very drunk on that milk. They also have another kind of drink made of water and honey, for there is no wine in that country, least of all among the commons, who lead a wretched life. They eat only once a day, and then very little. A man of this country eats more in one day than two of them do in three. And if a messenger comes from a foreign land to the Emperor, he will have food only once a day, and then very little.

When they go to war, they behave in a very warlike and wise manner, and do all they can to win, and conquer their enemies. Each one carries two or three bows, many arrows and a great battleaxe. The nobles carry short sharp swords at their sides; they have breastplates and helmets made of cuir-bouilli, and armour for their horses of the same material. They slay anyone who flees in battle. When they besiege a castle or walled town, they promise the besieged such fair terms that it is a wonder to hear them; for they will grant whatever conditions they ask. But as soon as the besieged have capitulated, they slay them and cut off their ears, and souse them in vinegar to make a dainty dish for their great lords. It is their intention to bring all lands under their rule.

They say that their prophecies tell them that they will be defeated by a people using arrows, and that those people will convert them to their religion. But they do not know which people that will be, ⟨and so they allow all nationalities and men of all kinds of religions and faiths to live among them without hindrance. When these people make their idols, or statues of their friends to act as a perpetual memorial of them, they make them naked; for they say that true love has no covering, and that no one should love anything merely for its outward beauty; one should love the disposition of the person and the good virtues nature has adorned him with.⟩ It is very dangerous to pursue the Tartars when they flee in battle; for they will shoot to their rear and kill men as well as if they were in front of them. When they are to fight, they keep so closely and tightly together that where there are in fact twenty thousand men, one would suppose there to be not over ten thousand. They conquer other lands easily and bravely, but when they have won them they do not hold on to them well. They prefer camping in tents in the plains to living in towns or castles. They have a low opinion of any people's intelligence except their own. Among them olive oil is of great value, for they say it is a sovereign medicine. All the Tartars have small eyes and small, thin beards. They are usually treacherous, for they keep no promises they make. They can endure better than any other people suffering and discomfort and difficulty in travel; for they learned how to in their own country, where they live with great wretchedness and scarcity.

When any of them is dying they stick a spear in the earth by him; and when he draws near to death, everyone leaves the house until he is dead; and when he is, they carry him into the open plains and bury him in the earth. And when the Emperor is dead, they set him in a chair in the middle of his tent; they set before him a table covered with a cloth, and on it bread and meat and other dishes, and a cup full of mares' milk. They put by him a mare and her foal, and a horse saddled and bridled, and they put on the horse as much gold and silver as he can carry. Beside this tent they dig a huge grave, and put in it the tent with the Emperor and all the other things, and bury them together. And they say that when he arrives in the next world, he shall not be without a horse, a house, gold or silver; the mare, they say, shall give him milk to drink and bring forth many horses for him, so that he will be well provided in the next world with everything he needs. For they believe that when they are dead they shall in the next world eat and drink and have dalliance with women as they have here. And from the time that the Emperor is laid in the earth no man must be so bold as to mention him in the presence of his friends. [And frequently they have them put in the earth secretly, by night, in wild places, and replace the grass to grow over the pit; or they cover the pit with sand and gravel, to the end that it should not be known where the grave is and that his friends should never be reminded of him. Then they say he has been caught away into another world, where he is a greater lord than he was in this.]*

And when this Emperor is dead and buried in the way I told you of, the seven tribes gather together and elect his son or the nearest man of his blood to be Emperor. And they say, 'We desire and pray and choose that you be our Emperor and sovereign lord.' And he answers and says, 'Will you be obedient to my commandments in all things that I tell you to do, without argument?' And with one voice they reply, 'We shall.' And he says to them, 'Know then that from henceforward my voice will be of as great strength, as sharp and cutting, as my sword.' And then he is set on a black felt cloth, with which they lift him up and put him on his throne and crown him. And then the cities and towns of that land send him presents, and at that time he can reckon to get three score cartloads and more of gold and silver, not counting jewels and gold and precious stones that great lords give him, which pass man's estimation. This is not counting, too, horses and cloths of gold and camaka [goat or camel-hair] and silk without number.

27

Of the kingdom of Tarshish and of the lands and kingdoms towards the northern parts, coming down from the land of Cathay

This land of Cathay is in deepest Asia, and in the west it borders the kingdom of Tarse [Tarshish], of which one of the Three Kings who visited Our Lord in Bethlehem was King. All who come of his lineage are Christian. In the land of Tarshish they never eat flesh nor drink wine. On this, the western, side of that kingdom, is the land of Turquesten [Turkestan], which reaches as far west as the kingdom of Persia and north as far as the kingdom of Khorasan. In the country of Turkestan are only a few cities, the best of them being Eccozar [Farab]. There are great broad pastures, but little corn; and so the common folk

* Omitted in Egerton, present in Cotton, here supplied from MS Royal 20 B.X.

of that land are all herdsmen and live in the open in tents, and drink a kind of beverage made of water and honey.

On this side of that land is the kingdom of Khorasan, which is fertile and good, but there is no wine. On the east of it is a great desert, stretching for more than ten days' journey. The best city of that land is called Khorasan, and the land is called after it. The people of that country are good warriors and very bold. On this side is the land of Cumania, from which a people in Greece called Cumanians were driven. It is one of the great kingdoms of the world, but it is not all inhabited, for in one part of that land it is so cold and in another so hot that no one can live there. And there are so many flies in that land that a man does not know where to put himself. In that land there are few trees that bear fruit. The people live in tents and dry the dung of their animals and burn it because fuel is scarce.

This land extends towards Prussia and Russia. Through it runs the river of Ethill [Volga], which is one of the great rivers of the world. At certain times of the year it is frozen so hard that men fight great battles on it, on horseback and on foot, often 100,000 men at once. A little way from that river is the Great Sea Ocean, which they call Maure [the Black Sea]. Between the two lies the greater part of the land of Khorasan. Towards the upper part of that land is the Mount Caspye [Caucasus]. And between that mountain and the great Black Sea is a narrow pass, on the route to India. And so King Alexander had a city built, called Alexandria, to guard the country, so that no one should pass without permission; that city is now called Porte de Fer [the pass of Derbend, Alexander's Iron Gate]. The principal city of Cumania is called Sarak or Sarachy [Serai]. This is one of the routes to India. But except in winter not many men go this way; this pass is called Berbent [Derbend]. Another way is to go through Turkestan from Persia; but that entails many days' journey through wildernesses. The third way is to go from Cumania via the Great Sea Ocean [the Black Sea, then thought to be an arm of the Great Sea Ocean] and through the kingdom of Abcaz [Abkhasia]. Know that all these kingdoms and lands as far as Prussia and Russia, and many others bordering them, are held by the Great Khan. He is indeed a lord great in power and territory.

28

*Of the empire of Persia; of the land of darkness;
and of the other realms from Cathay to the Greek Sea*

I have told you now of the lands and kingdoms in the north reaching
from the land of Cathay to Prussia and Russia, where Christian men
dwell; now I shall tell you of other lands and kingdoms between Cathay
and the Sea of Greece, reaching to Christian lands in that direction.
And since, after the Great Khan of Cathay and Prester John, the
Emperor of India, the Emperor of Persia is the greatest potentate, I shall
speak of him and his kingdom first. Know that he has two kingdoms, of
which one starts in the east at the kingdom of Turkestan and stretches
west as far as the River Phison [Oxus, not Ganges here], one of the four
rivers coming from Paradise. To the north it reaches to the Caspian, and
south to the deserts of India. This land is good, fertile, with many
people and cities in it. The two principal cities are called Bactria
[Bokhara] and Seormegraunt [Samarkand]. The other kingdom
reaches from the River Oxus to the west as far as the lands of Media and
Greater Armenia, to the north to the Caspian, and southward to India.
It too is a plenteous and kindly land. There are three principal cities
in it – Nessabon [Nishapur], Saphaon [Ispahan] and Sarmassane
[Samarkand?].

And then there is the land of Armenia, which once was split into four
kingdoms. This is a great, fertile and good land. It begins at Persia and
stretches west to the land of Turkey; in breadth it reaches from the city
of Alexandria now called Porte de Fer to the land of Media. In this land
of Armenia are many fair cities, but the most well-known is Tabriz.

Then there is the land of Media, which is very long, but not very
wide. It begins at Persia and India the Lesser, stretches west to the
kingdom of Chaldea, and north to Lesser Armenia. This land of Media
is very mountainous, with little flat land. Saracens and other kinds of
people called Cordynes [Kurds] live there. The principal cities are Seras
[Shiraz] and Kermen [Kermanshah].

Next is the kingdom of Georgia, which starts in the east at a mountain called Abior [Elbruz]. Many different nations live there, and the
land is called Halamo [Alania]. It reaches to Turkey and the Great Sea
[Black Sea]; to the south it borders Greater Armenia. There are two
countries in this land; one is called Georgia and the other Abkhasia.
Each has a king, and both are Christian; but the King of Georgia is

subject to the Great Khan. The King of Abkhasia is subject to no man, for his land is naturally strong and he defends himself well against all men.

In this land of Abkhasia there is a great marvel. There is a country there nearly three days' march in circumference, called Hamson [Hamschen]. That country is quite covered by darkness, so that people outside it cannot see anything in it; and no one dares go in for fear of the darkness. Nevertheless men who live in the country round about say that they can sometimes hear the voices of men, and horses neighing, and cocks crowing, and know thereby that some kind of folk live there, but they do not know what kind of folk they are. They say too that that darkness is there by a miracle of God which He showed there on behalf of Christian men; they find it written down among other wonders and marvels in old histories. Once there was a wicked tyrant who was Emperor of Persia, and he was called Taures [Shapur II]. This Emperor persecuted all the Christians in his empire; he travelled far and wide with a great army – to destroy them or force them to sacrifice to his idols. And many Christians were living in that country, who because of the persecution of that tyrant forsook all their goods and riches and fled, and would have made their way to Greece. When they had all gathered together in a fair plain which is called Megon [Moghan], the Emperor, who had been told of their flight, was lying before them with his army to fall upon them and kill them. When the Christians saw them coming towards them, they were much afraid, and kneeled down and beseeched God to help them and save them from their enemies. Immediately there fell a thick darkness which surrounded the Emperor and his army, so that they could not go away anywhere; and they still live in that darkness and always will. The Christian men went where they wanted; and so they could say thus, with the prophet David, *A Domino factus est istud et est mirabile in oculis nostris*, that is, 'By Our Lord is this done, and it is wonderful in our sight.'* ⟨It strikes me that this miracle and others like it should move Christian folk to have more devotion towards God than they do nowadays; for without doubt, if there were not so much wickedness and sin amongst Christian men they would be sovereign lords of the world. For God is always ready to help and succour his loyal servants, who serve him properly with a pure heart, so that he will give them the upper hand over their enemies, as the prophet says, *Quomodo persequebatur unus mille, et duo fugarent decem milia*, that is, 'One of thy true servants pursued a thousand unbelievers, and two chased ten thousand.'† And David said, 'A

* Psalm cxviii, 23.   † Deuteronomy xxxii, 30.

thousand shall fall at thy side, and ten thousand at thy right hand.'*
And how this shall be he says later in Holy Writ, *Quia manus Domini fecit
hoc*, that is, 'For the might of the Lord does all this'.† Thus it may be
openly demonstrated that if we would be good men, our enemies
might not stand against us.) Out of this land comes a river that by
sure signs shows that men live there but nevertheless no man dare
enter.

And you must know that in these kingdoms of Georgia and Abkhasia
and Lesser Armenia good devout Christian men live. They confess and
receive absolution once a week; some confess and are given absolution
each day. In this they show more devotion than we do, who are hardly
confessed and absolved once in a year.

Next to this land is the realm of Turkey, which borders on Greater
Armenia. Therein are many countries, for example Lycony [Lycaonia],
Saure [Isauria], Cappadocia, Bryke [Phrygia], Quificion [Lydia], Pytan
[Bithynia] and Geneth [Paphlagonia]. In each one of these countries are
many fine cities. This land of Turkey reaches to the city of Sakara
[Adalia], which stands on the Greek Sea; it is a large and good country,
as I said before. Also, among these lands is the country of Chaldea,
which stretches from the hills of Chaldea in the east to the city of
Nineveh on the Tigris; in the north it begins at the city of Maraga
[Maragah] and reaches the Great Sea Ocean in the south. The land of
Chaldea is mostly plain, and there are few rivers.

Next to the land of Chaldea is Mesopotamia, which starts in the east
at the Tigris at a city called Mosell [Mosul], and reaches in the west to a
city called Rochays [Roha, Edessa] on the Euphrates; in breadth it
stretches from the mountains of Armenia to the deserts of Lesser India.
It too is a flat country, good and fertile, with few rivers. There are two
high mountains in it, of which one is called Symar [Sindjar] and the
other Lyson. It borders the land of Chaldea.

Know that Ethiopia on the east borders the great desert, on the west
the land of Nubia, on the south Mauretania, and on the north the Red
Sea. Mauretania reaches from the mountains of Ethiopia to Upper
Libya; on the south it lies along the Great Sea Ocean, and to the north it
borders Nubia and Upper Libya. In Nubia Christian men live, and it
borders the lands and deserts of Egypt that I spoke of before. Then
there is Libya, Upper and Lower, which reaches to the Spanish Sea. In
that country there are many different peoples and nations. Now I have
told you of the many countries on this side of the great kingdom of
Cathay, of which many are subject to the Great Khan.

* Psalm xci, 7.   † Job xii, 9.

29

Of the countries and isles which are beyond the land of Cathay;
and of different fruits there;
of the twenty-two kings shut in within the mountains

And now I shall tell you of the lands and countries that are beyond
Cathay. A man who goes from Cathay towards India the Greater and
the Lesser will go through a kingdom called Cadhilhe [Kao-li, possibly
Korea], which is a great land. There there grows a kind of fruit as big as
gourds, and when it is ripe men open it and find inside an animal of
flesh and blood and bone, like a little lamb without wool. And the
people of that land eat the animal, and the fruit too. It is a great marvel.
Nevertheless I said to them that it did not seem a very great marvel to
me, for in my country, I said, there were trees which bore a fruit that
became birds that could fly; men call them bernakes [barnacle geese],
and there is good meat on them.* Those that fall in the water live and fly
away, and those that fall on dry land die. And when I told them this,
they marvelled greatly at it. In this land too there are great apples of
noble smell and taste; and a hundred or more of them are found in a
bunch; the leaves of the tree are two feet long, and some longer. And in
that country are trees bearing cloves and nutmegs and great nuts of
India [coconuts] and other different spices. There are vines that bear
such large bunches of grapes that a man can hardly carry one of them.

In this same land are the hills of Caspian which are called Uber [*ubera
aquilonis*, 'breasts of the north wind', the Caspian mountains]. The
Jews of the Ten Lost Tribes are shut up in these hills; they are called
Gog and Magog, and they can get out on no side. King Alexander drove
them here, for he intended to shut them up with the work of his men.
When he saw he could not, he prayed to God that He would finish what
he himself had begun. And although he was a heathen, God of His
special grace heard his prayer and closed the hills together, and they
are so big and high that they cannot be passed. And on the other side is
the Caspian Sea; but no one can escape on that side because the sea
comes up out of the earth under these hills, and runs on one side of the

* The old legend, recounted by Giraldus Cambrensis and Vincent of Beauvais
among others, had it that the geese, whose breeding habits were not well
known, grew from the stalked barnacle *lepas anatifera*, which has some slight
resemblance in shape and markings to a (minuscule) barnacle goose.

country through a great desert, reaching as far as the land of Persia. Even if it is called a sea, it is not one in fact, but a lake, the biggest in the world. So if the folk that are enclosed there desired and attempted to cross that sea by ship, they would not know where they would arrive and would not understand [any language except their own. And so they cannot get out]. And know that now the Jews have no land of their own to live in in all the world except among those hills. Even so they pay tribute to the Queen of the Amazons, and she has those hills guarded very well so that they do not cross them into [her] country, which borders those hills. Nevertheless it sometimes happens that one of them climbs over those hills and gets out, but no great number of them could climb out together because of the great height and the difficulty of the climb. And there is no other way out except by a little [path] made by men's diligence. That track is about four miles long, and then there is a great desert where no water or shelter is to be found for men because there are dragons and snakes and other poisonous animals; so except in winter no man can travel that way. This narrow path they call Clyrem; and as I said the Queen of the Amazons has it guarded very carefully. If it should happen that any of them get out, they can speak no language except Hebrew and so cannot speak with other men when they come among them. Folk in the country nearby say that in the time of Antichrist those Jews will sally out and do much harm to Christian men. And so all the Jews in the different parts of the world learn to speak Hebrew, for they believe that the Jews who are enclosed among those hills will know that they are Jews (as they are) by their speech when they arrive. And then they will lead them into Christendom to destroy Christian men. For those Jews say they know by their prophecies that the Jews enclosed among the hills will issue out and the Christians will be under their sway, just as they have been under Christian domination. And if you would know how they will find a place to get out, I shall tell you what I once heard said. In the time of Antichrist a fox will make his earth in the very place where King Alexander had the gates of the hills shut up, when he enclosed this people. And this fox will dig for so long in the ground that at last he will emerge among those people. When they see him, they will marvel at him greatly, for they never before have seen an animal like that. (Nevertheless they have all kinds of animals except the fox among them.) They will be so intrigued by this fox that they will chase him hither and thither; and they will pursue him until they come to the hole whence he came out. Then they will dig after him for so long that they will come to the gates that Alexander had stopped up with great stones and cement, and then they will break down these gates and find the way out.

From this land men go to the land of Bactria, where there are many wicked and cruel men. In this land there are trees that bear wool, like that of sheep, from which they make cloth. In this land too there are many hippopotami, which live sometimes on dry land and sometimes in the water; they are half man and half horse. And they eat men, whenever they can get them, no meat more readily. And in that land are many griffons, more than in any other country. Some men say they have the foreparts of an eagle and the hindparts of a lion; that is indeed true. Nevertheless the griffon is bigger and stronger than eight lions of these countries, and bigger and stronger than a hundred eagles. For certainly he will carry to his nest in flight a great horse with a man on his back, or two oxen yoked together, as they work together at the plough. He has talons on his feet as great and as long as the horns of oxen, and they are very sharp. Of these talons men make cups to drink out of, as we do with the horns of bulls; and the ribs of his feathers they make into strong bows to shoot with.

From the land of Bactria men go many days' journey to the land of Prester John, who is Emperor of India; and his land is called the isle of Pentoxere.

30

Of the royal estate of Prester John; and of a rich man who built a wonderful castle and called it Paradise

This Emperor, Prester John, has many different countries under his rule, in which are many noble cities and fair towns, and many isles great and broad. For this land of India is divided into isles on account of the great rivers which flow out of Paradise and run through and divide up his land. He also has many great isles in the sea. The principal city of the isle of Pentoxere is called Nise; the Emperor's seat is there, and so it is a noble and rich city. Prester John has under him many kings and many different peoples; and his land is good and wealthy, but not so rich as the land of the Great Khan of Cathay. For merchants do not travel so much to that land as to the land of Cathay, for it is too long a journey. And also merchants can get all they need in the isle of Cathay – spices, golden cloth, and other rich things; and they are reluctant to go to Pentoxere because of the long way and the dangers of the sea. For there are in many places in that sea great rocks of the stone called adamant, which of its nature draws iron to itself. And because no ships that have iron nails in them can sail that way because of these rocks, which would attract the ships to them, men dare not sail there. The ships of that part of the world are all made of wood with no iron. I was once in that sea, and I saw what looked like an island of trees and growing bushes; and the seamen told me that it was all great ships that the rock of adamant had attracted and caught there, and that all these trees and bushes had grown from the things that were in the ships. So because of these dangers and others like them, and because of the distance, they go to Cathay. And yet Cathay is not so near that those who set out from Venice or Genoa or other places in Lombardy do not spend eleven or twelve months travelling by land and sea before they arrive in Cathay. The land of Prester John is many days' journey further. Merchants who do go there go through the land of Persia and come to a city called Hermes [Ormuz], because a philosopher called Hermes founded it. Then they cross an arm of the sea and come to another city called Soboth or Colach [Cambaye]; there they get all kinds of goods, and as great plenty of parrots as there is of larks in our country. In this country there is little wheat or barley, and therefore they eat millet and rice, honey and milk and cheese and all sorts of fruits. Merchants can travel safely enough from there if they wish to. In that land are many parrots, which in their language they call *psitakes* [psitacci]; of their nature they talk just like a man. Those that talk well have long broad tongues, and five toes on each foot; those that do not talk at all – or not much – have only three toes.

This same royal King Prester John and the Great Khan of Tartary are always allied through marriage; for each of them marries the other's daughter or sister. In the land of Prester John there is a great plenty of precious stones of different sorts, some so big that they make from them dishes, bowls, cups and many other things too numerous to mention.

Now I shall speak of some of the principal isles of Prester John's land, and of the royalty of his state and of what religion and creed he and his people follow. This Emperor Prester John is a Christian, and so is the greater part of his land, even if they do not have all the articles of the faith as clearly as we do. Nevertheless they believe in God as Father, Son and Holy Ghost; they are a very devout people, faithful to each other, and there is neither fraud nor guile among them. This Emperor has under his rule seventy-two provinces, each one ruled by a king. These kings have other Kings under them, and all are tributary to

Prester John. In the land of Prester John there are many marvels. Among others there is a vast sea of gravel and sand, and no drop of water is in it. It ebbs and flows as the ocean itself does in other countries, and there are great waves on it; it never stays still and unmoving. No man can cross that sea by ship or in any other way; and so it is unknown what kind of land or country is on the far side. And though there is no water in that sea, yet is there great plenty of good fish caught on its shores; they are very tasty to eat, but they are of different shape to the fish in other waters. I, John Mandeville, ate of them, and so believe it, for it is true.*

And three days' journey from that sea are great mountains, from which flows a large river that comes from Paradise. It is full of precious stones, without a drop of water. It runs with great waves through the wilderness into the Gravelly Sea, and then it disappears. Each week for three days this river runs so fast that no man dare enter it; but on the other days people go into it when they like and gather the precious stones. Beyond that river towards the wilderness is a great plain, set among the hills, all sandy and gravelly, in which there are, as it seems, trees which at the rising of the sun begin to grow, and a fruit grows on them; they grow until midday, and then they begin to dwindle and return back into the earth, so that by sunset nothing is seen of them; this happens each day. No man dare eat of this fruit, or go near it, for it looks like a deceptive phantom. That is accounted a marvellous thing, as well it may be.

In this wilderness are many wild men with horns on their heads; they dwell in woods and speak not, only grunting like pigs. And in some woods in that land are wild dogs, that will never come near to man, any more than foxes do in this country. There are birds, too, that of their own nature speak and call out to men who are crossing the desert, speaking as clearly as if they were men. These birds have large tongues and five claws on each foot. There are others that have only three claws on each foot, and they do not speak so well or clearly. These birds are called parrots, as I said before.

This same King and Emperor Prester John, when he goes to battle against his enemies, has no banner borne before him; instead there are carried before him three crosses, of fine gold, which are very large and tall and encrusted with precious stones. Ten thousand men at arms and more than a hundred thousand foot soldiers are detailed to look after

* An instance, not common in Egerton, of the asseverating interpolation that became frequent in later texts. The sentence is in neither MS Royal 20 B.X nor Cotton.

each cross, in the same way as men guard a banner or standard in battle or wherever. And this number of men is always assigned to the guarding of these crosses whenever the Emperor goes to battle; this is not counting the main army, or certain lords and their men who are ordered to be in the Emperor's own division, and also not counting certain wings whose job it is to forage. And when he rides with his private company in time of peace, there is carried before him a wooden cross, without gold or painting or precious stones, in remembrance of the Passion of Christ who died on a wooden cross. He also has carried in front of him a golden plate full of earth, as a token that notwithstanding his great nobleness and power he came from the earth and to the earth shall he return. And there is carried before him another vessel full of gold and jewels and precious stones, like rubies, diamonds, sapphires, emeralds, topazes, chrysolites and many others, as a token of his nobility, power and might.

I shall now tell you of the arrangement of Prester John's palace, which is usually at the city of Susa. That palace is so wealthy, so noble, so full of delights that it is a marvel to tell of. For on top of the main tower are two balls of gold, in each of which are two great fair carbuncles, which shine very brightly in the night. The chief gates of the palace are of precious stones, which men call sardonyx, and the bars are of ivory. The windows of the hall and the chambers are of crystal. All the tables they eat off are of emeralds, amethysts and, some, of gold, set with precious stones; the pedestals that support the tables are, in the same way, of precious stone. The steps up which the Emperor goes to his throne where he sits at meals are, in turn, onyx, crystal, jasper, amethyst, sardonyx, and coral; and the highest step, which he rests his feet on when at meat, is chrysolite. All the steps are bordered with fine gold, set full of pearls and other precious stones on the sides and edges. The sides of his throne are of emerald, edged in fine gold set with precious stones. The pillars in his chamber are of gold set with precious stones, many of which are carbuncles to give light at night. Nevertheless every night he has burning in his chamber twelve vessels of crystal full of balm, to give a good sweet smell and drive away noxious airs. The frame of his bed is of sapphire, well set in gold, to make him sleep well and to destroy lustful thoughts – for he only lies with his wives on four set occasions in the year, and even then for the sole purpose of engendering children.

This Emperor also has another palace, rich and noble, in the city of Nise, and he sojourns there when it pleases him; but the air is not so good there nor as healthy as it is at Susa. Throughout all Prester John's lands men eat only once a day, as they do in the court of the Great Khan. You must know that every day in his court Prester John has more than thirty thousand people eating, not counting those who come and go; but thirty thousand people neither there nor in the court of the Great Khan consume as much in one day as would twelve thousand in our country. This Emperor always has seven kings in his court to serve him; and when they have served for a month, they go home and another seven kings come and serve for another month. And with those kings there always serve seventy-two dukes and 360 earls and many other lords and knights. And each day in his court twelve archbishops and twenty bishops dine. The Patriarch of Saint Thomas is there rather like a Pope. All the archbishops and bishops and abbots there are kings and lords of great fiefs. Each one of them has some office in the Emperor's court; for one king is porter, another steward, another chamberlain, another steward of the household, another butler, another server, another marshal – and so on, through all the positions that there are in his court. So he is very richly and honourably served. His land is four months' journey in breadth; in length it is without measure. Believe all this, for truly I saw it with my own eyes, and much more than I have told you. For my companions and I lived with him a long time and saw all I have told you, and much more than I have leisure to tell.*

Next to the isle of Pentoxere, which is Prester John's, is another long and broad isle called Mulstorak [Malazgirt];† it is under Prester John's lordship. In this isle there is great plenty of goods and riches. Once there was there a rich man called Catolonabes [Hasan ben Sabbah], and he was powerful and marvellously cunning. He had a fair strong castle, standing on a hill, and he had strong high walls built round it. Inside the walls he made a beautiful garden and planted in it all kinds of trees bearing different kinds of fruit. He had all kinds of sweet-smelling and flowering herbs planted too. There were many fair fountains in that garden, and beside them lovely halls and chambers, painted marvellously delicately in gold and azure with different stories; there were different kinds of birds, worked by mechanical means, which seemed quite alive as they sang and fluttered. In that garden he put all the kinds of birds and beasts he could get to please and delight a man. He also put

---

* These two sentences, not in the French or Cotton, are another interpolation.

† What follows is an account of the stronghold of the extreme Ismaili Muslim sect, the Hashishi'yun or Assassins, founded in 1096. Their power was broken by the end of the thirteenth century. Their chief fortress was Alamut in the Elbruz Mountains.

there beautiful maidens, not older than fifteen, the loveliest he could find, and boys of the same age; they were all clad in clothes of gold. These he said were angels. He also had three lovely wells made of precious stones enclosed in jasper and crystal, and other precious stones set in gold. He built conduits under the earth so that, when he wished, one of these wells would run with honey, another with wine, and another with milk, from these conduits. This place he called Paradise. And when any young noble of the country came to him, he led him into this Paradise and showed him all these things I have mentioned. He secretly had minstrels in a high tower where they could not be seen, playing on different instruments of music. He said they were God's angels, and that that place was the Paradise God grants to those He loves, saying, *Dabo uobis terram fluentem lac et mel*, which means, 'I shall give you a land flowing with milk and honey.'*

Then this rich man gave these youths a kind of drink which quickly made them drunk; then they were more blinded than before, and thought they had indeed been in bliss. He then told them that if they would put themselves in danger of death for his sake, when they were dead they would come to his Paradise and would evermore be of the age of the maidens, that they would evermore live with them and have pleasure and dalliance with them and they should still remain always virgin; and that after a certain time he would put them in a yet fairer Paradise, where they would see God in His majesty and bliss and joy. Thereupon they all agreed to do what he wanted. Then he would tell them to go to such and such a place and slay some lord or man of the area who was his enemy; they were to have no fear, for if they were killed he would put them in Paradise. Thus he had many lords of the country assassinated; and many of these young men were killed in the hope of having the Paradise that he promised them. Thus through his deceit he avenged himself on many of his enemies. When the lords and rich men of the land perceived the malice and guile of this Catolonabes, they banded together and attacked his castle, slew Catolonabes, and destroyed all his wealth and the beautiful things in his Paradise, and razed his castle; still the wells are there and one or two other things, but not the riches. It is not long since it was destroyed.

* Leviticus xx, 24.

31

Of the head of the devil in the Vale Perilous;
and of the customs of the peoples in different isles round there

A little way from that place towards the River Phison [Ganges] is a great marvel. For there is a valley between two hills, about four miles long; some men call it the Vale of Enchantment, some the Vale of Devils, and some the Vale Perilous. In this valley there are often heard tempests, and ugly, hideous noises, both by day and by night. And sometimes noises are heard as if of trumpets and tabors and drums, like at the feasts of great lords. This valley is full of devils and always has been, and men of those parts say it is an entrance to Hell. There is much gold and silver in this valley, and to get it many men – Christian and heathen – come and go into that valley. But very few come out again – least of all unbelievers – for all who go therein out of covetousness are strangled by devils and lost. In the middle of the valley under a rock one can clearly see the head and face of a devil, very hideous and dreadful to see; nothing else is seen of it except from the shoulders up. There is no man in this world, Christian or anyone else, who would not be very terrified to see it, it is so horrible and foul. He looks at each man so keenly and so cruelly, and his eyes are rolling so fast and sparkling like fire, and he changes his expression so often, and out of his nose and mouth comes so much fire of different colours with such an awful stench, that no man can bear it. But good Christian men, however, who are firm in the faith, can enter that valley without great harm if they are cleanly confessed and absolved and bless themselves with the sign of the Cross; then devils will not harm them. Even if they do get out without bodily hurt, they will not escape without great fear; for devils appear openly to them, menace them, and fly up and down in the air with great thunders and lightnings and awful tempests. Good men as well as evil will have great fear when they pass through, thinking that perhaps God will take vengeance on them for their past sins. My companions and I, when we came near that valley and heard all about it, wondered in our hearts whether to trust ourselves totally to the mercy of God and pass through it; some turned aside and said they would not put themselves in that danger. There were in our company two Friars Minor of Lombardy, who said they would go through that valley if we would go with them; so what with their encouragement and the comfort of their words, we confessed cleanly and heard Mass and took Communion and went into the valley, fourteen of us together. But when we came out we were only nine. We knew never what became of the remainder, whether they were lost or turned back, but we never saw them again. Two of them were Greeks and three Spaniards. Our other companions, who would not cross the Vale Perilous, went round by another way to meet us. And my companions and I went through the valley, and saw many marvellous things, and gold and silver and precious stones and many other jewels on each side of us – so it seemed to us. But whether it really was as it seemed, or was merely illusion, I do not know. But because of the fear that we were in, and also so as not to hinder our devotion, we would touch nothing we saw: for we were more devout then than we ever were before or after, because of the fear we had on account of devils appearing to us in different guises and of the multitude of dead men's bodies that lay in our path. For if two kings with their armies had fought together and the greater part of both sides been slain, there would not have been a greater number of dead bodies than we saw. And when I saw so many bodies lying there, I was very astonished that they were so healthy, without corruption, as fresh as if they had been newly dead. But I dare not affirm that they were all true bodies that I saw in that valley; I believe that devils made so many bodies appear so as to frighten us; for it is not likely that so great a multitude of folk should have really been dead there so freshly that there was no smell or corruption. Many of those bodies I saw seemed to be wearing the clothing of Christian men; but I well believe they came there from covetousness of the gold and other jewels in that valley, or because false hearts cannot stand the great fear and dread that they had on account of the horrible sights they saw. And I assure you that we were often struck to the earth by terrible great blasts of wind, thunder and tempests; but through the grace of Almighty God we passed through safe and sound.

Beyond that valley is a great isle where the folk are as big in stature as giants of twenty-eight or thirty feet tall. They have no clothes to wear except the skins of beasts, which they cover their bodies with. They eat no bread; but they eat raw flesh and drink milk, for there is an abundance of animals. They have no houses to live in, and they will more readily eat human flesh than any other. Thanks to them no pilgrim dare enter this isle; for if they see a ship in the sea with men aboard, they will wade into the sea to take the men. We were told that there is another isle beyond that where there are giants much bigger than these, for some are fifty or sixty feet tall. I had no desire to see them, for no man can go to that isle without being promptly strangled by those monsters. In these isles among these giants are sheep as big as oxen, but their wool is thick and coarse. I have often seen those sheep; and some men have often seen those giants catch people in the sea and go back to the land with two in one hand and two in the other, eating their flesh raw.

There is another fair and good isle, full of people, where the custom is that when a woman is newly married, she shall not sleep the first night with her husband, but with another young man, who shall have ado with her that night and take her maidenhead, taking in the morning a certain sum of money for his trouble. In each town there are certain young men set apart to do that service, which are called *gadlibiriens*, which is to say 'fools of despair'. They say, and affirm as a truth, that it is a very dangerous thing to take the maidenhead of a virgin; for, so they say, whoever does puts himself in peril of death. And if the husband of the woman find her still virgin on the next night following (perchance because the man who should have had her maidenhead was drunk, or for any other reason did not perform properly to her), then shall he have an action at law against the young man before the justices of the land – as serious as if the young man had intended to kill him. But after the first night, when those women are so defiled, they are kept so strictly that they shall not speak to or even come into the company of those men. I asked them what the cause and reason was for such a custom there. They told me that in ancient times some men had died in that land in deflowering maidens, for the latter had snakes within them, which stung the husbands on their penises inside the women's bodies; and thus many men were slain, and so they follow that custom there to make other men test out the route before they themselves set out on that adventure.

Another isle is to the southwards in the Great Sea Ocean where there are wicked and cruel women, who have precious stones growing in their eyes. They are such a nature that if they look upon a man with an angry intention, the power of those stones slays him with a look, as the basilisk does.

Near there is another isle, where the women make great sorrow when their children are born and great joy when they are dead. They call their friends together and make a feast and take the dead child and throw it into a great fire and burn it. And women who loved their husbands well, when they are dead, throw themselves with their children into the fire to be burnt. It is their opinion there that they are purged by the fire, so that no corruption shall ever after come by them, and, purged of all vice and all deformity, they will pass to their husbands in the next world. The cause why they weep and sorrow at the birth of their children and rejoice when they die is that when they are born into this world they come to sorrow and trouble, and when they die, they go to the joy of Paradise, where rivers of milk and honey and plenty of all kinds of good things are, and a life without sorrow. In this isle the King is always elected; they do not choose the richest or noblest man, but him who has the best character and is the most just and true, they make their King. They also ensure that he is an old man and not young. In that isle too are very righteous judges; for they do justice and right to every man, to poor as to rich, and judge every man according to his guilt and not according to his state or degree. The King also may not put anyone to death without the assent and advice of all his barons. If the King himself commits a trespass, like killing a man or some other such notable thing, he shall be killed for it. But he will not be killed by a man's hand; rather they shall forbid any man to be so bold as to keep company with him, or speak to him, come to him, or give him food or drink. And so he dies for pure need, hunger, thirst, and the sorrow in his heart. No one who is convicted of a trespass is spared, neither for riches, high estate, dignity, high birth, nor for any kind of gift; every man shall have according to his deeds.

Beyond this isle there is another isle in the sea, where there is a great number of people. They never eat the meat of hares, geese, or hens; nevertheless they have many of them and rear them just for the pleasure and the sight of them. But they eat the meat of other animals and drink milk. In this country they marry their own daughters, and their sisters, and their female relatives, and live ten or twelve or more together in one house. Each man's wife shall be common to the others who live there; each of them takes other wives, one on one night, one on another. When any of the wives bears a child, it will be given to him who first lay with her who is the mother; and so there is no one who knows whether the child be his or another's. And if one says to them that thus they may father another man's child, they answer that so will other men do their own.

In that country and throughout the whole of India there are a lot of crocodiles, which, as I told you before, are a kind of long-bodied serpent. At night it is in the water, and during the day it lies on the dry land on rocks or in crannies in the ground; in winter they eat no meat, but lie as if they were half dead. This serpent will kill men and devour them; and when it eats it moves the upper jaw and not the lower, and it has no tongue. Each year in that land they sow a kind of seed which grows up into small bushes; from them they gather cotton in great quantity. There is also a kind of wood which is so hard and strong that if a man burn it and cover its coals with ash, the fire will keep in for a twelvemonth or more. This tree has a marvellous number of leaves. And there are some trees that will neither burn nor rot. There are also hazels that bear nuts as big as a man's head.* There are trees that bear cotton, as in many other countries. There are animals, too, which they call *orafles*; and in Arabia they call them *gyrfaunts* [giraffes]. It is a handsome beast, well dappled, of the same height, or more, as a great horse; his neck is twenty cubits long, and his crupper and tail are like those of a hart. He is well able to stand on the ground and see over the top of a house. In that land there are many chameleons, which is a small animal the same size as a [little wild goat];† it neither eats nor drinks, but goes along always with its mouth open, for it lives on air. Often it changes colour, going into all colours except white and red: now it will be of one colour, and then suddenly of another. [There are also there great serpents, six score feet long; they are of different colours – striped, red, green and yellow, blue and black, and speckled all over.]‡ There are others which have a crest like a cock's on their heads and walk almost upright on their feet; they are four or more feet long easily. They usually live in the rocks and mountains and hills. Always they have their jaws open, whence they spit their venom. There are also wild swine of several colours, as big as oxen in this country; they are all brindled like fawns or does. [And there are also hedgehogs, as big as wild pigs are here; we call them porcupines.]§ And there are lions quite white, big and strong. There are also other kinds of animals, as big as horses; they are called *louherans*, and some call them *touez*, and others *odenthos* [the rhinoceros]. They have black heads and three horns on the brow, as sharp as swords; their bodies are yellow. They are marvellously cruel beasts, and will chase and kill the elephant. There is also another cruel and dangerous kind of animal, of the size of a bear, and their heads are like bears' heads. They have six feet, and on each foot are two claws, long, huge and sharp. In the body they are like bears, but their tails are like lions' tails. There are also rats bigger than hounds; and geese all red except for the head and neck, which are black; they are much bigger than our geese. There are also many other kinds of beast in

* Coconuts. The other trees are probably ebony.

† So in the French and in Cotton. Egerton reads 'raa' which Letts in his edition read as 'rat'. It would match the size of the chameleon better, indeed.

‡ From MS Royal 20 B.X. Omitted in Egerton.

§ Omitted in Egerton, supplied from MS Royal 20 B.X.

that country and in the countries round about, of which it would be too long to tell all the natures and appearances.

32

Of the goodness of the people in the isle of Bragman; of King Alexander; and why Prester John is so called

Beyond this isle there is another, large, fertile, full of people. They are good folk, honest, and of good faith and good living according to the nature of their faith. And even if they are not Christian, nevertheless by natural instinct or law they live a commendable life, are folk of great virtue, flying away from all sins and vices and malice, and they keep the Ten Commandments well. For they are not proud nor covetous, they are not lecherous nor gluttonous. They do nothing to another man they would not have done to themselves. They set no store by the riches of this world, or by possession of earthly goods. They do not lie, nor swear oaths for no reason, but simply say a thing is, or is not; they say that he who swears is about to deceive his neighbour. This isle these people live in is called the Isle of Bragman [Brahmin]; and some men call it the Land of Faith. Through it runs a great river, which is called Thebe. Generally all the men of that isle and of other isles nearby are more trustworthy and more righteous than men in other countries. In this land are no thieves, no murderers, no prostitutes, no liars, no beggars; they are men as pure in conversation and as clean living as if they were men of religion. And since they are such true and good folk, in their country there is never thunder or lightning, hail nor snow, nor any other storms and bad weather; there is no hunger, no pestilence, no war, nor any other common tribulations among them, as there are among us because of our sins. And therefore it seems that God loves them well and is well pleased by their manner of life and their faith. They believe in God who made all things, and worship Him with all their power; all earthly things they set at nought. They live so temperately and soberly in meat and drink that they are the longest-lived people in the world; and many of them die simply of age, when their vital force runs out.

When Alexander the conqueror reigned, and conquered all the world, he came to that land and sent letters to them who lived there, saying he would come and destroy their land unless they would be subject to him as other lands were. And they wrote letters back to him of this tenor: 'What thing could satisfy that man to whom all the world is not enough? You will find nothing here with us that would be a reason for making war on us; we have no worldly riches, nor do we desire to have any. All the places of our land and all our goods, movable and immovable, are common to every man. All our riches are our meat and drink wherewith we sustain our bodies; our treasure is peace and concord and the love that is between us. Instead of elaborate dress, we use a cheap cloth to cover our worthless carrion. Our wives, too, are not proudly and richly arrayed to please our eyes, for we consider such adornment a great folly, applying to the wretched body more beauty than God has naturally given it; our wives desire no more beauty than nature has given them. Our land serves us for two things: our livelihood while we live and for burial when we are dead. And up to this time we have always been at peace, of which you would now despoil and disinherit us. A King we have among us, not to right any man's wrongs – for among us no man does another wrong – but simply to teach us to be obedient. We need to have no judges among us, for none of us does to another except what he would have done to himself. Therefore you can take from us nothing but our peace, which up to this time has always been amongst us.' And when King Alexander had seen their letters and read them, it seemed to him in his heart that it would be a great pity and great unmanliness to hurt or trouble such folk; and he granted them a guarantee of peace, and bade them to continue with their good living and follow their good customs without having any fear of him, for he would not harm them.

Near that land is another called Oxidrace, ⟨and another that is called Gynoscriphe, where for the most part they follow the customs of the Brahmins, living innocently in love and charity each with another. They go always naked. Alexander the conqueror came to their lands; and as soon as he saw their manner of life and their loyalty and love to each other, he said he would not harm them, but told them to ask of him what they would, and he would give it them. They answered and said that worldly riches they would neither ask for nor have, but only meat and drink wherewith the feeble body might be sustained. For the goods and riches of the world, they said, are not lasting, but deceptive. But if he could give them things that were everlasting and not mortal, they would thank him much. The King answered them and said that he could not do so, for he himself was mortal as they were. 'Wherefore, then,' said they, 'do you gather the riches of this world, which is transitory and cannot endure? For whether you will or not, they will leave you, or you them, as happened to them who were before you.

And out of this world you will take nothing with you, but naked as you came hither shall you pass hence, and your flesh shall turn back into the earth from which it was made. And therefore you should not think that anything can endure for ever, except God who made all the world. And yet, not having any regard to this, you are so presumptuous and proud that, just as if you were God, you would make all the world subject to yourself; yet you do not know how long your life will be, nor the hour of your going.' When Alexander heard these words, and others like them, he marvelled greatly and was greatly ashamed and went away from them and did them no hurt.) And even if these people do not have the articles of our faith, nevertheless I believe that because of their good faith that they have by nature, and their good intent, God loves them well and is well pleased by their manner of life, as He was with Job, who was a pagan, yet nevertheless his deeds were as acceptable to God as those of His loyal servants. And even if there are many different religions and different beliefs in the world, still I believe God will always love those who love Him in truth and serve Him meekly and truly, setting no store by the vainglory of the world – just like these folk and Job. And so Our Lord says by the Prophet Ysai [Hosea], *Ponam eis multiplices leges meas*, that is, 'I shall put on them my laws manifold.'*
And also in the Gospel He says, *Alias oues habeo, que non sunt ex hoc ouili*, that is, 'I have other sheep which are not of this fold',† as if he said, 'Other servants I have besides those under the Christian law.' And with this agrees the vision which was shown to Saint Peter in the city of Jaffa, when an angel came from Heaven and brought with him all kinds of animals and reptiles and birds, and told him to take and eat; and Saint Peter answered and said, 'I never eat unclean beasts.' And the angel replied, *Quod Deus mundavit, tu ne immundum dixeris*, that is to say, 'Call thou not unclean that which God has cleansed.'‡ This was done as a token that men should despise no men for the difference of their laws. For we know not whom God loves nor whom He hates; and therefore when I pray for the dead and say my *De Profundis*, I say it for all Christian souls and also for all the souls who need praying for. And of this folk I will say thus much: I believe they are fully acceptable to God, they are so true and good. There are many prophets among them and have been since antiquity; for in their isles was once the Incarnation of Christ predicted, how he should be born of a virgin – it was three thousand years and more before the time of His Incarnation. They firmly believe in the Incarnation of Christ, but they do not know the manner of His Passion.

* Misquoted from viii, 12.   † John x, 16.   ‡ Acts x, 15.

Beyond this isle is another that is called Pytan, where the folk neither plough nor sow the land, and neither eat nor drink. Nevertheless they are a very fair people, well coloured, well shaped, according to their stature; for they are little, like dwarfs, somewhat bigger than the pygmies. This people lives on the smell of wild apples that grow there; and if they go far from home, they take some of these apples with them, for as soon as they lose the smell of them they die. This people is not fully rational; they are very simple, like beasts. Near there is another isle, where the people are covered in feathers and rough hair, except for the face and the palms of the hands. They travel as well in water as on land; and they eat meat and fish raw. Here there is a great river, two miles broad; it is called Wymare. Beyond that river there is a great wilderness, so I was told; I saw it not, nor did I cross the river. But men living near the river told us that in those deserts are the Trees of the Sun and Moon, which spoke to King Alexander and told him of his death. Some say that the people who look after those trees eat the fruit of them and the balm that grows there, and live four or five hundred years through the virtue of that fruit and that balm. For there there grows plenty of balm, as in no other place I could hear of, except in Egypt next to Babylon, as I told you before. My companions and I would gladly have gone there; but, as we were told, a hundred thousand men at arms would hardly be able to cross that wilderness because of the great numbers of wild beasts that there are in that wilderness, like dragons and different kinds of serpents and other ravening beasts, which kill and eat all they can get. In this land I have just mentioned there are many elephants, all white; some are blue, and of other colours, quite numberless. There are also many unicorns and lions and other hideous beasts. Many other isles there are in the empire of Prester John, and many marvels; there is also great wealth and noble treasures, precious stones and other jewels, but it would take too long to tell of them all.

Now I shall tell you why this Emperor is called Prester John. There was once an Emperor in that land who was a noble and brave prince; he had many knights with him who were Christian, like he has who is now Emperor. And one day this Emperor thought that he would like to see the manner of the service in Christian churches. At that time Christian men occupied many countries towards those parts, that is to say, Turkey, Syria, Tartary, Palestine, Arabia, Aleppo and all Egypt. And so it fell that this Emperor and a Christian knight who was with him entered a church in Egypt on the Saturday in Whit week, when the Bishop was holding an ordination service. The Emperor watched the service, and the way priests were made, and how solemnly and devoutly they were ordained. He then asked the knight what sort of people these were who were being ordained, and what they were called; the knight said they were priests. Then the Emperor said that no longer would he be called King or Emperor, but priest instead, and that he would take the name of the first priest who came out of the church. It happened that the first priest to come out of the church was called John; and so that Emperor and all the other Emperors since have been called Prester John, that is, Priest John. In the land of Prester John there are many good Christian men, living good lives, of good faith and religion; they are natives of the country. They have priests among them who sing Mass for them, but they make the sacrament of leavened bread, as the Greeks do. Also they do not say their Mass in exactly the same way as our priests do; they only say the *Pater Noster* and the words of the consecration with which the sacrament is made, as Saint Thomas the Apostle taught them long ago. They know nothing of the ordinals and additions of the court of Rome that our priests use.

33

Of the mountains of gold, which the ants watch over;
and of the four rivers that come from the Earthly Paradise

East from the land of Prester John is a large fertile land called Taprobane [Ceylon]. There is a rich and noble King in that isle, subject to Prester John. He is chosen by election. Here there are two summers and two winters in a single year, and harvest also twice in a year. And at all times of the year their gardens are full of flowers and their meadows green. Good and rational people dwell in this isle; there are many good Christian men among them who are so rich that they do not know the total of their goods. In former times, when people sailed there from the land of Prester John, they used ships of such a type that they needed twenty days to sail thither; but in the ships we use now they can do it in seven days. And as they sail they can often see the bottom of the sea in several places, for it is not very deep.

On the east there are two isles near this one, of which one is called Oriell and the other Arget [Pliny's Chryse and Argyre]; in those two isles the earth is full of gold and silver ore. And they are near the Red Sea, where it enters the Great Sea Ocean. And in those isles no stars can clearly be seen shining, except for one they call Canapos [Canopus]; nor can the moon be seen there except in the second quarter. In this isle of Ceylon are great hills of gold, which ants busily look after, purifying the gold and separating the fine from the unfine. Those ants are as big as dogs are here, so that no man dare go near those hills for fear that the ants might attack them; however, men win that gold by a trick. For the nature of the ants is that when the weather is hot, they will hide in the earth from mid-morning till after noon; and then the men of that country come with camels and dromedaries and horses, load them up with that gold, and go away before the ants come out of their holes. At other times of the year, when the weather is not hot and the ants do not hide in the earth, they use another trick to get this gold. They take mares who have young foals, and hang on each side of each mare an empty container with the mouth of it uppermost, trailing near to the ground, and then send them forth early in the morning to pasture round the hills where the gold is, keeping the foals at home. Then these ants, when they see these empty containers, go and fill them with gold; for it is the nature of the ant to leave nothing empty near them – there is no hole or cranny or anything else that they will not fill. And when it is thought that the mares are fully laden with gold, the men let the foals out, and they neigh after their dams. Then the mares hear their foals neighing and hurry quickly to them, laden with gold. And in this way men get a great deal of gold; for the ants easily tolerate all sorts of animals, man excepted.*

Beyond these isles I have told you of, beyond the deserts in the empire of Prester John, going still east, there is no inhabited land, as I said earlier; only wastes and wilderness and great crags and mountains and a dark land, where no man can see by night or day, as we were told. That dark land and those deserts last right to the Earthly Paradise, in which Adam and Eve were put; but they were only there a little while. And in the east of that place the earth begins. But that is not our east, where the sun rises for us; for when the sun rises in those countries, it is midnight in our land, because of the roundness of the earth. For, as I said before, God made the earth quite round, in the middle of the firmament. The hills and the valleys that are now on the earth are the

* At this point follows a curious interpolation on Thule and a miracle of Saint Thomas of Canterbury. It is not found in any text except Egerton, and clearly has nothing to do with the author of the book. I have therefore omitted it. Its only slight interest lies in the further evidence it shows of the way redactors sometimes added what they thought to be germane material to the text they were handling.

result only of Noah's flood, by which soft earth was moved from its place leaving a valley, and the hard ground stayed still and became a hill.

Of Paradise I cannot speak properly, for I have not been there; and that I regret. But I shall tell you as much as I have heard from wise men and trustworthy authorities in those countries. The Earthly Paradise, so men say, is the highest land on earth; it is so high it touches the sphere of the moon. For it is so high that Noah's flood could not reach it, though it covered all the rest of the earth. Paradise is encircled by a wall; but no man can say what the wall is made of. It is all grown over with moss and with bushes so that no stone can be seen, nor anything else a wall might be made of. The wall of Paradise stretches from the south to the north; there is no way into it open because of ever burning fire, which is the flaming sword that God set up before the entrance so that no man should enter.

In the middle of Paradise is a spring from which come four rivers, which run through different lands. These rivers sink down into the earth inside Paradise and then run many a mile underground; afterwards they rise up out of the earth again in distant lands. The first of these rivers is called Phison or Ganges; it rises in India below the hills of Orcobares [Himalayas?], and runs eastwards through India into the Great Sea Ocean. In that river are many precious stones and plenty of the wood called *lignum aloes*, and much gold in the gravel. This river is called the Phison because many waters collect and join it, for 'Phison' means roughly 'gathering'. It is also called Ganges after a king who was in India, whom men called Gangaras; because it runs through his land it was called Ganges. This river is clear in some places, disturbed in others, in some places hot, in others cold. The second river is called Nile or Gyon; it rises out of the earth a little way from Mount Atlant [Atlas]. Not far thence it sinks down again into the earth and runs underground until it comes to the shore of the Red Sea, and there it rises again out of the earth and runs all round Ethiopia, and so through Egypt until it comes to Alexandria the Great; there it enters the Mediterranean. This river is always disturbed and is therefore called Gyon; for 'Gyon' means the same as 'troubled'. The third river is called the Tigris, that is, 'fast running'; for it is one of the swiftest rivers of the world. It is called Tigris after an animal of the same name, which is the fastest animal on foot in the world. This river rises in Armenia under the Mount Parchoatra and runs through Armenia and Asia to the south, and then turns into the Mediterranean Sea. The fourth river is called Euphrates, which is as much as to say 'bearing well'; for many good things grow along that river. That river runs through Media, Armenia and Persia. And men say that all the fresh rivers of the world have their beginning in the spring that wells up in Paradise.

You should realize that no living man can go to Paradise. By land no man can go thither because of the wild beasts in the wilderness, and because of the hills and rocks, which no one can cross; and also because of the many dark places that are there. No one can go there by water either, for those rivers flow with so strong a current, with such a rush and such waves that no boat can sail against them. There is also such a great noise of waters that one man cannot hear another, shout he never so loudly. Many great lords have tried at different times to travel by those rivers to Paradise, but they could not prosper in their journeys; some of them died through exhaustion from rowing and excessive labour, some went blind and deaf through the noise of the waters, and some were drowned through the violence of the waves. And so no man, as I said, can get there except through the special grace of God. And so of that place I can tell you no more; so I shall go back and tell you of things that I have seen in the isles and lands of the empire of Prester John, which, relative to us, are below the earth.

34

Of the customs of the Kings and others living in the isles
adjacent to Prester John's land;
and of the honour which the son does to his dead father

There are other lands – if anyone wished to travel through them – by which men could travel right round the earth, and return, if they had the grace of God to keep to the right route, to their native countries which they set out from. So, in time, they would girdle the earth. But it would be a very long time before such a voyage was finished; and few men try it, because there are so many dangers, by sea and by land, besetting men who travel in foreign lands which would most likely fall on those who intended to make that long journey of circumnavigation. Still, it could be done well enough by God's grace. But men leave that long route and return from those isles I have mentioned via other isles surrounding the land of Prester John and the isles that are in his empire. In so returning, they come to an isle called Casson [Shansi]; and that isle is nearly sixty days' journey in length and more than fifty in breadth. It is the best land in those parts except for Cathay; and if merchants visited it as regularly as they do Cathay, it would be better. For cities and good towns are there so thick on the ground that when a man leaves one city he immediately sees another city or good town in front of him, whatever direction he takes. This isle is very bountiful in all kinds of spices and all kinds of other goods, especially those that pertain to man's livelihood. There are many great woods full of chestnut trees. The King of this land is very rich and mighty, and holds his land of the Great Khan of Cathay, for that is one of the twelve provinces that the Great Khan has under him, as I told you before; not counting his own land and other small isles. From this land men go to another isle which is called Ryboth or Gyboth [Tibet]; that too is subject to the Great Khan. This is a good land, bountiful in corn, wine, and many other things. Men of this land have no houses to live in, but live instead in tents made of black felt. The principal city of that land is walled with black and white stones, all the streets are paved with the same kind of stones. And in that city no man is so bold as to shed blood – neither of man or beast – on account of their devotion to an idol that is worshipped there. In this city lives the Pope of their religion, whom they call Lobassi. He distributes all the honours and benefices that belong to their idols; and all the priests and ministers of the idols are obedient to him as our priests are to our Pope.

In this land it is a custom everywhere that when any man's father is dead and his son wants to honour him, he sends for all the kinsfolk, his good friends, priests of their religion, minstrels and others; and they carry the body to a hill with great solemnity and great rejoicing. When they get there, the most important priest strikes off the dead man's head and lays it on a great platter of silver, or of gold if he is a rich man, and gives it to his son. And then all his friends sing and say many prayers, and then the priests and religious men of their cult hew the body into small pieces and say many prayers. And birds of that land, familiar with this custom, gather there and hover around them – vultures, eagles, ravens, and other raptors; the priests throw this flesh to them, and they carry it a little way off and eat it. And then, just as priests in our country sing for the souls of the dead *Subuenite, sancti Dei*, so those priests there sing with a loud voice in their language, 'Regard and see how good a man this was, whom the angels of God come to fetch to Paradise.' Then the son and all his friends think that his father has been greatly honoured when the birds have eaten him. And the more birds that arrive the more joy have all his friends, the more they think the dead man is honoured. Then the son goes home taking all the friends with him, and he gives them a great feast; each one tells the others in their mirth how ten or sixteen, or twenty birds came, just as if it were a great cause for rejoicing to them. Then the son boils his father's head, and the flesh from it he distributes among his special friends, giving each one a little bit, as a dainty. And from the cranium of the head he has a cup made, and he drinks from it all his lifetime in remembrance of his father.

From this land, coming in this direction through the land of the Great Khan for ten days' journey, is another good isle, whose King is rich and mighty. And in that land there is a lord who is marvellously rich; yet he is neither prince nor duke nor earl. Nevertheless many a man holds his land of him, and he is a lord of great wealth. Each year he has brought to him three thousand horses laden with corn, and as many with rice. This lord leads a marvellous life. For he has fifty maidens who serve him each day at his meals and his bed, and do what he wills. And when he sits at his meals, they bring him meat, always five dishes at once; and while bringing them they sing a lovely song. They cut up his meat in front of him and put it in his mouth as if he were a child; for he cuts none and touches none with his hands, which he keeps always on the table in front of him. For he has such long nails on his fingers that he can hold nothing with them. It is accounted very noble, and a great honour, to have such long nails in that country. Therefore they let their nails grow as long as they can and cut them not. Some let them grow so long that they grow all round the hand; they think it is very noble, a mark of great gentility. The mark of nobility in women there is to have small feet; and so as soon as they are born, they bind their feet so tightly that they cannot grow as big as they should. These damsels I mentioned, as long as their lord is sitting at table, are always singing near at hand. When he has eaten enough of the first course, they bring five other dishes before him, singing all the while. And so they do to the end of the meal. And in this way this lord leads his life, following the ancient custom of his ancestors, which custom his successors will follow in the same way. And thus they make their belly their god, so that they achieve no worthiness or bravery, living only in pleasure and delight of the flesh, like a pig in a sty. This rich man also has a very beautiful rich palace, where he lives, of which the wall is two miles in circuit. Therein are many fine gardens; and all the pavement of the halls and chambers is of gold and silver. And in the middle of one of the gardens is a little hill, whereon is a little palace with towers and pinnacles all of gold; therein he will often sit to disport himself and take the air, for it serves no other purpose.

From this land men come through the land of the Great Khan, of which I told you before, and so I do not need to go over it all again. Know that in all those lands, realms and nations, except for those inhabited by men lacking reason, there is no people which does not hold some of the articles of our faith. Even if they are of divers beliefs and creeds, they have some good points of our truth. And generally they believe in God who made the world, and Him they call God of Nature; and thus is the prophecy made true that says, *Et metuent eum omnes fines terre*, that is, 'And all the ends of the earth shall fear Him;'* and in another place, *Omnes gentes seruient ei*, that is, 'All people shall serve him.'† But they cannot properly talk of God, especially of the Trinity, because they have had no instruction. They know nothing of the Son, nor of the Holy Ghost; but they can speak of the Bible and especially of the book of Genesis and other books of Moses, and sometimes of the sayings of the twelve Prophets. And they say that those creatures that they worship are not gods, but they honour them for the great virtues that are in them, which may not be without the special grace of God. And about idols and simulacres they say that there is no people that does not have simulacres; they say that especially as they see Christian men with crucifixes and images of Our Lady and of other saints, doing honour to them. But they do not know that we do not worship those images of stone or wood for themselves, but in remembrance of the saints for whom they were made. They say also that angels speak to them in their idols, and perform miracles. They say truly, for they do have an angel inside them; but there are two sorts of angels, that is, one good, one bad, as the men of Greece say, Chaco [κακός] and Calo [καλός]. Chaco is the bad angel and Calo the good. But that is no good angel that is in their idols, but a bad one – that is, a devil who answers them and tells them many things to deceive them and maintain them in their idolatry and their error.

There are many other countries and other marvels which I have not seen, and so I cannot speak of them properly; and also in the countries I have been to there are many marvels which I have not spoken of, for it would be too long to tell of them all. And also I do not want to say any more about marvels that there are there, so that other men who go there can find new things to speak of which I have not mentioned. For many men have great delight and desire in hearing of new things; and so I shall cease telling of the different things I saw in those countries, so that those who desire to visit those countries may find enough new things to speak of for the solace and recreation of those whom it pleases to hear them.

* Psalm lxvii, 7.   † Psalm lxxii, 11.

And I, John Mandeville, knight, left my country and crossed the sea in the year of Our Lord Jesus Christ 1332; I have travelled through many lands, countries and isles, and have been on many honourable journeys, and many honourable deeds of arms with worthy men, although I am unworthy; I am now come to rest, a man worn out by age and travel and the feebleness of my body, and certain other causes which force me to rest. I have compiled this book and written it, as it came into my mind, in the year of Our Lord Jesus Christ 1366,* that is to say in the thirty-fourth year after I left this land and took my way to those parts.

[And forasmuch as many men believe nothing but what they see with their own eyes, or that they can imagine with their own natural wit, on my way home I made my way to Rome to show my book to our Holy Father the Pope. And I told him of the marvels I had seen in different countries, asking that he with his wise council would examine it, with different people who are in Rome, for in that city there are always men living who come from all the nations of the world. And a little while afterwards, when he and his wise council had examined it all the way through, he said to me that certainly everything was true that was in it. For he said he had a book in Latin that contained all these things and much more, after which book the *Mappa Mundi* has been made; and he showed me that book. And so our Holy Father the Pope has ratified and supported my book in all points.]†

Wherefore I pray that all those who read (or hear this book read) will pray for me, and I shall pray for them. And to all those who say devoutly for me a *Pater Noster* and an *Aue*, so that God may forgive my sins, may God grant a share in my pilgrimage and all other good deeds that I have done or may do in time to come up to my life's end. And I, as far as in me lies, do make them partakers in those good deeds, praying

---

* 1322 for setting out and 1356 for the writing in Cotton and Defective.

† This paragraph is a clumsy interpolation found only in the English versions of the *Travels* and one late-fifteenth-century Latin MS. The contradiction of the author's statement about writing his book at home in his old age is obvious; moreover, the popes did not return to Rome from Avignon until 1377, despite Urban V's ill-fated attempt. I have argued elsewhere ('Sir John Mandeville's Visit to the Pope: the Implications of an Interpolation', *Neophilologus* 54 (1970), pp. 77–80) that the interpolation might be used to attach a *terminus post quem* of 1377 to any English translation now known. In addition, its concern for papal approval might suggest that one important redactor recognized the controversial nature of some of the statements in the book, and, in the rapidly polarizing religious atmosphere of the time, sought to protect his work.

to God of whom all grace comes, that He fill with His grace all those who hear or read this book, and save them and keep them in body and soul, and after this life bring them to the country where there is joy and endless rest and peace without end. Amen.

Here ends the book of John Mandeville.

APPENDIX I: THE ALPHABETS

Several texts of the *Travels* include a number of alphabets of the various countries described. Scribal transmission, both in the copying of Mandeville and in the texts from which the originals of the alphabets might have been drawn, has made many of the examples of them corrupt to a degree. They are here reproduced (redrawn) from the Egerton MS, whose forms are more corrupt than those of the Paris text of 1371.

Mr Letts, in his *Sir John Mandeville, The Man and His Book*, concluded that the Greek was genuine with some corruptions; the Egyptian was genuine Coptic, but garbled; the Hebrew accurate in the names of the letters but corrupt in the forms; the Saracen was based on a corrupt Runic; and the Persian and Chaldean were doublets based (probably) on Nestorian-Syrian.

Obviously their usefulness is extremely limited. But it was not at all unusual for travel writers of this and later periods to introduce into their narratives alphabets or even small compendia of useful phrases. (Sometimes, as in the later expansions of Mandeville, or some sixteenth-century satiric Utopias, these are clearly fictional.) The inclusion of alphabets in the *Travels* thus indicates that the author has considered the common characteristics of the form he has consciously adopted, and may indeed have intended them as additional means of convincing his readers of the seriousness of his material. They, unlike us, would have had only a slight chance of checking them. All the indications are, as Mr Letts pointed out, that Mandeville took the alphabets from the best sources available to him: this, judging by the rest of the book, is what we would expect.

APPENDIX II: ISLES, COUNTRIES
AND DIRECTIONS

The reader may have been puzzled by the retention in the translation of
phrases like 'downward from Jerusalem', 'on the left side', 'the upper
part of that land', 'isles' and so on. The problem is that there is no way
of translating these terms, indicative of now exploded geographical
conventions, into modern ones based on our implicit assumptions of
modern maps and directions. Like us, Mandeville is holding a picture
in his mind; but it is not our picture.

Had Mandeville not written but drawn his picture of the world, what
might it have looked like? He would have had two overlapping and not
entirely consistent ones. The first, heavily and explicitly confirmed in
the book, is of the earth as a globe at the centre of the firmament of
Heaven, everywhere traversable, and with a gravitational pull (as we
would call it) towards the centre; so the Antipodeans walk upright as
we do and not on their heads. But when we come to the surface of the
world, whose spherical shape we today often represent as a plane,
another conception supervenes. Medieval maps of the world (as distinct from detailed portolano charts of parts of the coastline) still tended
to be schematic, of the 'T in O' type. The lands of the earth were
represented as enclosed within a circle of the Great Sea Ocean, to

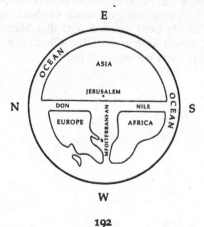

which all seas and rivers eventually flow. (Other large bodies of water – the Mediterranean, the Black Sea – are often called the Great Sea as well. Nomenclature is vague indeed at this period.) East is at the top, and the land masses are split by the Mediterranean, and the rivers Don and Nile, into three – Europe, Asia and Africa.

Thus the 'upper' part of a country is towards the top of the map. To get back to Europe from Cathay you would, on this convention, 'descend'. The 'left side' would be left as you looked at the map – therefore, the north. The Earthly Paradise is logically (and symbolically) enough at the top – for have we not all fallen away from there? Jerusalem occupies the crucial centre. Add to this the conception of the rotundity of the earth, and you get a schematic picture of climbing up the hemispherical land mass from the left to the symbolic high point and summit – Jerusalem – as a way of saying that you are travelling from northern Europe to the Holy City. It is clearly some mixture of the ideas of flatness of the map and rotundity of the earth that is behind the unease Mandeville feels about the term 'east' in paragraph 3 of chapter 33, where he seems to be attempting to marry the two ideas.

The development of measuring skills and surveying techniques from this very century onwards revolutionized the geographical conceptions of Europeans. The directional relationships of places to each other could not be accurately worked out so that they could be represented schematically with an accuracy that could be translated into compass bearings and miles walked. Hence the vagueness of terminology, particularly in distant lands. The word 'isle' can certainly mean 'island'; but often it suggests no more than 'a group of people living as a recognizable entity somewhere in the uncharted wastes whose borders and juxtapositions to other groups are ill defined'. It is therefore best to leave the word as it is; and it is obviously pointless to try to fix Mandeville's places on any modern map. Editors have tried in the past, and the result has often been ludicrous. The most helpful visual aid to Mandeville's *Travels* is to look at one of the numerous *Mappae mundi* still surviving. The excellent one in Hereford Cathedral dates from around 1300, and shows the schematic 'T in O' representation, and other features as described above. It also includes pictorial images of a number of things Mandeville describes in the East including the 'orrea' (barns) of Joseph. The vagueness at that time of terms we use today is perfectly illustrated by the legends on the map. And the vision of the surface of the earth as moralized symbol is starkly shown by the way the earth's four quadrants are boldly labelled MORS – death surrounds all.

SUPPLEMENTARY EXPLANATORY NOTES

Mandeville, like many writers of his generation, assumes a familiarity far more automatic and detailed than is likely in a reader today with the events of the Bible, especially in the historical books, and with the Psalms, which formed an important part of the liturgy. In brief explanatory notes, glossing everything is impossible: but as in the text I have glossed names into a form traceable in the Authorized (King James) Version of the Bible, diligent use of a concordance will clear up any areas of confusion or obscurity.

p. 44. *the common people . . . nothing without lords*: Mandeville here picks up a common note in the complaint writing of the Middle Ages, the failure of each of the Three Estates – those who work, those who fight and those who pray – who are mutually dependent on each other. His main fire here and, increasingly, later is directed against those who should lead both spiritually and temporally but who neglect their responsibilities. For a fuller discussion, see the documents invaluably anthologized by L. & J. Riley Smith, *The Crusades* (London, 1981).

    general passage: In other words, a crusade. The idea of the Crusade as Holy War guaranteeing salvation for those taking part was first enunciated by Urban II at the council of Clermont in 1096 – which announced the First Crusade. While the Crusade movement may in part have resulted from the appeal of the Byzantine Emperor Michael to the Pope for help after his disastrous defeat at Manzikert by the Seljuks in 1071, it was used as a clever ploy to try to turn outwards the violence endemic in European society. It is important to recognize the longevity of the Crusade idea – it was not dead even in the sixteenth century – and that a crusade is, in effect, an armed pilgrimage, literalizing the metaphor of the soldiers of Christ first used in Ephesians vi. This crusading background is important to Mandeville's book and its readership – he was, after all, writing at a time when crusades were virtually continuous in the eastern Mediterranean, in Spain, in Prussia and Lithuania: many English people – including the future Henry IV – fought on them, and Chaucer's Knight, we are told, has been on almost all of them, which is of course impossible. But that is another story . . . See also J. Riley Smith (ed.), *The Oxford Illustrated History of the Crusades* (London, 2001), and *A History of the Crusades* (London, 1999).

p. 45. *Of the way from England to Constantinople*: By this time the pilgrimage routes were well developed, and marked by chains of facilities for travellers like hospices, some of which can be seen on the ground today. Mandeville's enumeration is broadly accurate for a traveller coming from Northwest Europe.

p. 46. *Constantinople*: The Eastern Roman Empire had already undergone periods of drastic decline and renaissance. In 1204 the Crusade destined for the Holy Land to help the Frankish Kingdom of Jerusalem recover Jerusalem, lost to Saladin in 1187, diverted to Constantinople and sacked it to pay the Venetians, who were providing the transport. A Latin Emperor (Baldwin) was installed for a short period, before the Byzantine recovered their sovereignty, and a flood of relics, immensely valuable as attractants of pilgrims and pilgrims' offerings, was looted from the ancient city for the benefit of Latin Christendom. On relics, see J. Sumption, *Pilgrimage* (London, 1975) *passim*.

a statue of Justinian the Emperor: This stood till 1492; the orb was replaced in 1325 after being blown down in 1317.

the Cross of Our Lord: Fragments of the Cross abounded in medieval Europe, as did fragments of the Crown of Thorns. It was once calculated that the fragments of the Cross, collected, would build a small ship. The most serious early scholarly discussion of the Cross is in Lipsius, *De Cruce* (1593).

the Cross of Our Lord was made of four kinds of trees: Medieval people lived in a world of symbol and significance now largely forgotten. The properties (= nature and powers) of everything from stones to stars were well codified: cf. Bartholomew the Englishman's *On the Properties of Things*, ed. M. C. Seymour et al. (*On the Properties of Things: John Trevisa's translation of Bartholomaeus Anglicus*, Oxford, 1975–88). Further, the reading of scripture was invariably in the light of an interpretative system of types and antitypes – typology – where an event or person in the Old Testament symbolically related to other events or persons, and especially to the fulfilment of that shadow or symbol in the New: thus the Burning Bush is a type of the Virgin Birth, Jonah is an antitype of Christ, Melchisedek's (see p. 82) offering bread and wine is a type of the Mass.

p. 47. *Saint Helena*: Her Invention of the Cross is first to be read of in St Ambrose in 495, 150 years after she died. The legend becomes part of the vast collection of edifying saints' lives and miracle stories collected by Jacopo da Voragine (1230–98) as the *Aurea Legenda*, or *Golden Legend*. This huge book is indispensable to the understanding of the narratives of much medieval and Renaissance religious art.

Helena's supposed father is King Coel (Cole), according to Geoffrey of Monmouth's version of British history made *c.* 1135, which was universally accepted in the Middle Ages. She also makes a brief appearance in the Venerable Bede and in the Welsh *Mabinogion*.

p. 48. *the King's chapel*: The Sainte Chapelle in Paris, built by St Louis in 1246 to house the relics he had redeemed from the Venetians (not the Genoese), to whom the Latin Emperor had pawned them.

p. 49. *The Emperor of Germany*: The Holy Roman Emperor.

the shaft of the spear with which Christ was pierced: The Holy Lance was discovered, somewhat mysteriously, when the First Crusade was besieged in Antioch in 1098, and it boosted morale, and complicated politics, mightily. For an entertaining summary, see S. Runciman, *The History of the Crusades, I: The First Crusade* (Cambridge, 1951), pp. 240–53. Another supposed Holy Lance was shown to the leaders of the First Crusade in Constantinople.

Hellespont: A common confusion in the period. The Bosphorus is meant.

p. 50. *Hermogenes*: The name is a corruption of Hermes Trismegistus, the mythical sage who was supposed to have written the books of magical and mystical lore known as the Hermetic corpus – a corpus of enormous influence in Neoplatonist thought in the fifteenth and sixteenth centuries.

The Holy Ghost proceeds not from the Son: The Nicene Creed has the clause 'I believe in the Holy Ghost, who proceedeth from the father and the Son'. That *Filioque* (= 'and from the Son') clause, which Constantinople would not accept, was the cause of the split, enduring to this day, between the Eastern Orthodox and Latin Churches in 1054.

pp. 50–51. *as much power as our Pope . . . none of them*: John XXII (d. 1334) attempted to reunite the churches, but Patriarch Andronikos III refused.

p. 51. *Our Lord never ate bodily food*: The Greek Church does not say this, which is a mark of the Docetist heresy.

p. 53. *Hippocrates*: Cos is associated from antiquity with the healers Hippocrates and Aesculapius. (Hippocrates' son was called Draco (= Lat. 'dragon'). The Knight of Rhodes would be a Hospitaller. The dangerous kiss is a common folklore motif.

p. 56. *Tyre*: Tyre, at the foot of the strategic pass known as the Ladder of Tyre, was held by the Franks of Outremer until the Kingdom of Acre, successor to the Kingdom of Jerusalem, fell finally in 1291. The scholarly William of Tyre's book, written from the perspective of a Frank born and living in Outremer, was used by Mandeville.

Dido: In Vergil's *Aeneid* Dido does indeed regard her relationship with Aeneas as marriage though he does not – or is not allowed to.

p. 57. *Jaffa*: The reception of pilgrims in the Holy Land in the fourteenth and fifteenth centuries was highly organized if not very comfortable, but they met a good deal of hostility from the natives. A good summary is in Louise Collis, *The Memoirs of a Medieval Woman: The Life and Times of Margery Kempe* (London, 1983 repr.) pp. 81ff.

Andromeda: A confusion of the maiden and the monster, common in the period.

Haifa: Onomastics was a favourite medieval game, and only occasionally had any accuracy.

Fosse of Mynon: The name comes from Memnon, killed at Troy by Achilles, whose statue (much later than the time of Troy, of course) stood near the mouth of the Belus. The fine sand is ideal for glassmaking, and the Prague MS (British Library MS Addit. 24189) of Mandeville shows it being so used.

Gravelly Sea: Mandeville mentions this again (p. 169), in the right place: the Takla Makan desert, 250 miles by 600 of shifting sands.

p. 59. *Benedicite*: The canticle 'O all ye works of the Lord, praise ye the Lord', for Matins.

p. 63. *the River Gyon . . . from the Earthy Paradise*: One of the four rivers of Paradise (see also pp. 86, 167, 184). The tradition of the four rivers – Phison or Ganges, Nile or Gihon, Tigris or Hiddekel, and Euphrates – flowing from Paradise reaches far back into Jewish exegesis of the Old Testament. In a virtually rainless Egypt, the annual rise and fall of the Nile, caused by the rains in the mountains of Ethiopia, was a mystery for centuries.

p. 64. *In the desert of the land of Egypt a holy hermit*: The story is told of both St Antony and St Paul the Hermit.

the Phoenix: The Phoenix is described in the Bestiaries (cf. the splendid version of Oxford MS Bodley 764 by Richard Barber, Woodbridge, 1999). In that world of multiple significances, it is a symbol of resurrection, of Christ. The Bestiaries draws on a long tradition reaching back to antiquity. The subtext of Mandeville's book, exemplified in little touches like this one here, is that the whole creation shows forth the wonderful works of God: cf. Psalm xix and Romans i, 19–20. This is a very important idea for Mandeville: see Introduction, pp. 26–7.

p. 68. *In Sicily is a kind of snake*: These inconvenient reptiles Pliny reports in North Africa, and the *Golden Legend* in Malta.

Gebel: Arabic *jibel*, 'mountain'.

p. 69. *Saint Katherine*: One of the most popular saints in medieval devotion and iconography – see the *Golden Legend* again, or, as second best, the *Oxford Dictionary of Saints*, for the full story. Her emblems are a wheel and a sword, with which she was martyred at Alexandria. The monastery at Mt Sinai, once a centre of scholarship, is still a major place of pilgrimage.

Lignum aloes: A very hard, aromatic wood: not to be confused with the New World species (*guaiacum*) that after the sixteenth century was given that name.

Elim: The wanderings of the Children of Israel, recounted in Exodus, were very well known indeed – indeed, a history adopted as, and symbolic of, their own by all the Christian nations of Europe.

p. 73. *Ury [Uriah]*: It is most unlikely that Uriah the Hittite, husband of Bathsheba (II Samuel xi) founded this city. More onomastic fantasy.

giants: Possibly a reminiscence of Goliath, but that there were giants in the earth once in that place the books of Deuteronomy, Joshua and Numbers agree.

p. 74. *the Dry Tree*: Associated with the Oak of Abraham, under which he sat when he received the Divine visitation, at Mamre. Many faiths held it holy. It was once hoped the Great Lord from the West would be Frederick II Hohenstaufen, the Emperor nicknamed *Stupor Mundi* ('Wonder of the World') who died in 1230.

p. 75. *the first roses and rose-bushes that were ever seen*: No obvious source, but a similar story is told of the daughter his second wife, Keturah, bore Abraham; and cf. for the *champ fleuri*, Guillaume de Machaut, *Dit du Lion* (1342).

pp. 76ff. *Of the pilgrimages in Jerusalem*: The proximity of the sites of almost every event in Holy Scripture is remarkable, but, in a pilgrimage culture, highly advantageous. This sort of enumeration of the sacred sites, the events associated with them and the grace they may obtain for the penitent pilgrim is typical of the pilgrim manuals.

p. 77. *The Church where is the Sepulchre of Our Lord*: Erected by the Byzantines, it was restored and enlarged after the earthquake of 1114. Traditionally Adam was buried on Calvary (the First Adam prefiguring the death and resurrection of the Second Adam).

p. 78. *Godfrey*: The first Frankish King of Jerusalem.

Saint Helena: see above, pp. 47, 195.

p. 79. *Midpoint of the world*: The belief can be traced back to St Jerome in the fourth century AD, and explains why medieval 'T in O' maps (see Appendix II) always have Jerusalem in the centre.

p. 81. *the foreskin of Our Lord*: A relic purporting to be this was deposited at Aix-la-Chapelle by Charlemagne.

Titus: Sacked Jerusalem, destroying the Temple of Herod the Great, in AD 70.

p. 82. *Moriac*: The rock of Moriah was thought to have survived the sack, and the first Caliph Omar, after taking Jerusalem in AD 637, decided that it was thence that Muhammad ascended to Heaven. The Dome of the Rock was built over it.

on this rock: The scholarly childhood of the Virgin is elaborated in many medieval accounts of her life, and in many paintings she is disturbed at her studies by the arrival of Gabriel.

p. 84. *he sent for his sister*: This unedifying story is in Josephus, *Antiqu. Judaeorum*.

p. 85. *Judas hanged himself*: In the West, traditionally on an elder tree.

p. 86. *Between Jerusalem . . . men could cross it*: Note the symbolism, utterly typical of the way people interpreted their world, of this passage: the brook recalls the Jordan, both real and symbolic (of death), the boundary of the promised land (Canaan and Heaven), Christ is both the bridge builder (*pontifex*) and the bridge itself, and the Cross the only route from one side to the other.

p. 87. *Mary the Egyptian*: Possibly a confusion for St Pelagia, virgin martyr; St Mary of Egypt was a reformed courtesan. The former, unlike the latter, seems to have had a church dedicated to her in the vicinity of Jerusalem.

p. 89. *the Dead Sea*: sometimes called the Lake Asphaltis. An occasion for another symbolic explicatory trope, which the *Gawain*-poet used in *Clannes*.

p. 90. *apples fine of colour*: 'Sodom apples' have a long symbolic career. In Milton's *Paradise Lost*, X.545ff. the devils are fooled by them.

p. 91. *Dinah*: Genesis xxxiv.

p. 92. *Saint Tecle [Thecla]*: Possibly St Thekla Protomartyr (of Iconium), greatly venerated in the Eastern Church (she is associated with St Paul in the Apochryphal *Acts of Paul and Thekla*), but some think Mandeville means the Benedictine Abbess of Kitzingen and Ochsenfurt (ob. *c*. 790), whom St Boniface, Apostle of Germany, persuaded to leave the community of Wimborne, Dorset, and travel to Germany.

the head of St John: The conflicting claims of relics to authenticity was a not uncommon phenomenon. Guibert of Nogent (see Sumption, *Pilgrimage*, pp. 42–4) cannot have been alone in finding this led to a certain scepticism about any claims at all.

p. 97. *doves instead of messengers*: Many travellers remark on the pigeon post. It was more usual to attach the message to the bird's foot.

Iacobynes [Jacobites]: The followers of Jacobus (= James) Baradeus, a sixth-century monk: the confusion with the Apostle James is understandable. Monophysites, they believed that Christ had only one nature, not the dual, fully human and fully divine, nature postulated by orthodoxy. The Syrians used the Greek liturgy, but were after 1181 in formal communion with Rome.

p. 99. *Nostre Dame de Sardenake [Saidenaya]*: This miraculous portrait was supposedly by St Luke.

p. 100. *a river, called the Sabatory*: An intermittent spring, mentioned by Pliny (*Historia Naturalis* xxxi.2). But Pliny has it ceasing on Saturdays.

p. 103. *This Tartary*: Mandeville is here relying on the remarkable account of John of Piano Carpini.

Batu: Khan of the Golden Horde.

pp. 104ff. Mandeville uses William of Tripoli, who seems to have spoken Arabic, extensively in what follows. It is important to realize that this is the fullest, and the most widely available, written account of Islam circulating in the later Middle Ages, and formed the opinion of those without firsthand experience.

p. 105. *fast for a whole month*: Ramadan.

pp. 107–8. *Now I shall tell you what the Sultan told me one day*: This colloquy with the Sultan is an important satirical device, and follows a similar incident described by Caesarius of Heisterbach in his *Dialogus Miraculorum* as having happened after the Fall of Acre in 1291 between an unnamed emir and William of Utrecht.

p. 112. *Quicunque vult*: Not properly a psalm, but a creed (actually by St Ambrose) spelling out the Trinitarian position, as part of the polemics against the Arian heresy. (But the Athanasius at Trebizond is not the person once supposed author of the Creed.)

pp. 112ff.: *Chastel Despuere: Le chateau de l'épervier*: Haiton of Armenia recounts the foundation of the Byzantine Empire of Trebizond by Alexius Comnenus in 1204, after the Crusaders had occupied Constantinople.

The lady is Melior, sister of Melusine, whose legend is connected by Jean d'Arras in his *Mélusine c.* 1387 with the House of Lusignan, who claimed the Kingdom of Jerusalem. The king is probably Leon II.

p. 113. *a knight of the Templars*: The bloody suppression of the Knights Templar, and confiscation of their vast wealth, was in recent memory: the last Grand Master, Jacques de Molay, was burnt by Philippe IV in 1314.

p. 116. *the Amazons*: Traditionally, on the borders of Scythia on the Black Sea. These formidable ladies make regular appearances in the Alexander Romances, and the reconstruction of their bodies for military efficacy is widely reported. But only Mandeville differentiates the part removed according to rank.

p. 118. *only one foot*: The classical *sciapodes* – see p. 137.

good diamonds grow: This account of the properties of the diamond is typical of medieval lapidaries. The stone has magical as well as physical properties, and the Egerton redactor is careful to give his references to authorities.

p. 120. *We are in a climate*: The seven climates are latitudinal bands, distinguished by the length of their longest day, running round the earth. The idea is derived from Ptolemy, and each is, supposedly, governed by a planet. The properties of the planets, through the substance that rained down from them – 'influence' – on to the earth, affected everything, from the growth of metals in the earth to the physical and mental make-up of individual people.

ships made without nails . . . never get away again: 'Stitched ships' – their planks sewn end to end with fibre or leather – were common into the twentieth century in the Gulf region, and this is in fact one of the oldest methods of shipbuilding. Iron can be hard to get: it doesn't grow on trees. The magnetic rocks are a frequent motif in romances and tales from across the globe – but some rocks, of course, do affect the compass, and when compasses come to be used (after about 1200 in Europe) such rocks can cause many a ship to run aground in the same place.

p. 121. *some worship simulacres and some idols . . . they can worship them before they meet anything else*: Not in Mandeville's source, this subtle passage seems to be his invention.

p. 122. *pepper grows in a forest*: It is difficult now to realize how valuable a spice pepper was. A 'peppercorn rent' was a serious amount of money. Pepper made possible the eating of slightly rotten meat – and much of what Europe ate would have had modern Health and Safety people gibbering with horror, or dreaming fondly of the prosecutions they might one day bring. The power of Venice rested in part on its control of the western end of the Spice Routes – low bulk, high value – from the East, and it was the chance of breaking the Venetian monopoly that made a sea route round Africa to the East so attractive to the Portuguese and the Spaniards.

p. 123. *a noble and beautiful well*: The ultimate source for the Well of Youth is the *Letter of Prester John*, but Mandeville's personalized account catches the imagination. Ponce de Leon and his companions thought they had found it – or, at least, that is what they thought they were hearing tales of – in Florida in 1520.

people worship the ox: A garbled account of the holy cows of Hinduism.

p. 124. *St Thomas*: The Apostle Thomas was said to have evangelized India, where indeed, from the very early days of the Christian era there has been a vigorous Christian community.

pp. 125–6. *Others come in pilgrimage . . . as I said before*: In this passage it is difficult not to see reflected, quite possibly without irony, the situation in many pilgrimage sites in the West. The offerings of pilgrims certainly did, and were expected to, maintain buildings and services, including charitable ones; people did perform sometimes grotesque and even self-destructive acts of penance. The Church looked somewhat askance at the more extreme forms of these, especially when they became communal. The authorities were wary of the hysteria, for example, that the flagellant movement could generate. It is tempting to see in this account of the Juggernaut, which really existed, a transposed account of later fourteenth-century European popular religion. Even the offering of children may reflect on the way very young children in Western Europe were committed by their parents to the religious life. Note, however, the criticism of the lack of true devotion in those who follow a true religion.

p. 127. *They scorn other folk who go clothed*: Nakedness is often a sign of innocence in medieval art, of course, but Mandeville's fondness for providing biblical authority for unusual moral and social behaviour is well exemplified in this passage. The domestication of the outrageous – which suddenly questions accepted norms – is well shown in the story of children fattened up for the table. Swift could not do it better . . . indeed, *A Modest Proposal* probably draws on this passage.

pp. 127–9. *the Star Antarctic*: This discussion, with its further stress on the practical possibility of circumnavigation, is of great importance if only because it was so widely disseminated through the extraordinary career of the *Travels* in MS and later in print. The star Antarctic is probably Canopus, which is visible only below 37°N. In higher southern latitudes it sets; further north than 33° 16′ it is circumpolar. Mandeville's elevations for Polaris in the places he cites are correct.

This passage draws on many sources, but its very engaging and personalized tone makes it sound convincingly firsthand and authoritative. Folk such as Columbus found here apparently practical confirmation of what they read as theory in Pierre d'Ailly's *Imago Mundi*, and John of Sacrobosco's [Holywood] *De Sphaera* – which Mandeville had just put back in the book press!

p. 129. *Let a man take a spear*: It does not work, of course, but the idea of Jerusalem as being at the 'top centre' of the world is ancient. The spear may be a reminiscence of Eratosthenes' observation that at midday at the summer solstice at Syene, Egypt, a spear cast no shadow (an observation he used to help calculate the circumference of the earth, as described in Vincent of Beauvais, *Speculum Naturale* VI.13) Mandeville's value for the circumference is too large, of course.

p. 132. *trees that bear flour*: The sago palm.

trees that bear poison: The Upas tree of Java.

precious stones of great virtue: Probably silicaceous concretions in the joints of the bamboo. Of course, special virtue had to be the attribute of such remarkable things.

p. 133. *there is a marvel*: Clearly, Mandeville is referring to the yearly run of fish to the spawning redds.

p. 134. *Cynocephales*: Note the stress on the rationality of these strange people. Another bit of remarkable cultural relativity.

p. 135. *wild geese with two heads*: Probably hornbills, the confusion about the plurality of heads ultimately arising from the enormous development of the bill.

p. 136. *a people of evil customs*: Once again, Mandeville redirects the material of his source (here, Odoric) and makes the outrageous, the ultimate taboo, seem almost reasonable.

p. 137. *many different kinds of people*: Of course, the illustrators loved it – see the cover of this book! These monsters go back to Pliny and Solinus, but what is noticeable is 1) no account of the East could do without them and still be believed (as Polo knew) and 2) Mandeville crams them together in a single page and makes far less of them than he might have done.

pp. 141ff. *the Great Khan*: The description at length of the Khan's court and wealth is a topos by this time. But this account of his realm sets up within the book the model of a well-governed state, to which, to their discomfiture, the states of the West may be compared. That the state is that of the Khan of a people that had Europe shaking in its shoes only a couple of generations before adds to the irony.

At the beginning of the thirteenth century the nomadic tribes of central Asia loosely called Mongols or Tartars (the latter name is actually derived from the Chinese for one of the Mongol tribes) were approaching some sort of crisis.

Pressure of population on resources – nomads need a lot of ground – led to stress and increasingly sanguinary encounters with their more settled neighbours. The tribes came together under the leadership of a remarkable individual known in the West as Genghis Khan, who assumed the title Ilkhan. Under him, the Mongols exploded into aggressive conquest of their neighbours in a series of lightning campaigns marked by extreme disregard for human life and at the same time the strictest adherence to ideals of honour, bravery and obedience. In the next decades they struck deep into Russia, Eastern Europe, Persia, China and Japan. The first Mongol thrust into an Islamic country coincided with the Crusades in Egypt, led by St Louis of France, between 1218 and 1221. Genghis Khan finally abandoned any attempt to venture west of Persia. With his death in 1227 at the age of sixty-seven, the pressure of the horsemen of the steppes on the Arab world, which was even more vulnerable than Europe, eased for some years. But there were periodic further incursions – in 1258, for example, the Khan, Hulagu, grandson of Genghis Khan, sacked Baghdad after he had taken Damascus and Aleppo, massacred the population and killed the Abbasid Caliph Mostassim without the shedding of blood: the Tartars seem to have believed the blood was the seat of the soul, and avoided its shedding except in battle. Hulagu was on the point of attacking Jerusalem when the death of Mangu Khan caused his return to a general assembly of the leaders of the tribes to elect a new Ilkhan (see p. 149). (The Caliphate was restored, and lasted till 1920.)

The terror the Mongol incursions caused is palpable in the contemporary chroniclers – European, Arab, Persian, Chinese and Japanese. The historian Matthew Paris, writing at St Albans, makes a bitter (rather good) pun, hoping that *Tartari ad sua Tartara detrudentur* – 'that the Tartars could be thrust into the Hell that belongs to them': the same pun was used by St Louis. But Christian Europe as a whole suffered far less than the Middle and Far East, where the Mongols replaced the Chinese ruling dynasty with a house of their own (whose greatest ruler was Kubilai, or Kubla), at whose court Marco Polo of Venice lived for seventeen years. Indeed, at first, Christendom hoped that the Mongol incursions might herald the first offensive against Islam of the legendary Prester John (see p. 167); later, as the Mongols, now settling into a more peaceful role, established what has been called the *pax Tartarica* for the best part of a century over a region stretching from the Black Sea to China, the Franciscans with papal support spearheaded a series of missions to the Khanate to attempt to convert the Mongols to Christianity and thus automatically make them allies against the Muslims. It was such missions that took William of Rubruck, Odoric of Pordenone and John of Piano Carpini on their remarkable travels.

p. 146. *eight score years*: The election of Genghis Khan to supreme power was in 1206 (Vincent of Beauvais gives 1202). (This suggests a date for the writing of the *Travels* before 1366.)

p. 148. *He told them to bind them tightly together*: Where Mandeville got this edifying story from is not known.

Mango: Mangu Khan was actually baptized in 1254. The Tartars were tolerant of all faiths in their dominions.

p. 149. *captured the Caliph . . . died from hunger and thirst*: See note to p. 141.

p. 150. *Of the organization of the court of the Great Khan*: This passage, describing the court of Kublai, had a considerable literary progeny, not least in Coleridge.

p. 158. *women of that land . . . as well as men*: Another bit of subverting of gender assumptions.

p. 161. *Porte de Fer*: Alexander supposedly built a gate to shut in Gog and Magog lest they should overrun and destroy the world.

p. 163. *That country is quite covered by darkness*: The region of 'Megon' (Mughan), west of the Caspian, is subject to seasonal dense fog, and this may have saved the Christians fleeing from the persecution of Shapur II. But the account may also owe something to stories of the winter darkness of the Arctic.

p. 165. *There there grows a kind of fruit*: The Vegetable Lamb is described by Odoric, who does not claim to have seen it. By making the whole exchange firsthand, and citing the commonly believed story of the barnacle geese, at which 'they marvelled greatly', Mandeville vastly increases the immediacy and also reinforces his developing arguments both of the relativity of perception and of the common nature that rules everywhere.

p. 166. *pay tribute to the Queen of the Amazons*: Note that the safety of Europe depends on the regiment of these women who subvert everything Europe stands for.

p. 167. *trees that bear wool*: cotton, then virtually unknown in Europe.

Of the royal estate of Prester John: The legend of Prester John, the Christian Emperor of India, is first mentioned by Otto von Freisingen in 1158. A letter describing his great power and wealth, supposedly from him to the Christian princes of the West, was circulating by 1164 (Mandeville used this letter). There was a Christian ruler in the Far East, Wang Khan of the Keraits, who was identified with Prester John by William of Rubruck and later by Odoric. The other strand in the legend are the garbled accounts that came to Europe of the Christian Negus of Abyssinia. The existence of a substantial Nestorian Christian community in Turkish and Mongol dominions is not in doubt.

The search for Prester John, in the hope of making common cause with that Christian potentate against Islam, was prominent in the thinking of many statesmen down to the end of the sixteenth century: finding Prester John was one of the three main motives driving the Portuguese explorations to the East, into the preparation for which Mandeville's book had an important input as the fullest and most accessible account.

Pentexore: This could be, and probably is, the result of a scribal miscopying of 'Prester John'. History often is affected by bad handwriting or Chinese whispers.

p. 168. *great rocks of the stone called adamant*: See above, note to p. 120. The islands may well be mats of floating vegetation brought down by the rivers.

p. 169. *the gravelly Sea*: The Takla Makan desert. See also note to p. 57.

p. 171. *Catolonabes*: The name is corrupted from the title *Sheikh-al-Jibal*, 'Lord of the mountain'. Hulagu destroyed all the fortresses, and broke the power, of this murderous sect in the Persian dominions in 1256; in 1273 Baibars tackled the Syrian branch.

p. 172. *a kind of drink*: Probably hashish (*cannabis sativa*), hence 'assassin'.

p. 173. *the Vale of Devils*: See, on this splendidly handled little story, introduction pp. 20–21.

one can clearly see the head and face: Dr Seymour makes the convincing suggestion that Odoric, whom Mandeville adapts at this point, may have seen a Buddha sculpted on a rock face.

p. 175. *the custom is that when a woman is newly married ... stung the husbands on their penises inside the woman's bodies*: N. M. Penzer, *Poison Damsels, Thieves, Sacred Prostitution and the Romance of Betel Chewing* (New York, 2002) is an entertaining and scholarly study. The sources of this curious custom of a sort of *droit de seigneur* in reverse are obscure, and may go back to a garbled understanding of Herodotus (IV.172). Cultures where women are offered to strangers as a mark of hospitality are not unknown – Polo reports something similar in Tibet and in the province of Kain-do – but these women are rather more menacing than that.

gadlibiriens: Possibly a corruption of French *cuintebrise*. The snakes have a phallic significance, obvious for those so inclined.

as the basilisk does: A fabulous beast with eyes whose glance could kill. Looks could kill in that natural history.

pp. 176ff. The catalogue of fabulous beasts, with their habits credible or not, owes a good deal to the Bestiaries (see note to p. 64 above). The inclusion of this material is *de rigueur*, but it also underlines a key notion in the book, that what European eyes see as strange and marvellous might have a similar view of the European.

pp. 178ff. *Of the goodness of the folk in the isle of Bragman*: The Alexander Romances frequently use the motif of the great conqueror confronted by the simple goodness of people who want nothing, and Alexander's letter to their ruler (sometimes called Dindimus) is often quoted. The people whose values completely subvert European assumptions of worth and importance becomes a topos of travel writing as it develops – *Utopia* and *Gulliver's Travels* are clear descendants. The supposed response of the Brahmins offers a perfect opportunity for satirical attack. The function of this passage in this book, however, is slightly more complex: the Brahmin's direct-speech letter, which condemns by implication the priorities of the worldly, balances the Sultan's attack on the failings specifically of Christendom. The attack is going deeper, beyond the failings of a specific society, to the failing of a much more widely represented value system. Furthermore, this is very much a society where good is measured in works, and we are told as a starter 'and therefore it seems that God loves them well'. This runs close to a questioning of the doctrine of salvation by Grace, which the Church asserted, and in its insistence (as with Job) of there being those outside the Church whom God loves it is flat counter to the orthodox Roman view that *nulla salus extra ecclesiam* – 'there is no salvation outside the Church.'

p. 179. *Gynoscriphe*: The Gymnosophists (= 'wise ones who are naked') are a doublet of the Brahmins, and they too win the exchange with Alexander, who asks them a question like the one he asked Diogenes the Cynic, and gets a reply much longer but not substantially different.

p. 180. *And so Our Lord says by the prophet Ysai . . . the manner of His Passion*: The array of biblical texts is impressive, and certainly seems to support the idea that Mandeville is attacking the exclusive claims of the Pope.

p. 183. *when the sun rises in those countries*: Once more, as he moves to his conclusion, Mandeville stresses the roundness of the earth, and that one Nature rules everywhere, however strange its works might seem to eyes unfamiliar with any particular region, including Europe.

p. 184. *In the middle of Paradise*: Though, as Mandeville has just said and Milton repeats, the world changed at the Fall and at the Flood, belief that there was still somewhere the site of the Earthly Paradise died slowly. The Alexander Romances have Alexander attempt a journey thither. In the 1680s P. D. Huet, Bishop of Soissons, wrote a learned treatise on it which was translated for an English audience in 1694, and in 1714 a doctoral dissertation on it was defended in the University of Uppsala. The ultimate source, so to speak, of the four rivers that flow from Paradise is Genesis ii, 10.

p. 186. *In this land it is a custom everywhere*: Another example of Mandeville giving rational explanations for behaviour that Europeans would find repellent. Also clear is the parallel with the ritual and the theology of the Mass.

p. 188. *All people shall serve him*: Another emphasis on the subversive idea that there are several routes to salvation. Mandeville recalls, too, his early discussion (p. 121) of idols and simulacres, this time emphasizing its applicability to the practice in the Christian West.

SELECT BIBLIOGRAPHY

General Background

Atiya, A. S., *The Crusade in the Later Middle Ages* (London, 1938)

Bernard, J. H., *Guide Book to Palestine, A.D. 1350*, Palestine Pilgrims' Text Society, Vol. IV (London, 1894)

Burchard of Mount Sion, *A Description of the Holy Land*, ed. A. Stewart, Palestine Pilgrims' Text Society, Vol. XII (London, 1896)

Capgrave, J. *þe Solace of Pilgrimes: A Description of Rome ca. A.D. 450*, ed. C. A. Mills (London, 1911)

Cordier, H, *Mélanges d'histoire et de géographie orientales* (Paris, 1914–23)

Cottle, B., The *Triumph of English 1350–1400* (London, 1969)

Furnivall, F. J., The *Stacions of Rome and the Pilgrims' Sea Voyage* (London, Early English Texts Society, 1867)

Kimble, G. H. T., *Geography in the Middle Ages* (London, 1938)

Langlois, C. V., *La connaissance de la nature et du monde au Moyen Âge d'après quelques écrits français à l'usage des laïcs* (Paris, 1911)

Laurent, J. C. M., *Peregrinatores Medii Aevi quattuor* (Leipzig, 1864)

Ohler, N., *The Medieval Pilgrim* (London, 1989)

Riley Smith, J. (ed.), *The Oxford Illustrated History of the Crusades* (London, 2001)

Riley Smith, L. and J., *The Crusades* (London, 1981)

Sumption, J., *Pilgrimage* (London, 1975)

Webb, D., *Pilgrims and Pilgrimage in the Mediaeval West*, (London and New York, 1999)

Yule, Sir H., *Cathay and the Way Thither*, 2nd edn rev. H. Cordier, 4 vols. (Hakluyt Society, London, 1913–16)

Editions of the Texts

a) The Cotton Text: ed. M. C. Seymour (Oxford, 1967)

— ed. P. Hamelius, 2 vols. (Early English Text Society, London, 1919 and 1923)

b) The Egerton Text: ed. Sir G. F. Warner for the Roxburghe Club (London, 1889)

— ed. M. Letts for the Hakluyt Society, 2 vols. (London, 1953)

c) Seymour, M. C. (ed.), *The Defective Version of Mandeville's Travels* (Early English Text Society, Oxford, 2002)

d) Deluz, C., *Le Livre des Merveilles du monde de Jean de Mandeville* (Louvain, 2001). A critical edition of the Insular version

Discussions of the Travels, *the Author, the Book's History and Other Relevant Matters*

Bennett, J. W., *The Rediscovery of Sir John Mandeville* (Oxford, 1954)

Campbell, M. B. *The Witness and the Other World: Exotic European Travel Writing 400–1600* (Ithaca and London, 1988)

Deluz, C., *Le Livre de Jehan de Mandeville: une 'géographie' au XIVe siècle*, (Louvain-la-Neuve, 1988)

Elner, J., and Rubiés, J.-P. (eds.), *Voyages and Visions: Towards a Cultural History of Travel* (London, 1999)

Greenblatt, S. J., *Marvellous Possessions* (Chicago, 1991)

Higgins, I. M., *Writing East: The 'Travels' of Sir John Mandeville* (Philadelphia, 1997)

Howard, D. R., 'The World of *Mandeville's Travels*', *Yearbook of English Studies* 1 (1971)

Lawton, David, 'The Surveying Subject and the "Whole World" of Belief: Three Case Studies', *New Medieval Literatures* IV (2001)

Letts, M., *Sir John Mandeville: The Man and His Book* (London, 1949)

Moseley, C. W. R. D., 'The Metamorphoses of Sir John Mandeville', *Yearbook of English Studies* 4 (1974)

de Poerck, G., 'La tradition manuscrite des *Voyages* de Jean de Mandeville', *Romanica Gandensia* 4, (Ghent, 1955)

Seymour, M. C., 'The Origin of the Egerton Version of *Mandeville's Travels*', *Medium Aevum* 30 (1961)

—(ed.), 'Sir John Mandeville', in *Authors of the Middle Ages 1: English Writers of the Late Middle Ages*, (Aldershot, 1994)

Zacher, C. K., *Curiosity and Pilgrimage* (Baltimore, 1976)

INDEX

Page references in *italics* refer to the Introduction.

Index

Arabians, 72
Aram, *see* Haran
Ararat, 113
Archades, plain, 102
Archiprothopapaton, 123
Are of Gosra, *see* Zerah of Bosra
Arget (Argyre), 182
Aristotle, *19*, 50
Ark of the Covenant, 82, 91
Arkes, *see* Arqa
Armenia (Ermony), 44, 79, 97, 100, 112, 163, 164, 181, 185
Arnon, Mount, 89
Arqa (Arkes), 100
Artah (Artoise), 102
Artiron, *see* Erzerum
Ascalon, 61, 76
Ascopardes (Sudanese?), 71
al-Ashraf (Melechimandabron), Sultan, 60
al-Ashraf Khalil (Melechesserak), Sultan, 60
Asia, 145, 184, *passim*
Asia Minor, 79
asphalt, 89
Asphaltis (Asfaltit), Lake, *see* Dead Sea
Assassins, Valley of, 23, 171, 204
Athanasian Creed, 112, 199
Athanasius, Bishop of Alexandria, 112, 199
Athos, Mount, 49, 50; clarity of air (supposedly because reaches second highest of concentric Elements: Earth, Water, Air, Fire), 50
Atlas (Alloche, Atlant), Mount, 63, 184
Augustine, Saint, *28*, 98
Averroës, 27
Ayas (Laiazzo, Lairais), 112
Ayre, *see* Darum
Azary (Azarias), 58

Baalbek (Maubek), 102
Babel, Tower of, 61, 116, 145
Babilan Khan, *see* Boal
Babylon the Great, 61, 62
Babylon 'where the Sultan dwells', *see* Cairo
Baco, *see* Batu
Bacon, Roger, 26
Bactria (Bactrice), 111, 167
Bactria, *see* Bokhara
Baghdad (Baldak, Susis), 61, 149; sack of, 202
Baibars (Melechdaer, Benochdaer), Sultan, 60, 203
Balach (Balak), 89
Balahaam (Balaam), 89
Balbeor, *see* Belbays
Baldak, *see* Baghdad

Baldwin, King of Jerusalem, 78, 91
Bale, *see* Berke Khan
Balkhash, Lake, 147
balm, 65ff., 89, 181
bamboo, 132, 201
bananas (long apples), 65
Bandinanah (Flabryne), 122
Barach (Barak), 94
Baraqa (Melechsayt), Sultan, 60
Barbara, Saint, 58
barnacle geese, 165
Baroch (Sarchie), 122
Bartholomew the Englishman, 118, 195
Basan, 96
basilisk, 204
Bathsheba (Bersabee), 72-3
Bathyn, *see* an-Din, Sultan
Batu (Baco), 103
Batu (Cadu) Khan, 157
Bede, Venerable, 195
Bedouin (Bedoynes), 59, 72
Beersheba (Bersabee), 72, 76, 97
Behaim, Martin, 32
Beirut (Beruch), 56, 57, 100
Bekaa (Bochar), Valley, 100
Belbays (Balbeor), 58
Belgrade, 45
Belyan, Mount, *see* Altai
Belyon, River, *see* Abellin
Benjamin, 76
Benochdaer, Sultan, *see* Baibars
Berke (Bak) Khan, 157
Bernáldez, Andrés, *9*
Bersabee, *see* Beersheba; Bathsheba
Beruch, *see* Beirut
Bestiaries, 197, 204
Beth *see* Yezd
Bethany (Bithyria), 49
Bethany in Judea, 87, 88
Bethel (Luza), 81, 91
Bethlehem, 74, 76, 77, 114
Bethphage, 87
Bethsaida (Betsayda), 93
Bethsamoron, *see* Constantinople
Bethshan (Bethaaym, Citople, Scythopolis), 94
Betron, *see* Bosra
Betsayda, *see* Bethsaida
Bithynia (Pytan), 49, 164
Black (Great) Sea, 111, 161, 162
blood drinking, 134
Boal (Babilan?) Khan, 157
Bochar, *see* Bekaa Valley
Boem (Bohemia), 128
Boniface VIII, Pope, 25
Boniface, Saint, 198

Index

Borach Khan, *see* Ibaka Bek
Boradyn, *see* al-Afdal, Sultan
Bokhara (Bactria), 161
Borneo (Pathen? Thalamass?), 132
Bosphorus, 196
Bosra (Betron, Botron), 62, 90
Boteniga, 131
de Bourgogne, Jean, *10*
Braban(t), 128
Bradenople, *see* Adrianople
Bragmans (Brahmins), *25*, 178ff., 204
Brindisi (Brunduse), 68
Brome, Richard, *9, 34*
Brunduse, *see* Brindisi
Bryke, *see* Phrygia
Bulgaria (Pannony, Bulgary), 45
Bunyan, John, *17*
Burchard of Mount Sion, *19, 26*
Burgoyne (Burgundy), 68
Burgu, *see* Cuyuk Khan
Burning Bush, 70
Byzantium, *see* Constantinople

Cadhilhe, *see* Kao-li
Cadrige, *see* Khadija
Cadu, *see* Batu Khan
Caesarea (Gerare), 58
Caesarea Philippi, 97, 103
Caesarius of Heisterbach, 199
Caffilos, 134
Caiaphas (Cayphas), 48, 57, 65; *see also* Haifa
Cain, 73, 96, 99; Mount, 96
Cairo (Babylon where the Sultan dwells) 58, 59, 62, 63, 67, 68, 69, 93, 100, *passim*
Calabria (Calabre), 57, 68
Calamy (Mailapur), 114
Calanok, *see* Indo-China
Calcas, *see* Carki
Caldee, *see* Chaldea
Caleb (Caleph), 73
Caliph, 202; meaning of, 59; of Baghdad, 149
Calistra, *see* Thera
Calvary, 47, 77
Camalach, *see* Khan-balik
Cambaye (Colach, Soboth), 168
cambille, 74
Campagna, 68
Cana, *see* Thana
Cana in Galilee, 93
Canaan, 116
Canapes (Canopus), Star, 181, 201
cannibalism, 134, 187; in Lamory, 117
Canopak, 58
Canopus, *see* Canapes

Canterbury Tales, 15
Canton (Latoryn), 138
Capadoce, *see* Cappadocia
Capernaum (Capharnaum), 93, 96
Cappadocia, 101, 164
Cardabago, 114, 114n.
Caremoran, *see* Hwang-ho, River
Carki (Calcas), 49
Carmana (Theman?), 115
Carmel, Mount, 57
Carmelite friars, 57
Carnaa, *see* Persepolis
Caromosan, *see* Hwang-ho, River
Carpeteya, *see* Scarpanto
Carras, *see* Mount Real
Carthage (Dydoncato), 56
Carygan, *see* Tuku-Timur Khan
Caspian Mountains, 161; *see also* Caucasus
Caspian Sea, 111, 117, 162, 165, 203
Cassach, *see* Kashan
Cassay, *see* Hangchow
Casson, *see* Shansi
caste marks, 131
Castle of Pilgrims, 103
Catalan Atlas, 31
Cathay, 62, 141ff., 165, 167, 168, 185, 186; attitudes to religion and Christianity, 144; conquered by Genghis Khan, 147
Catolonabes, 203; *see also* Hasan ben Sabbah
Caucasus (Caspye Mountains), 161; (Mount Athos), 49
Cayphas, *see* Caiaphas
Cayphas (town), *see* Haifa
cedars of Lebanon, 90
Celsite, *see* Merv
Ceylon (Taprobane, Silha), 135, 182
Chaanguys, *see* Genghis Khan
Chaghatai (Chahadoy) Khan, 157
Chaldea (Caldee), 44, 61, 62, 109, 111, 112, 116, 117, 164
chameleons, 177
Channel, *see* Edessa
Chapelle, Sainte, 195, 198
Charauk Khan, 157
Chariton (Markaritot), Saint, 77
Charlemagne, 81, 198
Chasak, *see* Kashan
de Chateaubriand, Comte, *35*
Chaucer, Geoffrey, *13, 15, 16, 17, 29, 40, 194*
Chebisa, *see* Kubilai Khan
Chermes, *see* Ormuz
Chibense, *see* Nanking
children: fattened for table, 127; sacrificed to idols, 27, 124–5
Chios (Silo), 53
Chippron, *see* Soprony

Index

Dindimus, 204
Diogenes, 204
dirpe, see Dry Tree
Dismas, 55; cross of, 46
Dispolis, *see* Lûdd
Djebeil (Gibilet), 102
dog-headed men, 134–5, 201
Don (Thanay), River, 111
Dothan (Dothaym), 92
doves as messengers, 198
Dry Tree (*dirpe*), 74, 197
Dundeya, *see* Andaman Islands
Durazzo (Duraz), 68, 101
Dydoncato, *see* Carthage

Earth, size of, 201
Easter Fire miracle, 77
Ebron, *see* Hebron
Eccozar, *see* Farab
Edessa (Channel, Edisse, Rochays, Roha)
    102, 124, 164
Edward I of England, 60
eels in India, 120
Effrem, *see* Ephraim Syrus, Saint
Egerton MS, owners, 41
Egypt (Egipte), 44, 46, 58, 59, 63ff., 76, 79,
    108, 117, 164; fertility of, 65
Elbruz (Abior), Mountain, 162
Eleazar, 99
elephants used in war, 133
elevation of stars, 128
Eli (Hely), 91
Elijah (Helyas), 56, 57, 95
Elim, 69
Eliople, *see* Heliopolis
Elisha (Helizeus), 88, 92
Elizabeth, Saint, 86
Elkanah (Helchama), 91
Elphy, *see* Qalawun, Sultan
Em(m)aus, 86, 101, 103
Emperor of Persia, 156
Endor, 94
Eneas, *see* Aeneas
Engeddi, 89
England, 45, 119, 130
English letters, 110
Ephesus, 53
Ephraim Syrus (Effrem), Saint, 62
Ermony, *see* Armenia
Erzerum (Artiron), 113
Estates, Three, 194
Ethill, *see* Volga
Ethiopia (Ethiope), 44, 62, 63, 64, 111, 117,
    118, 164, 184
Ethiopians, afflictions of, 117
Etna (Gebel), Mount, 68

Et-Tih (Acchelek), desert, 58
Eucharist, 84
Euphrates, River, 61, 111, 113, 164, 184;
    diverted by Cyrus, 61 (cf. Herodotus I,
    189, 191)
Europe, 145
Eustace, Saint, 102
Eve: grave of, 73; *see also* Adam

Fabri, Felix, 12
Famagusta (Famagost), 55, 101
Farab (Eccozar), 160
Fare, *see* Messina
feasts, at Khan's court, 150ff.
Fenice, *see* Phoenicia
Ferne (Ilgun?), 102
Ferne, River, *see* Pharphar
Field of Blood (Acheldemak), 85
Field of Flowers at Bethlehem, 74ff.
Filioque clause in Creed, 196
fish, swarming to shore, 133
Flabryne, *see* Bandinanah
Flagramy, 103
Flaxania, *see* Naxos
Flood, Noah's, 77, 113, 184
Florach, 102
Florida, 32
Fosse of Mynon (cf. nearby statue of
    Memnon), 57, 196
Franciscans, 98, 202
Frederick II, 197
Frobisher, M., *9*, 32
Fuggers of Augsburg, 32
funeral customs: at Caffilos, 134; at Quilon,
    124; at Thana, 122; in Tartary, 159; in
    Tibet, 186

Gabaon, *see* Shobek
Gabriel, 94, 104, 109
Galilee, 90, 91, 93ff., 99
Galile(e), Mount, 87
Galilee, Sea of, 96
Gangaras, King, 184
Ganges (Phison), River, 162, 173, 184
Garisym, *see* Gerizim
Gaulonitis (Traconye), 96
Gawain poet, *28, 34, 41*,198
Gaydon, *see* Tatu
Gaza, 57, 58
Gebal (Gebel), 102
Gebel, *see* Etna
Geen, *see* Genoa
geese, barnacle, 203
Gelboe, *see* Gilboa
Gemlik (Chivotot, Cibotus), 53
Geneth, *see* Paphlagonia

213

Index

Genghis Khan (Chaanguys), 146–7
Gennesaret (Gerassen), Lake, 96
Genoa (Geen), 68, 92, 101, 112, 120, 141, 168
Genoese (Januenes), 48, 53, 101, 120
Geoffrey of Monmouth, 195
George, of Cappadocia, Saint, 98, 100, 101
Georgia, 163, 164
Gerare, see Caesarea
Gerassen, see Gennesaret
Gerizim (Garisym), Mount, 92
Germany (Almayne), 45, 103, 128
Gesen, see Goshen
Gethsemane, 86
giants, 73, 174
Gibilet, see Djebeil
Gideon, 94
Gihon (Nile), River, 62, 196
Gilboa (Gelboe), 90, 94
ginger, 123
giraffes, 177
globe, size of, 130
Godfrey of Bouillon (Boloon), 78, 198
Gog and Magog, 28, 165, 203
Golden Legend, 41, 197
Golgotha, 77
Gomorrah, 89, 116
Goshen (Gesen), 63
Gower, John, 11, 16, 27, 40
Graften, see Silistria
Gravelly Sea (cf. sands and wadis of desert), 57, 114, 169
Great Khan of Cathay, 10, 141ff.; allied to Prester John, 168; fighting with King of Java, 132; hawking, 152–3; hunting, 141; name, 145; palace, 141; state, 142ff.; table manners at court of, 143; *see also* 62, 103, 135, 139, 140, 167, 168, 186, 201ff.
Grece, see Crete
Greece (Cresses), 45, 46, 100, 101, 163
Greek Emperor, 112; control of Church, 52; dominions, 49; palace of, 50; relics possessed by, 48, 49
Greek Sea (Mediterranean), 164, *passim*
Greff, see Corfu
Gregory, Saint, 98
Gregory XI, Pope, 41
griffons, 167
Guibert of Nogent, 198
Gulliver's Travels, 18, 35, 204
Guylford, Sir Richard, 22
Guys, see Kuyuk Khan
Guytoga, see al-Adil, Sultan
Guyuk (Burgu) Khan, 157

Gyboth, see Tibet
Gymnosophists, 25, 178–80, 204 (Gynoscriphe, Oxidrace)
Gyon (Gihon), River, see Nile

Hadrian (Adrian), Emperor, 81
Haifa (Cayphas), 57, 103, 196
Haiton of Armenia, 19, 20, 21
Hakluyt, Richard, 31, 33
Halamo, see Alania
Halaon, see Hulagu Khan
Hall, Joseph, 9, 25, 34
Halope, see Aleppo
Ham, 145
Hamath (Dameth), 59
Hamelius, P., 24
Hamschen (Hamson), 163
Hangchow (Cassay, Kinsay), 24, 138ff.
Hannah (Anna), 91
Hanway, Jonas, 34
Haran (Aram), 90
Harran (Aran), 62
Hasan ben Sabbah (Catolonabes), 171
hashish, 204
hawthorn's virtues, 48
Hayla, see Ai
Head, Richard, 34
heathen, common ground with, 188
Heber, see Aber
Hebron (Ebron), 73, 74, 76, 91
Helchama, see Elkanah
Helena, Saint, 78, 83, 195; daughter of Coel, 47; finds the Cross, 47
Heliopolis (Eliople), 64
Helizeus, see Elisha
Hellespont, 196
Hely, see Eli
Helyas, see Elijah
Henry of Lancaster, 11, 39, 40
Henry, Prince of Portugal, 16, 32
Henryson, Robert, 14
hens, wool-bearing, 138
Heraclea (Riclay), 102
Hercules, 121
Hereford Map, 15
Hermes, see Ormuz
Hermogenes, (Hermes Trismegistus), 50, 196
Hermon, Mount, 93, 95, 96
Herod, the Great, King, 58, 83–4
Herod Agrippa, 84
Herod Antipas, 84
Herodotus, 11
Higgins, Iain, 30
Hilarion, Saint, 55
Hilary of Poitiers, 98

214

Index

Index

John of Trevisa, 195
John, Saint, Hospice of, 80, 86
Johnson, Samuel, *34, 39*
Jonathan, 94
Jong, *see* Peking
Jopp(a), 57
Jordan River, 88ff., 96, 103
Joseph, 58, 66, 76, 91–2
Joseph of Arimathea, 79
Joseph, Saint, 94
'Joseph's Barns', 66
Josephus, 198
Joshua (Iosue), 73, 87
Josias (Jehoram?), 94
Judas Iscariot, 85, 86, 106, 198
Judas Maccabaeus, 76, 101
Judea (Judee), 46, 76, 89
Judgement, by Saint Thomas's hand, 124
Judgement, Last, 95
Juggernaut, *23, 25*, 125–6
Julian the Apostate, Emperor, 81, 91
Julius Caesar, 78
justice of the heathen, 176
Justinian, Emperor, 195; statue, 46

Kao-li (Cadhilhe, Korea?), 165
Kashan (Cassach, Chasak), 75, 114
Katherine, Saint, 69–71, 197
Kedron, brook, 86
Kempe, Margery, 196
Kermanshah (Kermen), 162
Khadija (Cadrige), 109
Khan, election of, 160
Khan, Genghis, 202
Khan, Great, *see* Great Khan
Khan Hulagu, 202
Khan Mangu, 202
Khan Wang of Keraits, 203
Khan-balik (Camalach), 153
Khorasan (Corodan), 109, 160–61
King Alisaunder, 15
Kings, Three, 75, 114, 118, 160
Kinsay, *see* Hangchow
Koran, 27, 75, 105ff.
Krak (Carras), 91
Kubilai (Chebisa) Khan, 149
Kuchu Khan (Nachaly?), 157
Kunya (Stancon), 101
Kurds (Cordynes), 161
Kus (Couston), 63
Kuyuk (Guys,Thyak) Khan, 148, 157

Lacuth, *see* Latakia
Laiazzo, *see* Ayas
Lamech, 96
Lamory, *18, 27; see* Sumatra

Lance, Holy, 49, 195
Langland, William, *17*
Lango (Cos), 53
Lanteryn, *see* Linching
Larrais, *see* Ayas
Latakia (Lacuth), 102
Latoryn, *see* Canton
Latron (Mount Modyn), 102
Lay (Lake of Nicaea, confused with River Sangarius), 102
Lazarus, 87
Lebanon (Liban), 97, 100
Lemnos (Lempnia), 49, 50
lemon juice: to deter crocodiles, 135; to deter snakes, 113
Leo I, Emperor, 69
lepers, *11–12*
Lesbos (Tesbiria), 49
Lettow, *see* Lithuania
Liban, *see* Lebanon
Libro del Conoscimento, 40
Liby(a), 44, 164, *passim*; and Antarctic Star, 128
Lidda, *see* Lûdd
Liège, *10*
lignum aloes, 69, 154, 197
Limassol (Lymettes), 55
Linching (Lanteryn), 141
Lithuania (Lettow), 103
Little Cilicia (Sem Cecil), 97
Livonia (Nyfeland), 45,103
Livre de Merveilles, 30
Lombardy, 45, 101, 141, 168
Lombardy mile (approximately one English mile; half a great continental league), 57, 69, 97
Lombe, *see* Quilon
long apples (bananas), 65
Longemaath, 101
Lot, 89, 109, 116; grave of, 74; wife of, 90
Louis IX of France, 59, 195, 202
Lûdd (Lidda, Dispolis), 101
Ludolf von Suchem, *26*
Luke, Saint, 49, 99, 199
Lull, Ramon, *26*
Lusignan, house of, *41*, 199
Luza, *see* Bethel
Lycaonia (Lycony), 164
Lydgate, John, *26*
Lydia (Quificion), 164
Lymettes, *see* Limassol
Lyson, 164

Mabaron, *see* Coromandel
Mabinogion, 195
Macedonia, 49, 50, 118

Index

Mosul (Mosell), 164
Mount Joy, 86, 91, 101
Mount Modryn, *see* Latron
Mount Moriah (Moriac), 82, 198
Mount of Olives, 86, 87
Mount Real (Reall, Krak), 60, 91
Muhammad, *40, 62, 148*; and the hermit, 109; and wine, 75, 104, 107ff.
Mulstorak, *see* Malazgirt
Munchausen, Baron, *40*
Münster's *Cosmographia*, 31
Myra (Marc), 53
Mysael (Meshach, Mysak), 58

Naaman, 91
Naboth, 94
Nabugodonosor, *see* Nebuchadnezzar
Nachaly, *see* Kuchu Khan
Nachor (Nahor), 90
Nails, Holy, 79
Nairmount, 102
nakedness, 120, 127, 200
Nanking (Chibense), 139
Naphtali, 97
Naples, 68
Nashe, Thomas, *34*
an-Nasir (Melechinasser), Sultan, 60
Nativity, Church of, 75
Natumeran, *see* Nicobar
Naxos (Flaxania?), 49
Naym, 93, 94, 95
Nazareth, 91, 93ff.
Nebuchadnezzar (Nabugodonosor), 58–9
Negus of Abyssinia, 203
Nembrot, *see* Nimrod
Neopolis, *see* Shechem
Nessabon, *see* Nishapur
Newburgh, castle, 45
Nicaea (Nyke), 53, 102
Nicholas, Saint, 53
Nicobar Islands, 134–5
Nicosia, 55
Nile (Gyon, Gihon), River, 69, 111; from India, 63; inundations of, 62; subterranean course of, 184
Nimrod (Nembrot), 61, 145
Nineveh (Niniue), 116, 164
Ningpo (Menk), 141
Ninus, King of Babylon, Arabia, Egypt, 116
Nise, 167, 170
Nishapur (Nessabon), 162
Noah (Noe), 47, 57, 113, 114, 145; Ark, 113
Norway, 129

Nubia (Numidia), 64, 164
Nuremberg Chronicle, 31
Nyfeland, *see* Livonia
Nyke, *see* Nicaea

Ocean Sea, 111, 120, 117, 133, 161, 164; Appendix II
Odoric of Pordenone *11ff., 19, 20ff., 27ff., 30, 32, 40, 201, 203, 204*
Oertige, *see* Delos
Ogotai Khan (Cichota), 148
Old Man of the Mountains, *23*; *see also* Assassins and Catolonabes
Olympus, Mount, 50
Omar, Caliph, 198
Orcobares (Himalayas?), 184
Orda (cf. camp of Golden Horde), 103
Orda Khan (Creten?), 157
Ordu Khan (Ogodai), 157
Oriell (Chryse), 182
Ormanx, 102
Ormuz (Hermes, Chermes), 120, 168
Orontes, *see* Pharphar
Ortygia, *see* Delos
otters used for fishing, 138
Otto von Freisingen, 203, 204
Outremer, 196
Oxidrace, *see* Gymnosophists
Oxus (Phison), 162
ox-worship, 123–4

Palestine (Philistia), 57, 69, 76, 111, 181
Pannony, *see* Bulgaria
papacy, 205; Avignon, *24*
Paphlagonia (Geneth), 164
Paradise, Earthly, 63, 111, 113, 154, 169, 183–4; rivers of (cf. Nile), 86, 167, 184, 196, 197, 205
'Paradise' of the Assassins, 173
Parchoatra, Mount, 184
Paris, 81, 138
Paris, Matthew, 202
Paros (Minca), 49
parrots, 168, 169
Patera, 53
Pathen, *see* Borneo
Patmos, 53
Paul the Hermit, 197
Paul, Saint, 54, 99, 107, 198
Pegolotti, Balducci, *11*
Peking (Jong), 141, 149, 153
Pelagia, Saint, 198
Pentecost, 85
Pentoxere, 167ff., 203
pepper, 122–3, 200
Percipre (Perschembre?), 112

218

Index

219

Index

Index